AF505973

Democracy and Northern Ireland

Beyond the Liberal Paradigm?

Adrian Little
Lecturer in Political Theory,
University of Melbourne

First published 2004 by
PALGRAVE MACMILLAN
Houndmills, Basingstoke, Hampshire RG21 6XS and
175 Fifth Avenue, New York, N. Y. 10010
Companies and representatives throughout the world

PALGRAVE MACMILLAN is the global academic imprint of the Palgrave Macmillan division of St. Martin's Press, LLC and of Palgrave Macmillan Ltd. Macmillan® is a registered trademark in the United States, United Kingdom and other countries. Palgrave is a registered trademark in the European Union and other countries.

ISBN 1–4039–1248–3

This book is printed on paper suitable for recycling and made from fully managed and sustained forest sources.

A catalogue record for this book is available from the British Library.

Library of Congress Cataloging-in-Publication Data
Little, Adrian, 1969–
    Democracy and Northern Ireland : beyond the liberal
paradigm? / Adrian Little.
        p. cm.
    Includes bibliographical references and index.
    ISBN 1–4039–1248–3 (cloth)
        1. Liberalism–Northern Ireland. 2. Multiculturalism–Northern Ireland.
3. Democracy–Northern Ireland. I. Title.
JC574.2.G7L58 2004
320.9416–dc22   2003067761

10   9   8   7   6   5   4   3   2   1
13   12   11   10   09   08   07   06   05   04

Printed and bound in Great Britain by
Antony Rowe Ltd, Chippenham and Eastbourne

*'On the whole, there is no such thing as a right or a wrong;
the work lives and develops through the interplay of opposing
forces, just as in nature good and bad work together
productively in the long run'.*

*'one paves the way, lays foundations, supports, constructs,
and one organizes; all good things. But one does not arrive at
a whole.'*

Paul Klee

Contents

Acknowledgements

As usual, many people have contributed to the production of this book, none of whom can be held responsible for any remaining mistakes or misunderstandings. At Palgrave I would like to thank Alison Howson, Beverley Tarquini and Guy Edwards who helped me refine my initial proposal and the anonymous referees who commented upon it. I am also extremely grateful to the participants at the panel on 'Political Theory and Northern Ireland' which I convened at the Political Studies Association Annual Conference in Leicester in April 2003. My own paper there covered elements of Chapters Two and Three and I am fortunate to have had constructive comments on it from Alan Finlayson and Simon Thompson in particular. A draft of the entire manuscript was finally read by Paul Dixon, James Martin and Anna Hilton. Paul Dixon made a number of important points especially with regard to many of the practical issues in Northern Irish politics that are discussed at the outset of the book. As usual James Martin cast a critical eye over the theoretical arguments and the book may well not have emerged (certainly not as it has) without regular discussion of the issues on Friday lunchtimes in the Hobgoblin in New Cross Gate. Lastly, Anna Hilton read the manuscript assiduously and the book contains considerably more punctuation than it would have done without her efforts. I also thank her for her encouragement during a long, hot summer and for reminding me that class still matters.

Introduction

The meaning of democracy in Northern Ireland has always been contested but it has rarely been discussed in light of debates in political theory. Thus, whilst there is a huge body of literature studying the events of 'The Troubles', potential options for the future of Northern Ireland and, more recently, the course of the peace process, political theorists have been unusually reticent. Nonetheless, for a relatively small place, Northern Ireland has attracted a disproportionately large amount of coverage in both popular and academic literature compared to other parts of the world. Partly this can be explained by the unique circumstances of Northern Ireland. It has been called a 'place apart' and the seemingly intractable nature of the conflict there poses significant problems for those concerned with the nature of politics in deeply divided societies. Despite the advancements of the peace process, the enduring nature of the conflict and the uncertainties it embodies means that Northern Ireland remains fertile ground for political analysis.

Given the prominent literature on Northern Ireland then, it is surprising that very few political theorists have engaged with the problem and offered their insight into the difficulties which exist there. After all, politics in Northern Ireland is intimately bound up with the concepts that animate political philosophy: justice, rights, equality and so forth. For this reason it offers up an opportunity to examine how we operationalise these concepts in the practical circumstances of a divided society, but there appears to be a reticence amongst political theorists to engage in this task. At the same time, many of those who specialise in the area of Northern Irish politics have tended to analyse the problem in terms of the historical background to the conflict or the practical realities of the problems that occur in political life within the accepted parameters of the debate as it stands. In short, there has been insufficient attempt to integrate these literatures and find out what political theory can contribute to the analysis of Northern Ireland and the lessons it provides for normative political philosophy. The central aim of this book is to contribute to this process of reflecting theoretically upon Northern Irish politics.[1]

The focus in what follows falls upon recent developments in democratic theory and, in particular, the main contributions from liberalism which have established the theoretical framework of liberal democracy. What must be made clear from the outset is that there is no universal, homogenous model of liberal democracy which can be delineated. Liberal democracy has developed different systems and attributes in the varying countries in which it has emerged across the world. In this sense each of these countries is a 'place apart'. However, many of the same concepts are appealed to as the justification for the systems of governance which have emerged in different polities and Northern Ireland is no different to anywhere else in this respect. Indeed, such is the highly political nature of everyday life in Northern Ireland that discourses of rights, freedoms and justice abound. It is unusual, then, that the nature of the Northern Irish polity has barely been examined in the light of the major theories of liberalism. However, what becomes clear on undertaking such a task is the way in which liberal theories are undermined when applied to the practical realities of Northern Ireland. The major contention in this book is that the example of Northern Ireland demonstrates many of the weaknesses of liberal theories of democracy and that, whilst it is an extreme example, the flaws shown up by the application of liberal thought to Northern Ireland resonate with all attempts to practically apply liberalism.

In order to establish the practical basis on which different theories of democracy will be analysed, I will initially outline the provisions of the Belfast Agreement before analysing its implications. This is intended to provide a foundation for those theorists with little prior knowledge of recent Northern Irish politics. From there I go on to evaluate a number of perspectives in contemporary political theory using examples from Northern Ireland to highlight their strengths and deficiencies. This is designed to integrate the literature from political theory and that on Northern Ireland throughout the book. Thus, whilst some of the debates in political theory can be somewhat recondite at times, I hope to make them accessible to those who are not political theorists by assessing them in the light of the concrete realities of establishing democratic politics in Northern Ireland.

Liberalism and democracy

The main reason that liberal models of democracy prove so problematic lies in their focus on political agency and particularly that of the individual rather than issues of social structure. This criticism is particularly applicable to the influential model of political liberalism developed by John Rawls (1996). Rawlsian theory has inspired numerous debates within contemporary liberalism but perhaps most notable amongst them is his movement in his later work towards a more deliberative form of politics. This is construed narrowly as a system of procedures that are agreed upon to guide us through public debate. Politics, for Rawls, is the public space in which decision-making takes place free from the multiplicity of non-public moralities which are the hallmark of diverse, pluralistic societies. This initial model of deliberative democracy has been both criticised and built upon in the work of Jürgen Habermas (1998), who has constructed his position around a set of discourse ethics that can be separated from particularistic moralities. Here the focus is upon establishing a number of ethical principles that govern public deliberation and which everyone can agree to regardless of their substantive moral positions. Through following these procedures we can move towards consensual decision-making whereby the rationality of any decision is guaranteed by the procedural mechanisms that have been followed.

I argue that both of these approaches – the dominant ones in contemporary liberal thought – are problematic when it comes to understanding the practical problems of politics in Northern Ireland. They rely too heavily on the ideal-type of the rational individual and the capacity of individuals to separate the methods of politics from their substantive private or non-public beliefs. As we shall see, this demands a lot of any individual in any given society but is especially difficult to envisage in the context of Northern Ireland where interpretations of the political and liberal concepts of justice are closely bound up with 'private' concerns of culture, nationality, religion and so on. Moreover, both the Rawlsian and Habermasian models can be criticised for basing politics around the pursuit of some kind of consensus. I argue here that consensus is difficult to achieve in complex, contemporary societies and that its pursuit can lead to the emaciation of democratic politics. It is on this basis that the second half of the book examines theories that have placed greater emphasis on social structure as opposed to the sole focus on individual agency in the dominant forms of liberalism.

Democratic theory has been invigorated in recent years by theories concerned with the revitalisation of civil society. This has been particularly notable in the growth of theories concerned with concepts such as trust and social capital, as in the work of Robert Putnam (2000) and Onora O'Neill (2000) for example. Here attention is switched to the social context in which individual actors behave. Thus, rather than seeing citizenship and democracy as related to the formal relationship between individuals and the state, civil society theories concentrate on the wide range of intermediate institutions which characterise societies. These intermediate bodies are deemed vital to the health of democratic polities because they provide sustenance and meaning for people in their everyday lives. Advocates of civil society tend to argue that a strengthening of the intermediate section of modern democracies will provide an ethical framework which supports the relationship that individuals have with each other and the state. Whilst the focus on structural issues is an advance on the dominant liberal theories of democracy, the literature on civil society also contains some similar difficulties. The most significant of these is the sometimes overt and at other times more subliminal pursuit of consensus. The implication of civil society theory has often been that we will be better able to make consensual decisions if we shift powers of decision-making away from governments and the state and empower people and groups to make decisions for themselves. However, this book contends that this neglects the deep-seated nature of conflict and disagreement in diverse societies. In such circumstances a less hierarchical form of decision-making – whilst it might be desirable in itself – cannot guarantee a more consensual environment. Indeed, such is the ingrained nature of power and inequalities that many of the conflicts they engender will emerge in a strengthened civil society. In many respects then, civil society might provide a recipe for more social unrest and conflict rather than less.

The issue of political conflict and the centrality of power relations to contemporary politics have been advanced in recent years by the growth of identity politics and, in particular, recent debates within feminism. In the work of multiculturalists such as Bhikhu Parekh (2000) group rights form the basis of social justice where groups may be accorded separate rights on the basis of the demand of their differing cultures. Multiculturalism has had some recent impact in Northern Ireland although it is fair to say that the most influential discourses are of equal rights for groups rather than differentiated rights. Feminist theorists such as Iris Marion Young (2000) and Nancy Fraser (1997) have discussed issues of diversity and identity and argued that we need to understand individual identity on the basis of 'multiple intersecting differences'. This refers to the shift in some feminist theories away from universal categories (such as 'women') towards an understanding that all individual identities are comprised of a range of sources of the self. Thus, rather than essentialising the experiences and identities of all women under one catch-all category, we need to understand the particularistic nature of the cross-cutting identities that come together to make people who they are. Whilst gender may be a prominent source of individual identity, it is but one such source amongst many, including things like social class, ethnicity, culture, nationality, sexuality, disability, religion and so on. In all of these categories there are complicated relations of power and so the formation of individual identity is an extremely complex process that is over-simplified if we essentialise groups of people under one of these headings.

The anti-essentialist argument of some contemporary feminists is an important one in the context of Northern Ireland where too often political analysis has relied too heavily on the simplistic reduction of society into two opposed groups (be that nationalist/unionist, catholic/ protestant, and so on). Anti-essentialist feminism encourages us to view society as more complex and therefore challenges political strategies for peace which are based upon accommodating the claims of large, undifferentiated groups. That said, such has been the exclusion of women from politics in Northern Ireland, the strategy of feminist politics there has often been somewhat essentialist in character. This reflects the structural constraints that women have faced and an initial desire to increase the formal political activism of women and to encourage greater representation of and by women. This objective has borne some success in recent years but feminists in Northern Ireland may need to attend to Fraser's concern that a politics of recognition should also be accompanied by a politics of redistribution. From this perspective, we need to remember the importance of material inequalities in the generation of social power and the opportunity to participate in decision-making processes. From Fraser's point of view, we should not surrender the redistributive paradigm with regard to social and political inclusion in our pursuit of a politics of recognising difference. Again, this resonates with the example of Northern Ireland politics which has traditionally been élite-driven with limited participatory opportunities especially for the more deprived sectors of Northern Irish society.

The final perspective addressed in the book is that of radical democratic critics of liberalism. In terms of its implications for democracy, this position is articulated most significantly by Chantal Mouffe (2000). The centrepiece of this theory is that rather than pursuing consensus, democratic politics is primarily concerned with plotting a course through the problems and antagonisms which emanate from political conflict. Thus, any complex society will contain political divisions that are generated by the plurality of values contained therein. The health of that democracy can be gauged by the extent to which the values held by others are understood as those of legitimate adversaries rather than antagonistic enemies. Whilst conflict cannot be eradicated in complex societies, it can be ameliorated. Radical democracy argues for a more inclusive polity where divergent groups and movements have more input into decision-making. It is, then, opposed to the élitist nature of politics that is evident in places like Northern Ireland. Moreover, it recognises the significance of the redistributive paradigm in challenging élitism and establishing a more inclusive basis for participating in politics. The book contends that this provides us with a way of understanding some of the recent developments which have taken place in the peace process in Northern Ireland and hints at a new ethical framework for understanding democracy there. The weakness of radical democracy in the eyes of its critics is its inability to answer questions regarding institutional design. For this reason, it is fair to say that radical democracy is concerned more with how we actually understand 'the political' rather than the technicalities of the design of democratic political institutions. Nonetheless the contention of radical democracy is that we would be better able to resolve questions of institutional design if we had a more considered and radical conception of democracy.

Political theory and Northern Ireland

The outline of the argument in the book set out above suggests that debates in political theory have important implications for Northern Ireland. However, critics might ask what resonance the example of Northern Ireland has in terms of justifying or criticising particular normative political philosophies. After all, one could take up the argument that Northern Ireland is indeed a 'place apart' where the usual ethical principles and values of liberal democracy cannot operate in standard fashion. This argument is rejected here insofar as there is not a 'normal' model of society which is synonymous with liberal democracy. To this end, every society should be regarded as a 'place apart' where the values and institutions of liberal democracy will vary according to the contingent circumstances in which they emerge and develop. Thus, the recognition by some such as Mitchell (2001) that

Northern Ireland departs from the normal standards of parliamentary democracy can be applied to a greater or lesser extent to all liberal democracies.

The reason why Northern Ireland provides useful avenues for political theorists to explore lies in the overt nature of the political divisions and antagonisms which exist there. It is an example that throws a sharp light on the ways in which the existence of a plurality of moral and political values can generate conflict. That these conflicts have sometimes led to political violence in Northern Ireland should not detract from the lessons that can be learned about the potential for conflict emanating from value pluralism in any liberal democracy. In other words, the sometimes violent nature of conflict in Northern Ireland does not set it apart from other societies where political divisions do not manifest themselves in the same ways. The issue of violence should not blind us to the 'normality' of Northern Ireland especially in recent years. Whilst there might be a heightened awareness of political division, this does not necessarily make politics and violence the central aspect of everyday life. Indeed it is fair to say that, like many contemporary societies, the primary religion in Northern Ireland could be deemed to be consumerism.[2] The point is, then, that everyday life in Northern Ireland is not as clearly distinguishable from other societies as a cursory glance at political conflict might convey.

The example of Northern Ireland also suggests that we should be careful in the way that we employ ideal-typical formations in political theory. Whilst there is always a place for such thinking in normative political philosophy, this does not mean that ideal-types can be parachuted in to resolve the complex practical problems of divided societies.[3] In many respects it can be argued that theoreticians are behind politicians in places like Northern Ireland in understanding the practicalities of politics in complex situations.[4] In Northern Ireland the reality of politics in recent years has signified a degree of awareness (amongst pro-Agreement parties at least) that democratic politics are complicated, untidy and sometimes chaotic. This provides a salutary lesson to political theorists of the practicalities of democratic politics in real situations. Circumstances ensure that political procedures and institutions will always be contingent and subject to criticism and transformation in all societies. In short, political realities will always establish constraints upon the ways in which agents can act and this insight deserves greater recognition in the theoretical literature.

The thrust of the book, then, is to not only cast new light on the political conflicts in Northern Ireland from the vantage point of political theory, but also to identify the lessons that theorists should learn from the practicalities of Northern Irish politics. This suggests that a recognition of the complexities of democratic politics might lead us to think differently about what can be achieved in Northern Ireland. This is important because the Belfast Agreement of 1998 bears clear imprints of contemporary developments in liberal democratic thought. If, as I argue, there are problematic aspects of this particular strand of political theory, then it is not surprising that the political process since 1998 has been somewhat uneven. However, this does not mean that we should reject the Agreement; instead we can recognise that it is an example of the contingency of political procedures and institutions. The main claim of this book is that an alternative way of conceptualising democracy might enable us to understand the fitful and fluctuating nature of politics. This implies a rather different ethical framework for democratic politics than appears in most ideal-typical theories. At times actors in the peace process in Northern Ireland have provided evidence demonstrating awareness of changing ethical frameworks.[5] This, in itself, reflects the contingent nature of democratic politics and the lessons that are to be learned from Northern Ireland.

The underlying message of the book is the problems that emerge when we only understand Northern Ireland through the 'two traditions' paradigm, which homogenises vastly differentiated groups of people and essentialises culture (Little 2003; Finlayson 1997, 2001). As such it underestimates the diversity in Northern Ireland and the plurality of values and arguments that exist there. This underlines the dangers of essentialism in all societies. However, if we recognise the existence of value pluralism and its implications for democracy, there is an opportunity to forge a new hegemony. In Northern Ireland this implies challenging the hegemonic position of the 'two traditions' paradigm. By understanding the import of value pluralism on how we conceive 'the political', democratic politics becomes much more dynamic. Rather than seeking solutions to political problems, we can start to understand that democracy is energised by such conflicts. In terms of Northern Ireland, this implies that there is no fixed solution to the problem. The Belfast Agreement should be regarded as part of a process – even a starting point – of finding ways to manage and contain political conflict. This is an example for all liberal democracies that political institutions should not be regarded as permanent and immobile. Instead the health of any liberal democracy must be measured by the capacity it holds for criticism of its own procedures and its propensity for dynamic change.

1
Explaining the Belfast Agreement

The signing of the Belfast Agreement in 1998 was a pivotal moment in the history of Northern Ireland. It was significant because it was the first time in twenty five years that there had been an accommodation between major parts of the unionist and nationalist communities and, even more notably, this process was also agreed by republicans and representatives of loyalist paramilitaries as well. In the subsequent referendum on the provisions of the Agreement, seventy one per cent of the public voted in favour and there appeared to be a relatively high level of consensus by the standards of Northern Ireland. However these basic figures disguise some of the nuances of Northern Irish politics which help to explain the sluggish pace of political development since the Agreement. Whilst the vast majority of nationalists voted in favour of the Agreement, the unionist community was almost split in two between those who supported and those who resisted the new provisions. The Democratic Unionist Party (DUP) provided the most audible voice of opposition to the Agreement along with smaller unionist parties. Since 1998, the electoral fortunes of the DUP have been in the ascendant which suggests that opposition to the Agreement in the unionist community is on the increase. This trend has been confirmed by the vocal opposition emanating from dissident elements within the Ulster Unionist Party (UUP) despite the pro-Agreement stance taken by the party leadership. Clearly then, in terms of democratic theory, the simple majority in Northern Ireland who backed the Agreement is not in itself a sufficient basis for the unquestioned assumption of political legitimacy.

Aggregative understandings of democratic legitimacy cannot be used uncritically due to the deep cleavages within Northern Irish society. This implies that a more complex understanding of democratic legitimacy is needed in societies like Northern Ireland. The majority in favour of the Agreement in the 1998 referendum is not set in stone; instead it was the result of a set of contingent historical circumstances and the democratic legitimacy that it generated is therefore subject to change. Indeed there is clear evidence of this in the fluctuating levels of support for the Agreement that we have witnessed within unionism. This suggests that we need to understand that votes and elections are rather blunt instruments for measuring support and legitimacy for political initiatives like the Belfast Agreement. Even where political accords generate substantial levels of democratic consensus, the threat of violence remains and levels of violent activity continue to disturb the democratic process in Northern Ireland. The point here is that democracy is not a stagnant set of institutions that can be measured or endorsed through the signing of agreements or the holding of elections; rather it is an ongoing and dynamic process in which the degree of legitimacy of institutions will fluctuate according to the public mood and the broader context of Northern Irish society. This chapter will examine the provisions of the Belfast Agreement and will critically evaluate their implications. Moreover it will analyse the model of democracy that emerges from the Agreement and the strengths and weaknesses of the democratic arrangements that have been set in place. This will provide a backdrop to the rest of the book in the sense that different versions of liberal and democratic theory will be analysed in the light of the experience of Northern Ireland in establishing a new democratic polity.

The provisions of the Belfast Agreement

As with previous documents in the peace process of the late twentieth century, there are three main strands in the Belfast Agreement. These focus on the democratic institutions within Northern Ireland, the relationship between Northern Ireland and the Republic of Ireland, and the relationship between the Republic of Ireland and the United Kingdom more generally. In addition to these strands focusing on political institutions, the Agreement also invokes recommendations on 'Rights, Safeguards and Equality of Opportunity' which help to establish the liberal credentials of the Agreement. The Agreement also contains provisions that are unique to Northern Ireland insofar as it deals with specific issues concerning the decommissioning of weapons, security, policing and justice, and prisoners. Lastly, the Agreement makes specific reference to the validation and implementation of the new arrangements and the review procedures following the implementation of the Agreement. In what follows, I will initially describe the provisions of the Agreement before going on to subject them to critical analysis and to locate them within broader debates within democratic theory.

At the outset of the Agreement the liberal nature of the document is clear insofar as its introduction is couched in the language of toleration, human rights, mutual respect, and the resolution of difference. As tends to be the case with documents of this kind, there is little critical reflection upon the meaning of these concepts and, more importantly, how they might give rise to further division and conflict. Nonetheless the driving force of the Agreement is the commitment by all signatories to follow democratic politics, and recognition that, despite political differences, all aspirations have equal legitimacy. On the part of the governments of the United Kingdom and the Republic of Ireland there is an undertaking to legislate to change the constitutional status of Northern Ireland and to alter the Constitution of Ireland. As was the case during the initiatives in the build-up to the Agreement, the two governments also recognise the principle of majority consent for any change in the constitutional status of Northern Ireland, the need for majority consent in both parts of Ireland for any move towards reunification, and the legitimacy of the aspiration to reunification. Moreover, the governments are committed to introducing such measures in their respective parliaments if consent is given North and South and, whatever the constitutional arrangements, to upholding liberal principles of impartiality and 'the principles of full respect for, and equality of, civil, political, social, and cultural rights, of freedom from discrimination for all citizens, and of parity of esteem and of just and equal treatment for the identity, ethos and aspirations of both communities' (The Agreement, 1998: 2).

The most substantive part of the Agreement is the section on Strand One, namely, the democratic institutions to be established within Northern Ireland. The key institutional provision is for the formation of the Northern Ireland Assembly, which would be elected through the single transferable vote mechanism and would take responsibility for government departments that was previously exercised by the Secretary of State for Northern Ireland – powers that could be expanded in the future. The key to the Assembly would be power-sharing, whereby, subject to the need to abide by the European Convention on Human Rights, decisions would be taken on a cross-community basis. This would require parallel consent (a majority of both nationalists and unionists voting in favour of a particular measure) or 'a weighted majority (60%) of members present and voting, including at least 40% of each of the nationalist and unionist designations present and voting' (The Agreement, 1998: 5; see also O'Leary 1999: 69–71). Aside from the specific procedural mechanisms for ensuring a broadly representative Assembly and Executive, this is a controversial provision because it requires all members of the Assembly to register their 'designation of identity' as 'nationalist, unionist or other' (The Agreement, 1998: 6). As we shall see in due course, this throws up complications with regard to the straitjacket of the orthodox categories in Northern Ireland (i.e. the assumption of uniformity within the 'two traditions') and the ways in which designations might be changed for strategic reasons. This was demonstrated in November 2001 when three members of the Alliance Party (normally designated as 'other') in the Assembly redesignated themselves as unionists to assist the re-election of David Trimble as First Minister (Evans and Tonge 2003: 27).[1] The Agreement legislated for the establishment of an Executive Authority in the Assembly that would be comprised of a First Minister, a Deputy First Minister and ten departmental ministers who would all take their posts on the basis of the d'Hondt system (O'Leary 1999: 95–6) to ensure cross-party representation in the executive.[2] The Assembly as a whole would have the authority to pass primary legislation on devolved matters, with some powers remaining with the Secretary of State for Northern Ireland and the Westminster parliament retaining authority over non-devolved issues. Also of note would be the formation of a Civic Forum which would be a consultative body comprised of representatives of business, trade unions, and the voluntary sectors to advise on matters of social, economic and cultural significance.

Strand Two of the Belfast Agreement focuses on the relationship between Northern Ireland and the Republic of Ireland, and in particular, the formation of a North/South Ministerial Council. This reinforced the view that had been held by both the British and Irish governments that the Republic of Ireland should have an input involving cooperation and consultation on particular issues that had a cross-border content, such as tourism and agriculture. The Council would be comprised of the leaders of the executives from North and South (First Minister, Deputy First Minister and Taoiseach) along with relevant ministers from both the Dáil and the Legislative Assembly, depending upon the particular issue that was under consideration. However, democratic authority would remain with the Northern

Ireland Assembly and the Irish parliament respectively. Nonetheless, despite the statement of the authority of the Northern Ireland Assembly, this measure was an appeasement of nationalists who particularly welcomed the reinforced institutional role for the Republic of Ireland that built upon the measures initiated in the Anglo–Irish Agreement (1985). There is no definitive definition of which issues are of mutual interest in the document so there is scope for disagreement between the two authorities over which issues should be discussed under the auspices of the North/South Ministerial Council.[3] Moreover, the possibility was built into the provisions for the Council that decisions made by that body may be rejected by the Northern Ireland Assembly or the Irish parliament so, again, there is an understanding within the Agreement that conflict between the different institutions may be forthcoming. In many ways then, the provisions for the North/South Ministerial Council are rather vague and open to considerable conflict between the actual participants on the one hand, and also between the Council and the Northern Ireland Assembly and Irish parliament where democratic accountability actually lies.[4] The capacity of the Northern Ireland Assembly to reject agreements made by the Council appears to be a key factor for unionists concurring with the establishment of the latter when it was so clearly an institution that would be more attractive to nationalists. Nonetheless, as O'Leary notes, the legislation was framed in such a way that neither the Northern Ireland Assembly nor the Ministerial Council could function without the operation of the other. This was designed to ensure that both nationalists and unionists did not try to undermine one of the bodies to strengthen the other (O'Leary 1999: 80–83).

The third of the three main strands of the Belfast Agreement focuses on the relationship between the United Kingdom and the Republic of Ireland and contains the provisions for the establishment of the British–Irish Council (BIC). The aim of this council would be 'to promote the harmonious and mutually beneficial development of the totality of relationships among the peoples of these islands' (The Agreement 1998: 14). The British–Irish Council would be comprised of members of not only the British and Irish governments but also representatives from devolved institutions across the UK including not only Northern Ireland, Wales and Scotland, but also other institutions representing areas such as the Isle of Man and Channel Islands. Again, the idea would be to have ministers from each institution with a responsibility for a particular relevant issue to attend the council. Like the provisions of Strand Two, the idea would be to encourage consultation and, where possible, agreement on issues of common concern; not surprisingly, some of the issues of concern listed in The Agreement mirror those that would concern the North/South Ministerial Council. The emphasis on agreement in the British–Irish Council is less pronounced because, given the diversity of the institutions represented and the widely varying extent of their powers, it is much less likely that co-operation and concurrence would be forthcoming. Moreover, it was also recognised that the institutions to which representatives were accountable would have differing agendas. Thus, whilst the BIC would normally 'operate by consensus', it was also recognised that '[i]ndividual members may opt not to participate in such common policies and common action' (The Agreement 1998: 14). Under this part of the Agreement there is also a section on a new British–Irish Intergovernmental Conference which would supplant the provisions of the Anglo–Irish Agreement (1985). This would involve the Prime Minister and the Taoiseach and/or relevant Ministers and special advisers where appropriate. The important consideration here was that the Irish government would be able to put forward views on issues affecting Northern Ireland that were not devolved to the Northern Irish Assembly, and therefore that the government of the Republic would have an input on all-island or cross-border cooperation even on issues that had not been devolved. This was clearly a bow in the direction of nationalist opinion and it was a counter-balance to the appeasement of unionism that was evident in the formation of the British–Irish Council.

Whilst considerable attention has been devoted to these institutional arrangements of the Belfast Agreement, the most important aspects of the document in terms of theories of liberalism and democracy lie in the provisions in the section on 'Rights, Safeguards and Equality of Opportunity'. This element was notable not least because it provided a clearer statement of rights for people in Northern Ireland than was the case for their counterparts elsewhere in the United Kingdom. After acknowledging the commitment to mutual respect, civil rights and religious liberties for all, the signatories affirmed the following rights: to free political thought; to freedom and expression of religion; to democratically pursue national and political aspirations; to seek constitutional change by peaceful and legitimate means; to freely choose one's place of residence; to equal opportunity in all social and economic activity, regardless of class, creed, disability, gender or ethnicity; to freedom from sectarian harassment; and, for women in particular, to full and equal political participation (The Agreement 1998: 16). On top of this extensive list of human rights, The Agreement also commits the British government to the incorporation of the European Convention on Human Rights (ECHR) into the law of Northern Ireland. There is an important recognition in this part of the document that a vague aspiration on equal opportunity would not be sufficient, and for this reason there is a strong statement that public authorities would have a statutory obligation to ensure equal opportunities. This suggests an awareness that this had not previously been the case in the history of Northern Ireland. The strength of this statement is also evident in the wide definition of groups that would benefit from these equal opportunities as they would extend to 'religion and political opinion; gender; race; disability; age; marital status; dependants; and sexual orientation' (The Agreement 198: 16).

The other major plank of the 'Rights, Safeguards and Equality of Opportunity' provisions would be the establishment of a Northern Ireland Human Rights Commission which would supplement the ECHR to take account of the specific circumstances that pertain in Northern Ireland. In so doing, the Agreement states that this would constitute a Bill of Rights for Northern Ireland 'to reflect the principles of mutual respect for the identity and ethos of both communities and parity of esteem' (The Agreement 1998: 17).[5] Alongside these legislative measures in the United Kingdom, a new statutory Equality Commission would be established in Northern Ireland which would replace an existing range of commissions and agencies concerned with equality issues, and there was a provision that would allow the Northern Ireland Assembly to establish a Department of Equality if it wished to do so in the future. Moreover, the Republic of Ireland would seek to ensure that its citizens would have an equivalent range of human rights provisions as in Northern Ireland and would undertake consultation on constitutional amendments in order to achieve this objective. An important part of this process would be the establishment of a Human Rights Commission comparable to the one in Northern Ireland, and this would pave the way towards a joint committee to instigate measures guaranteeing fundamental rights for the entire population in Ireland.

Of course, a standard objection made with regard to human rights legislation and measures to ensure equality of opportunity is that these tend to be somewhat legalistic and that the formal existence of rights and equal opportunities does not guarantee that they are substantively experienced.[6] The Belfast Agreement manages not to fall into some of these difficulties because, in some areas, it is explicit about the problems faced by specific groups of people. For example, in a section on 'Reconciliation and Victims of Violence', careful consideration is given to the acknowledgement of the suffering of victims of violence. There is a recognition that some areas have been particularly badly affected by 'the Troubles' and that therefore there is a need to establish and support community initiatives to enable people to come to terms with their misfortunes. Thus, it is understood in the Belfast Agreement that community and voluntary organisations have a particularly important role to play in the redevelopment of communities that have been blighted by 'the Troubles' and, significantly, that resources will need to be allocated to this sector to enable it to perform its pivotal role in the reconstruction of Northern Irish society. Whilst organisations working within communities may well reflect the concerns of one particular section of society, the Agreement aspires to the promotion of a culture of tolerance and, with that, more integrated education and mixed housing. As we will see in Chapter five, this demonstrates an awareness of some of the difficulties in invigorating the community and voluntary sectors in a divided society like Northern Ireland.

The contextualisation of the rights, equality and freedom agenda in the Belfast Agreement continues in a section on 'Economic, Social and Cultural Issues'. Some of the provisions here are general in nature but others are very specifically directed towards the experiences of Northern Ireland. In the former category, the British government is committed to pursuing 'sustained economic growth and stability' and the promotion of social inclusion, alongside an economic development strategy that would embrace planning for the region. These sort of measures could be a feature of British government policy for any region in the United Kingdom, particularly given the commitments of the Labour government elected in 1997 and its devolution agenda. However, much of this section of the Agreement is concerned with the specific context that pertains in Northern Ireland. Thus, for example, the Agreement recognises a need to tackle the problems of a divided society and, in particular, the specific problems within the region that affect urban and rural areas and those in border areas. Not surprisingly, given the policies of the Labour government in place when the Agreement was constructed, there is a section on employment equality and the need to tackle unemployment as a basis of social inclusion and reducing the differences between the unemployment rates in the two communities.

When it comes to cultural aspects of rights and equal opportunities, much of the focus of the Belfast Agreement is on the issue of language.

In this vein it proclaims that all signatories 'recognise the importance of respect, understanding and tolerance in relation to linguistic diversity, including in Northern Ireland, the Irish language, Ulster-Scots and the languages of the various ethnic communities, all of which are part of the cultural wealth of the island of Ireland' (The Agreement 1998: 19). Whilst this appears to be an even-handed treatment of linguistic diversity across the two traditions and beyond, it soon becomes clear that this aspect of the Agreement is really concerned with the Irish language. Thus, the British government is committed to the following measures: to promote the Irish language where people want it and where it is appropriate; to facilitate and encourage its use in public and private life; to remove or diminish restrictions on Irish development; to greater liaison with the Irish language community; to facilitate it in the education system; to explore the expansion of access to Irish language broadcasting in Northern Ireland; to provide financial support for Irish language programme- and film-making; and to encourage the Northern Ireland Assembly to sustain the above commitments. It is important to reiterate that this approach is reserved for the Irish language; such substantive provisions are not explicitly extended to Ulster-Scots or Urdu or Mandarin. Thus, where the section on linguistic diversity indicates a universal dimension, in effect it is really directed towards the pressure from the Irish language community. In any case, the Agreement recognises the cultural and political significance of symbols and emblems and suggests that they should be used in a way that enhances mutual respect between traditions. In this sense, making a special case for Irish language does not breach the general intentions of the Agreement given that the Irish language is not, in itself, disrespectful towards the culture of other groups.

The remainder of the Agreement is less relevant to our argument as it deals with substantive matters specific to Northern Ireland rather than issues that may provide more generalised lessons for liberal democracy elsewhere in the world.[7] Nonetheless, it is worth providing some commentary on these aspects of the Agreement because they do pertain to the conditions under which any workable settlement in Northern Ireland could be implemented. These relate in particular to the areas of decommissioning, security, policing and justice, and prisoners. In terms of decommissioning, it is recognised as an indispensable aspect of the negotiating process and the signatories commit themselves to the disarmament of paramilitary groups. Thus, the participants are to work in 'good faith' and 'to use any influence they may have' to achieve full decommissioning of paramilitary organisations within two years of referenda on the Agreement in both parts of Ireland. Importantly, the document states that this should take place 'in the context of the implementation of the overall settlement' (The Agreement 1998: 20). Ultimately, as we have seen since the Agreement was signed, these clauses contain a level of ambiguity that has permitted the competing political actors to maintain different stances on the issue of the disposal of paramilitary weapons. Likewise, the responsibility for adjudicating on decommissioning is not entrusted to either government or the new institutions formed by the Agreement, but rather it is to be decided by the Independent International Commission on Decommissioning which was headed by the Canadian General John de Chastelain. Clearly, the rapid progress towards decommissioning envisaged in the Agreement has been much more difficult to implement in practice than was originally thought. Part of the difficulty here has been the ambiguity which surrounds the issue in the actual Agreement.

One example of this lies in the idea that decommissioning will take place in the context of the overall Agreement being implemented. In terms of security the British government commits itself to making progress (depending on the prevailing situation) on the reduction of the number and roles of Armed Forces, on the removal of security installations, on the removal of emergency powers in Northern Ireland, and the establishment of a 'normal peaceful society'. Progress towards these matters would be a subject of consultation with the Irish government which, for its part, would review relevant legislation in the Republic of Ireland. Again, the fact that these measures would be gauged according to the changing situation in Northern Ireland almost inevitably meant that nationalists would claim that progress was too slow whereas unionists would argue to the contrary. It is tempting to suggest that, as with decommissioning, it was only by couching these measures in vague terms that were open to more than one interpretation that it was possible to achieve agreement. This takes us to the third example of provisions that were particular to Northern Ireland, namely, policing and security. Whilst the Agreement sets out to state that every society is concerned with policing, the specific conditions in Northern Ireland underpin this part of the document. Although recognising the suffering and sacrifices of members of the Royal Ulster Constabulary (RUC) and their families, the Agreement explicitly states that the context of the peace process 'provides the opportunity for a new beginning to policing in Northern Ireland with a police service capable of attracting and sustaining support from the community as a whole' (The Agreement 1998: 22). Thus, the signatories want to develop a more representative police force that reflects the make-up of Northern Irish society and one that, in normal circumstances, would be unarmed.

The section on policing and justice also contains some interesting sentiments that, whilst unremarkable in many liberal democracies, signify the need for change in Northern Ireland. Here the language is characterised by concerns for fairness, impartiality, accountability, representativeness and effectiveness in policing. Thus, not only do the signatories recognise the need for a different type of police force, but they are also explicit in the pursuit of a police force that meets the criteria of public confidence and acceptability. These sentiments are extended to the criminal justice system as a whole as the Agreement aims to deliver a fair and impartial system of justice which can encourage and respond to the concerns of the community. To do this, the criminal justice system would need to inspire confidence throughout the community and would have to 'deliver justice efficiently and effectively' (The Agreement 1998: 22). Whilst these sentiments were clearly designed to appease nationalist critics of the RUC, it is also the case that they are open to interpretation regarding the extent to which they are being met. Thus, for example, the degree of public confidence is likely to vary over time depending on context and circumstance, and the level of efficiency and effectiveness is also open to question. This is not to say that these measures were undesirable, but rather that their implementation in practice might be more problematic than a cursory glance at the Agreement might suggest.

The last section which is particular to Northern Ireland relates to the treatment of prisoners. Both governments commit themselves to the implementation of an accelerated programme for the release of prisoners who were affiliated to an organisation that was maintaining an unequivocal ceasefire. It would be incumbent on The Secretary of State for Northern Ireland to keep the different organisations under review to ensure that their ceasefire was being maintained. The Agreement states that prisoners who met the criteria above would be released within two years of the passing of the requisite legislation by the two governments. Moreover, they both recognise that upon release prisoners need to be rehabilitated within the community and therefore programmes of support, especially with regard to education and training, would be required. This was clearly the bitterest pill for many politicians and ordinary people in Northern Ireland to swallow, but it was widely seen as the *quid pro quo* which would facilitate the process of decommissioning. Notwithstanding the breakdown of some of the paramilitary ceasefires and the fresh imprisonment of some of those deemed to be in breach of the provisions of the Agreement, the accelerated prisoner release programme took place within the envisaged time frame. Of course, this became even more controversial in the light of the impasse over decommissioning which has blighted political progress in the years after the Belfast Agreement. Nonetheless, the two governments realised that the relationship between prisoner releases and decommissioning was not directly reciprocal but instead had to be placed in the context of the overall Agreement. Moreover, *realpolitik* told the two governments and the parties that were not linked to paramilitary organisations that the prisoner release programme was essential if the political pathway for these movements was to become the dominant strategy at the expense of violence. This was never likely to be a process that would satisfy everyone and so it was approached with a degree of pragmatism by most of the parties involved in framing the Agreement as a necessary evil.

Overall, the Agreement can be viewed as an example of how difficult it is to enact liberal democratic theories in deeply divided societies. The Belfast Agreement is an exemplar of how the 'normalisation' of democratic politics in these types of society is heavily dependent upon the particular context within which the process takes place. In the case of Northern Ireland, it was accepted by the majority of the participants in the multi-party talks and the two governments that democratic politics, at least in the medium term, would take on a consociational form.[8] That is, there was wide recognition that power-sharing would be a feature of Northern Irish democracy, and that there could be no return to the simple majority thinking which had spawned the Stormont regime until 1972 and which continued to inspire some elements of unionist thinking in Northern Ireland thereafter. Once it was understood that a liberal democratic model could not be imported and applied to Northern Ireland, it was always clear that the arrangements that were established would be unique. Indeed, although lessons could be learned from consociational arrangements elsewhere in the world, whatever institutions were put in place would reflect the particular conditions that prevailed in Northern Ireland (as is the case in all polities). Nonetheless, whilst the Belfast Agreement did not match some pre-formed theoretical model, it is clear that key aspects of liberal democratic thinking did influence its creation. Thus, underpinning the Agreement, we see key liberal concepts such as toleration, rights and parity of esteem. The actual provisions borrow from democratic theory in their commitment to aspects of group rights, the need for political deliberation, the importance of intermediate groups, and so on. This is not accidental, but as we will see in the course of the book, all of these influencing features are moderated when they are practically applied in the Northern Irish context. Northern Ireland and the Belfast Agreement then, provide a useful example of how political theories can be difficult to enact in practice and how real political settlements will tend to borrow from a range of democratic theories rather than any one of them providing some kind of blueprint. Before proceeding to examine some of the key democratic ideas in contemporary political theory however, it is important to provide some critical analysis of the provisions of the Belfast Agreement in order to assess their import for political development in Northern Ireland.

Evaluating the Belfast Agreement: the limitations of consociationalism

In democratic terms consociationalism is a controversial strategy reliant as it is on somewhat fixed ideas of the divisions that exist within any given society. Nonetheless, for the last thirty years or so, it has been widely (though not universally) accepted in Northern Ireland that a feasible political settlement there would need to have a consociational impetus towards power-sharing. However, the longevity of these kinds of arrangements is not taken for granted by advocates of consociationalism. To this end Wilford argues that Arend Lijphart, the key architect of consociational thinking:

> did not intend that consociations were to be ends in themselves, rather that they could provide a means of moving towards a more 'normal' mode of competitive politics in the medium to longer term. In the shorter-run, a heavy premium is placed on mutual trust and confidence, initially among the relevant élites, which, *ceteris paribus*, descend to envelop contending communities. In this respect one may, perhaps, depict consociationalism as 'trickle-down politics'.   (Wilford 2001b: 4)

Taking this on board, it is important that consociationalism is understood as part of a democratic process rather than as a model for democracy in itself. However, that said, much of the literature and political argument surrounding the Belfast Agreement has tended to lapse from time to time into an unquestioning acceptance of the consociational model as the ideal format for democratic institutions in Northern

Ireland. Partly this is related to the way in which the Agreement itself has been constructed and thereafter the way in which it has been presented to the Northern Ireland populace. Whatever explanation is given, Wilford's point needs to be borne in mind whenever we address the relationship between consociationalism and democratic theory. The broader point to remember is that politics everywhere, not just in Northern Ireland, is a process. The dynamic of politics means that there will never be an end-state in which democracy is objectively achieved; the perceived health of democracy at any given time will depend on numerous contextual factors and it is a matter of political judgement as to whether the conditions in one particular instance are democratic at all. Certainly, the fluctuating fortunes of the peace process in Northern Ireland point towards changing dynamics within politics that undermine the notion of fixity in our understanding of democracy.

The main features of consociationalism in the management of ethnic conflict are 'a grand coalition between parties representing the main ethnic communities, minority veto rights, proportionality in public sector employment and expenditure, and segmental autonomy' (Wolff 2001: 12). Wolff notes that, whilst these kinds of initiatives had been a feature of the Sunningdale Agreement of 1973, the context of the Belfast Agreement was significantly different.[9] For example, not only were there relatively stable paramilitary ceasefires and a central role for political parties linked to paramilitaries in the 1990s, but there was also a more explicit international angle, provided in particular through the interest of the United States and conflict resolution initiatives elsewhere in the world. When these are coupled with the changing approaches of the British and Irish governments, it is clear that context is fundamental to our understanding of politics generally and agreements such as that in 1998 in particular. In practice, the political context of such agreements will therefore necessitate deviations from theoretical models such as the consociational theory proposed by Lijphart (1968, 1969). In Northern Ireland, the attraction of consociationalism is clear insofar as it is designed to provide political élites with the wherewithal to reach consensual decisions with the representatives of those from whom they or their supporters are divided in everyday society. Moreover, according to Lijphart's thinking, the system should be constructed in such a way as to encourage political élites to be moderate, although this will depend to a greater or lesser extent on the electoral system that is used (O'Leary 2001, 1999: 74). Nonetheless, there are dangers in systems that provide political élites with such powers. For example, the ways in which the UUP/SDLP (Social Democratic and Labour Party) control of the dyarchy of First Minister/Deputy First Minister under David Trimble and Seamus Mallon enabled those two parties to reinforce their position within the Executive are detailed in Wilford (2001b). Arguably, this was an outcome of the consociational model employed, but other parties such as the DUP and Sinn Féin complained that it contravened the spirit of the Agreement which had indicated a broader sense of power-sharing.

Northern Ireland is, of course, often seen as 'a place apart': a country dominated by Western liberal democratic values coupled with a highly divided social and political system. Given the need to contextualise theoretical models for political reality, perhaps it is not surprising that Northern Ireland's Assembly, as envisaged in the Belfast Agreement, bears little resemblance to the political systems of 'normal' democratic arrangements in the West. Indeed Paul Mitchell argues that in the light of the provisions of the Belfast Agreement:

> Northern Ireland is not really a parliamentary democracy at all. The usual minimal definition of a parliamentary democracy is that the executive is directly responsible to the legislature via confidence procedures ... Neither the quasi-presidential joint first ministers nor the Executive as a whole can be dismissed easily by the Assembly ... Thus, by institutional design the Agreement provides incentives toward power-sharing by not requiring policy agreement in advance. The Executive once formed is intended to be "stable" *vis-à-vis* the Assembly in that it cannot be easily dismissed.   (Mitchell 2001: 37)

Mitchell explicitly recognises that democracy in Northern Ireland is, at times, somewhat distant from the usual standards of democratic organisation in Western countries. Indeed political arrangements are intentionally designed to reach accommodation and stable government in Northern Ireland; their proximity to norms of liberal democracy are only a secondary consideration, if that. Importantly, Brendan O'Leary (2001: 49) notes that the Belfast Agreement diverged from traditional models of consociationalism insofar as the leaders of the participants represented national groups rather than ethnic or religious communities. Moreover, whilst it proposed an internal consociation to Northern Ireland, there were also several confederal and federal institutions and elements of co-sovereignty between the two governments. What emerged from the Belfast Agreement then, was a set of distinctive arrangements that had to be manufactured to match the contextual circumstances that prevailed in Northern Ireland. Indeed O'Leary (2001: 52–6) contends that the actual Agreement has been breached several times (including by the British government) and this can obviously raise questions about the legitimacy and democratic authority of the political developments since 1998. The amount of legalistic gymnastics in the framing of the Agreement stored up future difficulties which would undermine the Agreement itself when, almost inevitably, provisions were later breached.[10] In terms of democracy, it suggests that we need to be sceptical about such legalism and, moreover, that no document or Agreement is capable of encapsulating lasting democratic arrangements. The provisions of the Agreement are actually an historical artefact which capture the political decisions of the respective élites in terms of what they could sell to their membership at a given historical point. The Agreement establishes principles which may well turn out to be difficult to reverse, but this does not mean that it contains the definitive statement of how democratic institutions should be established in Northern Ireland: such arrangements will change and develop according to circumstances and different contexts in Northern Irish politics.

Such an understanding of politics is not commonplace in the literature on Northern Ireland but is evident in the work of Arthur Aughey on unionism (Aughey 2001). He notes that, whilst there has been a traditional culture of fatalism that permeates unionism, this is balanced by an element that understands the dynamics of contemporary politics and the contingent, transient nature of the political agreements that are forged:

> it is that very contingency of politics – a world without permanence – which engenders pessimism among many unionists. However, it may also engender its own qualified optimism. Political life, as a tissue of contingencies, is just as contingent for one's opponents as it is for oneself. Those who believe in historical inevitability … are more often than not … wrong-footed by history.   (Aughey 2001: 197)

For unionists like David Trimble this involved a calculation that the Belfast Agreement was, in that particular historical and political context, about as good as any agreement was going to get. With the restatement of Northern Ireland's position within the union, the *de facto* acceptance of partition by Sinn Féin and the need for a majority within the country to back any major constitutional change, it offered a shoring up of the unionist position, albeit with a greener dimension than many unionists would ideally prefer. To some extent then, the unionist acceptance of the Agreement advocated by Trimble was intended as a brake on any political dynamic towards Irish reunification. Whilst democratic politics always contains a dynamic of one kind or another, pro-Agreement unionists saw it as a means of establishing a new baseline that would influence the parameters within which that dynamic would be forged.

The Agreement then, was a strategy for the establishment of a new paradigm for democratic politics where the key understanding for unionists was, 'if we want what is valuable to stay the same some things will have to change' (Aughey 2001: 197). This understanding of the contingency of politics necessitated a strategy that accepted imperfection – this did not mean that unionist utopias were illegitimate but merely that they clashed with republican and nationalist utopias and that any agreement would require an adulteration of both. Thus, it is the failure to grasp the relationship between contingency and democratic politics that inspired rejectionism, even though many of the criticisms raised by rejectionists are not, in themselves, invalid or illegitimate. Where rejectionists err is in their understanding of strategy in democratic politics; the idea that ideal-type aspirations are achievable blinds rejectionists to the underlying political dynamics. The rejection is couched in short-termism insofar as it implies that the obstacles constructed by the rejection of agreement will prevent the development of an objectionable political settlement. This neglects the extent to which the dynamic of politics will ensure that life goes on and that there will have to be some kind of agreement in the future. Rejectionists fear any such agreement arguing that it will establish a new political paradigm that will inevitably dilute their objectives. Those who understand contingency in democratic politics understand that the participation in agreement in the short-term can have a long-term effect on the nature of future political developments. In short, what rejectionist unionists under-estimate is the extent to which their strategy might lead to more unpalatable outcomes in the long-term than those which are available through participation in the peace process in the short-term.

The contingency of democratic politics has often led to a rather unseemly side to Northern Irish politics. Dixon (2002a) notes how the two governments and the main political actors have engaged in a range of practices from lying to collusion in their efforts to bring their supporters with them. To some extent this is an inevitable dimension of politics in such a deeply divided society as Northern Ireland and it implies that the health of democracy should be measured by the extent to which these practices are kept to a minimum. It has of course required careful choreography and backstage activity in order to try and ensure the sharing of political risks. For Aughey, participating parties 'should accept risk management, or what might be called the principle of "simultaneity" – colloquially known as "jumping together" – as a way to avoid the politics of blame and to secure both parties from their critics. In Sicilian fashion, neither would lose face' (Aughey 2001: 199). Insofar as simultaneity is central to the furtherance of democratic politics in Northern Ireland, then the unseemly strategies identified by Dixon are a necessary evil. However, this also means that democracy needs to be understood in more complex terms than is sometimes the case in Northern Ireland. The simple dichotomy of violence and democratic means shrouds the extent to which the achievement of democracy will sometimes involve actions that may be widely regarded as morally dubious or improper. Of course, this is not necessarily a desirable or attractive spectacle but it does remind us that democratic politics rarely reach the pinnacles of democratic theory. The reality is marked by contingency and strategic decisions that are often borne out of necessity rather than the pious hopes of democratic theorists.

The importance of the context of political change also needs to be recognised in some of the literature on republican attitudes to the peace process. MacIntyre (2001), for example, notes how the political strategy of the Provisional leadership in the 1990s has diverged wildly from the traditional aspirations of republican ideology. In so doing he points to the changing discourses of the Provisional leadership and uses for his example the different utterances of Martin McGuinness and Gerry Adams in 1986 and their position in the late 1990s onwards. What this demonstrates is a change in strategy on the part of the Provisional leadership as to the best means to achieve their political objectives. MacIntyre sees the armed struggle as central to Republican ideology when, in fact, armed struggle is a method or strategy rather than a feature of a political ideology. Nonetheless he is correct to point out the differing construction of Provisional republicanism compared to the historic legacy that was bequeathed in the broader Irish republican movement. The point is that a changing socio-political context demands different types of political and ideological strategy. The new paradigm afforded by the peace process encouraged a more critical strategic thinking on the part of the Provisional leadership. MacIntyre chastises Jennifer Todd for failing to provide qualitative evidence that a 'new' republicanism emerged during the peace process (MacIntyre 2001: 216). That is as may be – the point for us is that a new strategic calculation entered into the republican equation. Ultimately, when it comes to *realpolitik*, whether this amounted to a 'qualitatively new phenomenon' is something of a moot point. In short, context is all and the Provisional leadership calculated that a fresh strategy was required for the new circumstances that emerged out of the long war. In the words of Ruane and Todd (1999: 57):

> McIntyre's argument rests on taking one binary opposition (anti-partitionism vs. partitionism) as the essential feature and organising core of republican ideology … But what if, rather than republicans rejecting anti-partitionism for partitionism, they instead have rejected this organising ideological dichotomy.

Essentially, what became clear in the discourses of the Provisional leadership during the 1990s peace process was a paradigm shift that recast the relationship between republican ideology and practical political strategy.

The other key dimension of the Agreement that is particularly controversial in the light of recent democratic theory is the requirement of Assembly members to designate themselves as 'nationalist', 'unionist' or 'other'. The dangers of such a process are well-documented but the predominant fear is that it will lead to an institutionalisation and reinforcement of communal divisions.[11] Clearly, such a process is strategically required by the power-sharing impetus which underpins the Agreement, but it also reproduces and substantiates the belief that ethnic divisions in Northern Ireland are static and intransigent, and that rather than challenging these assumptions we should establish institutions which contain them. Even those who believe that these ideas are not supportable in the longer-term have tended to 'acknowledge the problem, but see it as a necessary concomitant of meeting vital communal interests, one which is essential now, but may not be in the future' (Ruane and Todd 1999: 22). There is a need then, to deconstruct support for the Agreement and differentiate between those who advocate it because they believe in consociationalism as a justifiable democratic strategy, and those who recognise tensions between the Agreement and democratic principles but also see a pragmatic need to build upon the progress made during the peace process. The latter view is consistent with the understanding of democratic contingency and the imperfect nature of democratic arrangements in any society. The danger of equating the specific arrangements for power-sharing in the Belfast Agreement with the theory of consociationalism is that the latter becomes reified as a model for resolving political disagreement in deeply divided societies, when the reality behind the Agreement is much more pragmatic and less driven by academic theory.

A key deficiency of designation is the way in which it depicts static and unchanging forms of political agency. It underestimates the divisions within the 'two traditions' and their shifting political priorities and dynamics. As Dixon (2002b: 3) has argued, it misunderstands the importance of 'bringing politics back in'. Indeed Lijphart, the primary architect and advocate of consociational forms of democracy, openly acknowledges that it is a system reliant upon reinforcing the separate pillars of society and against an opening out of democratic social engagement between the conflicting groups. Dixon rightly contends that consociationalism embodies a somewhat pessimistic view of the people and their ingrained political attitudes and, as a result, it appeals to political élites to lead their constituencies towards accommodation rather than conflict. Thus the:

> 'pessimistic realism' of the consociational approach leads them to believe conflict can only be managed or regulated rather than resolved. Consociationalists do not seek to restructure or transform … the deeper causes of conflict but are so pessimistic that they are content to put the lid on a conflict and stabilise the situation. (Dixon 2002b: 4)

The problem with the consociational approach lies not so much in the recognition of antagonism but in a failure to understand the changing dynamics of political cleavage and antagonism. It assumes that political opponents and their views are entrenched and are incapable of development towards a less conflictual order. This is the 'realism' that Dixon alludes to in the self-understanding of the consociationalist. However, the existence of antagonism cannot be explained solely in terms of one over-arching dichotomous conflict. The nature of antagonism in Northern Ireland is multi-layered and is contingent upon the protagonists and the issues of division in different local contexts. This results in serious political divisions within each of the 'two traditions'. However, it is possible to agree with consociationalists that there will always be conflict without following the path of political élitism that they follow or the consensualism of

liberal civil society theory.[12] In many ways consociationalism reinforces social divisions by asking political élites to define themselves in
sectarian terms. It tries to segregate and divide groups in a society like
Northern Ireland where they live cheek by jowl. It leads to frustration
with élitist politics and exasperation with the political élites who are
not able to bring their constituencies with them at all times. In the
run up to elections politicians focus on the differences within their
sectarian bases in a way which often leads them to appeal to the
lowest common denominator. Because consociationalism does not
engage seriously with the question of how we are to change beliefs, it
reproduces a system where sectarian division is the actual problem. At
the same time, by focusing on only one aspect of social and political
division, it over-simplifies the wide range of conflicts that politicians
need to deal with by suggesting that *the* division is the *only* major
schism that needs to be addressed in the political system. In the case
of Northern Ireland, there is a resulting failure to deal with the traditionally élitist nature of politics there.

For Dixon (2002b) this consociational approach involves an
emasculated conception of democracy as well as an élitist conception
of politics and a pessimistic view of the people. The primary problem
is the way in which consociationalism views democracy in terms of
political institutions without an accompanying focus on political
identity and attitudes, ideology, culture and so on. Of course political
institutions are fundamental to the construction and understanding
of democracy, but there is a danger in the consociational model of
the artificial construction of two monolithic categories to contain a
diverse and changing population. These categories reject democratic
change in identity and agency and rely instead on traditional political actors to follow the path of accommodation and bring their constituencies with them. The evidence of the Northern Ireland peace
process is that this is difficult to do not least because they pay
insufficient attention to other sources of identity beyond the ethno-
national divide. In this vein Dixon (2002b: 5) contends that consociationalists neglect economic/class-based categories and the role of
ideology and culture in the Northern Irish conflict. Thus, there is a
predilection towards segregation in consociational models on the
basis that 'good fences make good neighbours' (Dixon 2002b: 6).
In this sense, consociationalists are not particularly interested in
cultural or ideological change as it complicates their design of political institutions to enable inevitably conflicting groups to live alongside each other. When this limited understanding of diversity is

combined with a general lack of clarity with which the label 'consociationalism' is used, then its hegemony over peace discourses in
Northern Ireland can be explained. For Dixon (2002b: 9) this is particularly notable with regard to the way in which consociationalists
have subsumed all forms of power-sharing under their auspices and,
in so doing, have imbued them with the 'élitist, conservative' bent of
consociationalism.

In terms of democratic theory, Dixon's most significant arguments
relate to the élitist nature of consociational thinking and the concomitant focus on traditional political agency as the source of progress.
This focus on political élites neglects the structural factors which
provide the backdrop to the environment in which political actors
engage with one another. Indeed, this prioritisation of agency over
structure is evident in substantial sections of the literature on the peace
process including, for example, MacIntyre's analysis of Provisional
republicanism above and the comparative literature which yearns for
Ulster's de Klerk or lazily denounces Ian Paisley as Northern Ireland's
equivalent of Ariel Sharon. This focus on political actors, and particularly leadership élites, serves to draw attention away from the structural
and contextual factors which contribute to the environment in which
they act. Contrary to the dominant consociational thinking, such
structural factors can open up opportunities for political élites as well
as constrain them. Whilst it is always worth retaining a sceptical line
about the peace process in Northern Ireland, it undoubtedly provided a
contextual background which enabled political élites to move to places
where they had not previously felt able to go. This was not merely
because they thought the peace process was a good idea, but that the
changing structural dynamics that emerged in the course of the process
provided new opportunities. In short then, structure and agency have
gone hand in hand in the peace process in Northern Ireland and therefore the health or ill-health of that process at any given time cannot
merely be explained in terms of what political leaders have decided to
do. As we know, the course of the peace process has been affected by
not only the changing circumstances of Northern Ireland but also
social and political developments across the world. To put it in Dixon's
words, we should develop an approach to democracy which compre-
hends that we need 'to consider the particularity/context of each
conflict, the dispersal of power among the various parties to a conflict
and examine the structural conditions which both constrain and
enable political élites to take steps towards accommodation' (Dixon
2002b: 16).

Conclusion: the paradox of the Belfast Agreement

A positive interpretation of the Belfast Agreement is provided by Wilford, who contends that '[b]olstered by a new regime of human rights and a commitment to a culture of equal opportunity, it has something for (nearly) everyone. Steeped in a pluralist, inclusive philosophy, the Agreement represented an imaginative attempt to move from a condition of zero-sum to positive-sum politics' (Wilford 2001b: 121). Certainly the Agreement promised pluralism and inclusivity but much of this was aspirational rhetoric rather than firm commitment. Ultimately it was concerned with a settlement of political élites and paid only lip service to others in Northern Irish society beyond the realm of formal politics. However, this seems to be almost inevitable; in order to work, the Agreement had to be framed in such a manner as to allow numerous interpretations. This was inevitable precisely because there were more than one or two constituencies from which it had to gain support. At the same time there were two over-arching themes that characterised the Agreement:

> On the one hand, it is a political deal, an elaborate mechanism for the sharing of power, designed to allow two communities with conflicting interests, aspirations and allegiances to coexist with justice and without violence. On the other hand, it is a framework within which the underlying conditions of conflict can be addressed by some form of transformative social process.   (Ruane and Todd 1999: 16–17)

For Ruane and Todd the strategy of the political deal was the aspect that was used to appeal to unionists, whilst the transformative dimension of the Agreement was the interpretation intended to mollify nationalist aspirations. Clearly this was a difficult task to pull off, and this explains why all the signatories had to accept provisions that were anathema to their traditional political strategies and objectives. Of course, these enabled their opponents to point to issues which signified how much they had been forced to relinquish in the political dialogue. For many people then, weighing up the sacrifices that were involved on all sides, the promise of a less violent society was the ultimate reason for supporting the Agreement. Above all, what the Agreement offered the people of Northern Ireland was a greater degree of normality than had hitherto been the case.

Whilst this driving force was fundamental to the support for the Agreement provided in the referendum, it was something of a hostage to fortune. The politicians in support of the Agreement had to talk up their achievements to their potential voters, and in so doing it is quite possible that expectations were raised to unrealistic levels. Ultimately politics can only do so much and the establishment of political institutions was never likely to eradicate the tensions and conflicts that permeate Northern Irish society. What it did suggest was that such tensions would be diluted and in several regards (not least the murder count) that was indeed the case. Whilst not the most inspirational rallying call, the possibility of a substantial decline in violence was to be a major legacy of the Agreement. Nonetheless, with some prescience, Ruane and Todd argued soon after its inception that the Agreement went 'a considerable way to contain conflict' but that it left 'aspects of the conflict of interests and of legitimacy untouched, while other issues in conflict may re-emerge as the Agreement is implemented' (Ruane and Todd 1999: 22). This prediction has been borne out in political developments since 1998 and this demonstrates the contingency of any democratic accord. Given the faltering progress of Northern Irish politics since the Agreement, it is important in the rest of the book to analyse the applicability of other models of liberal democratic theory to ascertain their relevance to the advancement of politics in Northern Ireland.

2
Political Liberalism

The provisions of the Belfast Agreement demonstrate a diverse range of political influences. It attempts to construct a range of institutions that can 'normalise' the Northern Irish polity. As such, those institutional arrangements are idiosyncratic insofar as they reflect the contextual dynamics of Northern Ireland and do not provide a blueprint for resolving political conflicts in other deeply divided societies. In many respects the pragmatic interests or entrenched dogmatism of politicians in Northern Ireland have shaped political developments in the province rather than any deep engagement with political theory. Nonetheless, it is clear that many of the key debates in liberalism and democratic theory have been played out during the peace process. It is the contention in the rest of the book that the example of Northern Ireland throws a sharp light on many of the failings of liberal democratic thinking. It is an extreme example of course, but the divisions and cleavages in Northern Ireland are merely intense manifestations of the kinds of schisms that characterise all contemporary diverse liberal democracies. Thus, the argument is that the problems of liberal democratic theory that are revealed by the analysis of Northern Ireland are also applicable to the extension of the theory in any society. The nature of those problems will vary according to the contextual situations and contingencies of different societies, but the underlying message remains that ideal-type liberal theory is very difficult to translate into political practice. Indeed, political necessity often means that, as in Northern Ireland, politicians are sometimes ahead of the game compared to normative political philosophers. To begin the argument it is important to engage with the work of the most significant liberal political philosopher of the second half of the twentieth century: John Rawls.

Rawls and *Political Liberalism*

The most developed and influential expression of contemporary liberalism can be found in the work of John Rawls, initially in *A Theory of Justice* (1971) and more recently in *Political Liberalism* (1993).[1] The latter builds upon the argument of the former and makes some important differentiations from the earlier position which have substantive ramifications for our understanding of politics in Northern Ireland. The initial Rawlsian argument puts forward a theory of justice which is established in the social contract tradition and hypothesises an imaginary 'Original Position' in which individuals, deprived of key aspects of self-knowledge which could impact upon their life chances (the 'Veil of Ignorance'), would agree to live together according to certain principles of justice. For Rawls, these principles would involve 'justice as fairness' and this would establish basic tenets of liberalism such as state impartiality. Importantly, Rawls did not suggest that this was a purely 'political' view of liberalism, but instead this thesis was presented as a comprehensive set of ideas upon which a liberal consensus could be developed. This argument in *A Theory of Justice* aroused numerous critical responses including the views that Rawls was prejudiced towards liberalism rather than being impartial, that his hypothetical model made too many assumptions about human motivation, and that the scope of his argument was too grand to accommodate the micro-level political diversity of contemporary societies. In short then, Rawls was accused of constructing an asocial model of liberal democracy that reinforced atomistic individualism (Little 2002a).

With the publication of *Political Liberalism* in 1993, Rawls provided a developed account of his thesis that took on board elements of these criticisms and established a different framework through which his position should be addressed. Where the original theory of justice appeared to be a comprehensive moral doctrine, Rawls now focused his attention on articulating a solely 'political' doctrine of liberalism. Thus, he wanted to make a contrast 'between comprehensive philosophical and moral doctrines and conceptions limited to the domain of the political' (Rawls 1996: xvii). In this sense, whereas *A Theory of Justice* envisaged a society in which citizens agreed with the principles of 'justice as fairness' as the most appropriate basis for social organisation, the later position implied that we only need agreement on the basic principles for political engagement. The reasons for this shift are relatively straightforward. Rawlsian liberalism had acquired criticism for the way in which it glossed over the nature of social diversity and the range of moral positions within society in the drive to reinforce liberal principles. In his later work Rawls recognised that not only was there a range of differing moral viewpoints in society, but also, crucially, that these perspectives may be incompatible with one another. For this reason it would be unrealistic to assume that justice as fairness could provide a consensual basis for social organisation; rather, Rawls wanted to put forward the case for a situation in which the nature and procedures of political engagement are agreed by groups of people with different moral viewpoints. Thus he argued that as long as there is a position of 'reasonable pluralism', liberals should construct an 'overlapping consensus' on the form of political engagement between different comprehensive moral viewpoints. In this sense, political liberalism 'assumes that, for political purposes, a plurality of reasonable yet incompatible comprehensive doctrines is the normal result of the exercise of human reason within the framework of the free institutions of a constitutional democratic regime' (Rawls 1996: xviii).

In *Political Liberalism* Rawls recognised that the problem for liberals is not simply in dealing with the fact of pluralism but in dealing with the outcomes of that pluralism. If pluralism is contextualised, then the incompatibility that Rawls identifies becomes more evident. It is not just that there are different moral viewpoints in a pluralistic society, but it is also the case that those perspectives may contradict one another or generate conflict and tension. In this sense, Rawlsian theory is more persuasive when it relinquishes the idea that 'justice as fairness' leads to a well-ordered society. This leads to the following basis of justice:

> the aim of political liberalism is to uncover the conditions of the possibility of a reasonable public basis of justification on fundamental political questions. It should, if possible, set forth the content of such a basis and why it is acceptable. In doing this, it has to distinguish the public point of view from the many nonpublic (not private) points of view. Or, alternatively, it has to characterize the distinction between public reason and the many non-public reasons and to explain why public reason takes the form it does ... Moreover, it has to be impartial ... between the points of view of reasonable comprehensive doctrines.   (Rawls 1996: xxi)

Whilst Rawls managed to circumvent the accusation that he posits liberalism as a comprehensive doctrine for justice in society as a whole, his newer position also generated a number of problems. The key questions which arise from his depiction of political liberalism concern (i) the substance of the overlapping consensus, (ii) the separation of reason into the public and non-public categories, and (iii) the idea of reasonableness which underpins his political model for a pluralistic society. Lastly, questions can also be raised about (iv) the constructivist methodology that Rawls employs whereby rational individuals agree on procedures which will generate the principles of political justice. The latter relies heavily on well-meaning, reasonable individuals engaging with one another according to agreed regulations as 'they have a basis on which public discussion of fundamental political questions can proceed and be reasonably decided, not of course in all cases but we hope in most cases of constitutional essentials and matters of basic justice' (Rawls 1996: xxiii). This appears an unlikely construction in many liberal democracies but in a divided society like Northern Ireland, it looks even less likely. To demonstrate the limitations of the Rawlsian model, I shall address the four issues raised above with reference to the practicalities of Northern Irish politics.

(i)   The substance of the overlapping consensus

Rawls saw the basis of a rational and just politics in the existence of procedures with which everyone in a diverse society could agree. This gave rise to the notion of an 'overlapping consensus' which was defined thus by Rawls:

> In such a consensus, the reasonable doctrines endorse the political conception, each from its own point of view. Social unity is based on a consensus on the political conception; and stability is possible when the doctrines making up the consensus are affirmed by society's politically active citizens and the requirements of justice are not too much in conflict with citizens' essential interests as formed and encouraged by their social arrangements.   (Rawls 1996: 134)

This definition recognises that in a diverse society not everyone will assent to political procedures for the same reason, but rather that these procedures will harness support from different groups for a variety of reasons. In this sense consensus does not imply that everyone agrees for uniform reasons; Rawls was aware that in a society of competing comprehensive doctrines such uniformity is impractical. However, in the interest of social harmony, diverse groups may agree to live together by certain procedures as they offer the least worst situation for their particular comprehensive doctrine. Not surprisingly, Rawls felt that liberal proceduralism provided just such a model that diverse groups could abide by. To some extent the Northern Irish peace process has involved an overlapping consensus of a kind, insofar as the process and the Belfast Agreement have been supported for differing reasons. Thus, some people have gone along with it as it promised a less violent though imperfect society, whereas others regard the process as one where their view of the conflict has prevailed. Of course, the history of Northern Irish politics over the last twenty years has been littered with political initiatives that suggest that neither side has triumphed, and the relative success of the Belfast Agreement is a mark of pragmatic acquiescence to political arrangements short of either side's ideal.

However, to call this state of affairs a 'consensus' is wide of the mark. First of all, substantial numbers of people in Northern Ireland disagree with the peace process and, even though a majority backed the Belfast Agreement in the referendum, arguably support has dissipated to some extent since then. A second reason to suspect the label of consensus when linked to the Northern Irish peace process is the lop-sided nature of support for the Belfast Agreement. Clearly it has harnessed much more support from nationalists than it has from unionists, and the dissipation of support referred to above is much more clearly identifiable in the unionist community.[2] The key point here is that even where elements of an overlapping consensus can be identified at a given time, those overlapping reasons are not set in stone. Thus, for example, those who saw the Belfast Agreement as a vindication of the growing electoral mandate of republicans and as a mechanism to further extend the role of the Republic of Ireland in the North may retain their reasoning for supporting the Agreement. On the contrary, those who provided support on the grounds of a defeat for republicanism or an ending to all forms of violence and terrorism have been more sceptical of the course the process has taken since the Agreement. In this sense any 'overlapping consensus' is subject to change and it is difficult to evaluate the extent of consensus at any given time.

The point is, then, that the prominent position that the idea of 'overlapping consensus' holds in Rawlsian thought can disguise the prevalence of disagreement and conflict and the normality of their place in a democratic system. Thus, with the evidence of Northern Ireland at hand, we can challenge the primacy of an 'overlapping consensus', and argue instead that it is the role of democratic politics to negotiate differences and conflicts. Certainly there needs to be some kind of agreement as to the institutions of a democratic polity, but these institutions must be subject to challenge and must contain the capacity for change. The danger of the idea of an 'overlapping consensus' is that it makes democratic politics too rigid and static and impedes political change because, at a given time, there has been a consensus on particular institutions. Moreover, 'overlapping consensus' contains the potential to silence or marginalise oppositional voices that one could argue are sometimes the lifeblood of a functioning democratic polity. Indeed Rawls recognises that political liberalism requires stability. The danger with this prescriptive model is that potentially it does not leave sufficient space for the requisite dynamism to adapt to changing social and political circumstances. Moreover, the presumption that 'in a constitutional democracy the public conception of justice should be, so far as possible, presented as independent of comprehensive religious, philosophical, and moral doctrines' (Rawls 1996: 144) underestimates the difficulties of divorcing conceptions of justice from comprehensive viewpoints. I will return to the difficulties of this view of justice as free-standing in the next section.

The other aspect of overlapping consensus to discuss is Rawls' view that it needs to sustain stability. For Rawls, the consensus must be capable of withstanding fluctuations in power within a society and this requires a constitutional consensus. This is a difficult demand to make of politics in Northern Ireland where there is not even consensus on the political space where constitutional jurisdiction should lie, let alone agreement about the nature of the institutions that have been put in place. It is important to add that this is not only the case in an unusual society like Northern Ireland, but these kinds of disputes about constitutional arrangements exist in most liberal democracies. For Rawls, a constitutional consensus evolves over time in liberal democracies but again this ignores the fact that in many societies major ruptures are still taking place that demand new constitutional arrangements. In this sense, it appears sensible to regard the provisions of the Belfast Agreement as transitional. Just as the Agreement superseded earlier constitutional arrangements so political developments will ensure that in time it is replaced by something else. This will not be the kind of smooth evolution that Rawls envisages but, instead, is likely to be a process of conflict and contestation just as the path to the Belfast Agreement was characterised by considerable upheaval (and indeed severe violence at times when political break-thoughs were imminent). In this sense, the stability that Rawls aspires to is unlikely to emanate in a changing and divided society like Northern Ireland.

(ii)   Separating public and non-public reason

It is noted above that Rawls might have been overly optimistic in his attempt to separate the idea of political justice from comprehensive moral viewpoints and in this section I will broaden the issue to address this problem in relation to deciding between what is public and non-public. To this end it is worth examining the definition of public reason provided by Rawls:

> Public reason is characteristic of a democratic people: it is the reason of its citizens, of those sharing the status of equal citizenship. The subject of their reason is the good of the public: what the political conception of justice requires of society's basic structure of institutions, and of the purposes and ends they are to serve.   (Rawls 1996: 213)

To summarise then, Rawls regarded public reason as the voice of citizens aimed at the good of the people and finds its expression though the model of political liberalism. As with much of the Rawlsian vision of political liberalism this makes ideal-type assumptions about the composition of liberal society. His vision of the way in which liberal democracies cohere is difficult to operationalise in the context of a complex society like Northern Ireland where, arguably, there is no public reason such is the inherent division within society. This is because the substance of reason in Northern Ireland cannot be easily separated from the comprehensive moral viewpoints held by political participants therein. Likewise, these comprehensive moral viewpoints are often expressed in terms of the good of a particular section of society defined by ethno-national allegiance with little concern for other groups. In this scenario people will be deeply resentful of any claim to public reason that does not correspond with their own comprehensive viewpoint. In other words, the vision of public reason put forward by Rawls relied upon the existence of an overlapping consensus. If, as I argued above, there are problems with the idea of an overlapping consensus in Northern Ireland, then the idea of a public reason that articulates the voice of the people for the good of all is difficult to establish. Lastly, if these aspects of public reason cannot be operationally articulated then the idea of establishing that reason in procedures and institutions is a distant target in societies like Northern Ireland.

To clarify this point it is worth examining the differentiation that Rawls made between public and non-public reason. The initial argument is that by definition public reason is a singular voice whereas he contended that there is a multiplicity of non-public reasons emanating, for example, from churches, pressure groups, professional organisations and so on: 'Nonpublic reasons comprise the many reasons of civil society and belong to what I have called the "background culture," in contrast with the public political culture. These reasons are social, and certainly not private' (Rawls 1996: 220). Rawls therefore contended that reason is inherently social and that there is no such thing as private reason. Thus, the separation that he wanted to apply is between the multiplicity of comprehensive viewpoints that exist within civil society (non-public reason) and the political principles and procedures that imbue government institutions with their authority (public reason). Whereas the former is, by definition, heterogeneous, the latter must be singular and uniform in political liberalism. The content of public reason then, emanates from the fundamental rights and freedoms enshrined in liberal democratic institutions and the equal opportunities they provide to influence the pursuit of the common good. For Rawls, this provided this political conception of justice with democratic legitimacy. However, when we unpack this model we see that Rawls understood that differing political values will result from the existence of a multiplicity of comprehensive moral doctrines in civil society. Where full agreement is not possible, though, a 'vote can be held on a fundamental question as on any other; and if the question is debated by appeal to political values and citizens vote their sincere opinion, the ideal is sustained' (Rawls 1996: 241). Ultimately then, Rawls had to revert to a majoritarian answer where differences occur, although this majoritarianism was dressed up in the language of sincerity and reasonableness. This should not detract us from the liberal democratic orthodoxy of what Rawls was proposing, and simple reversion to majoritarianism where intractable problems arise is not an option in Northern Ireland with its complicated historical baggage.

Rawls was wise not to articulate a clear public-private distinction when it comes to reason but his separation of the public and non-public runs into similar difficulties in Northern Ireland. For example, political institutions there have a limited and fluctuating degree of legitimacy. This changes according to social and political circumstances and the perceived workings of the relevant institutions. The perceptions involved in making judgements about these issues of legitimacy are closely bound up with the comprehensive moral viewpoints that Rawls distinguished from public reason. The distinction is not at all clear in Northern Ireland (or most other liberal democratic societies,

I might add). There is a leap of faith in Rawls' thought whereby the demand for reasonable engagement – or 'the duty of civility' – gives rise to an accepted public reason; in Northern Ireland it is difficult to imagine reasonableness or, even if it was an operative value, whether it would necessarily give rise to a uniform public reason as Rawls envisaged it.

(iii)   What is reasonableness?

Rawls took his inspiration from Kant in defining reasonableness in terms of 'the idea of society as a system of fair cooperation and that its fair terms be reasonable for all to accept is part of its idea of reciprocity' (Rawls 1996: 49–50). In this sense he regarded reasonableness in terms of cooperation between individuals who trust in others to reciprocate and similarly behave in a fair and cooperative manner. This requires individuals to be prepared to sacrifice their own ideals in the interest of reaching a working compromise whereby everyone can remain free and equal, even if their objectives have not been met. For Rawls, unreasonableness was manifest when individuals insist on maintaining their particular position and refuse to honour a cooperative position when it does not suit their particular interests. This position makes enormous claims on people in any society to surrender their ideals in the interest of a greater good or a 'majoritarian consensus'. However, Rawls contended that the representatives of citizens must be rational as well as reasonable insofar as rationality implies a 'unified agent ... with the powers of judgment and deliberation in seeking ends and interests peculiarly its own' (Rawls 1996: 50). In this vein he argued that the reasonable and the rational complement one another. Whilst these two aspects may appear to contradict one another, Rawls noted the reasonable is an attitude or characteristic that appears in the public sphere in a way that the rational does not. The public sphere of political engagement then, is based upon procedures of cooperation whereby rational agents engage with one another on the basis of fair cooperation and accept the outcomes of these procedures. Without the commitment to reasonableness then, the political would resemble a Hobbesian world of conflicting, self-interested rational actors. Importantly though, being reasonable does not entail selfless altruism; rather Rawls expects us to put forward our rational positions. Thus the 'reasonable society is neither a society of saints nor a society of the self-centered' (Rawls 1996: 54).

In many respects the Rawlsian demand for reasonableness is appealing for a deeply divided society like Northern Ireland. It asks people to adopt a cooperative approach and to set aside particularistic interests once agreed political procedures have been followed by political participants. However as a normative foundation for politics in divided societies it appears impractical.[3] The implementation of such a model in Northern Ireland *would* effectively ask political actors to relinquish their objectives in the name of a greater, cooperative good. In some circumstances of lesser importance such an approach may be workable, for example, when provided with choices of economic, social or public policies. However, political cleavages in Northern Ireland are closely bound up with issues of identity, and politics is often defined by the clash of opposing identities. To surrender one's rational interest for many political actors would be to relinquish the very foundations of one's political identity. Reasonableness as Rawls saw it demands too much of any political actor let alone one bound up within the highly conflictual politics of Northern Ireland. This is not to say that we should *encourage* people to be unreasonable but rather to say that the *normative demand for reasonableness* as a foundation of politics is difficult to implement in the context of a divided society. The Rawlsian position under-estimates the difficulties of antagonism, especially where politics is perceived as a zero-sum game whereby any perceived benefit accrued by one community is regarded as a loss by the other. The 'fair cooperation' and 'reasonableness' that Rawls advocates as normative principles are difficult to operationalise in the overarching climate of Northern Irish politics. Moreover, in a society where the legitimacy of various political institutions is questioned by different groups, the idea that procedural agreements require an acceptance of the impartiality of the decision-making process makes even more onerous demands upon an already ambitious conception of how politics should operate in a liberal democracy.

In short, a demand for reasonableness carries more weight if it is not burdened with the conditions that Rawls attaches to it. In divided societies like Northern Ireland reasonableness lies more in agreeing to listen to, debate with, or work with one's opponents rather than give up one's ideals in the name of the greater good. Of course, this is a much more contingent and pragmatic notion of reasonableness but it is all the more workable for that. It is this kind of reasonableness that has inspired the consociational arrangements of Northern Ireland, rather than the highly prescriptive Rawlsian model which attempts to second-guess the procedural outcomes of political engagement before interaction has actually taken place. Nonetheless, it is worth remembering that even this limited understanding of reasonableness has not always been a prevalent feature of recent Northern Irish politics and democratic politics also has to grapple with the issues that arise from people who do not want to adopt a 'reasonable' approach.

(iv) Constructivism

One final element of Rawls' political liberalism that needs to be discussed is his constructivist methodological approach. In *A Theory of Justice* Rawls used the concept of the 'Original Position' as a foundational point on which to establish fair procedures. In this sense Rawls argued that political relations should be established upon the grounds of particular procedures. Thus, the wider model of political liberalism is constructed upon a basic principle of 'justice as fairness'. This idea of constructing political procedures around basic concepts of justice is the main structural underpinning factor behind an 'overlapping consensus':

> The reason such a conception may be the focus of an overlapping consensus of comprehensive doctrines is that it develops the principles of justice from public and shared ideas of society as a fair system of cooperation and of citizens as free and equal by using the principles of their common practical reason. In honouring those principles of justice citizens show themselves autonomous, politically speaking, and this in a way compatible with their reasonable comprehensive doctrines.   (Rawls 1996: 90)

The problem with this standpoint in the context of Northern Ireland is that it tries to establish what it is that political actors should be agreeing about before political engagement has even taken place. This constructivist position, whereby founding principles are enshrined before politics, misunderstands how different political positions will disagree about the substantive meaning of the founding principles and therefore that the foundations and legitimacy of those principles will be uneven between different political actors. Even a commitment to a Rawlsian principle such as equal opportunities is a weak foundation on which to establish political dialogue when there are so many vague understandings of what equal opportunities actually entail. In reality these are political debates, matters of substance, that cannot be blithely asserted as the source of consensus. It is in the judgement of their substance that consensus or dissension will be generated. On top of this, political actors may change their minds over time about the political principles they support and the versions of them that they believe in.

Political constructivists like Rawls limit the scope of political debate by ring-fencing some (often ill-defined) principles around which particip-ants should agree. Not surprisingly these are liberal values in the case of Rawls, and it could be argued that they are prejudiced against non-liberal cultures and groups, such as women, which have often been excluded to a greater or lesser extent in liberal democratic polities.[4]

In Northern Irish politics we could argue that there have been found-ing principles on which political dialogue has been constructed. Thus, for example, it could be argued that involvement in talks was predic-ated upon a commitment to the Mitchell principles of non-violence and an undertaking on the part of all political actors to do all in their power to bring about a cessation of violence. Only on such a basis, the constructivist might argue, could democratic political engagement begin. But when we strip away the layers of this argument some falla-cies begin to emerge. Firstly, on the most practical level, political engagement between some of the key actors was under way long before the first paramilitary ceasefires had been declared which suggests that the basis of dialogue was not *a priori* but rather evolved over the time as a *result* of political engagement rather than as a *precursor* to it. Secondly, it would also be fair to say that much of the language used to bring forth political dialogue was suitably vague for the very reason that there was no agreement as to what a 'cessation of violence' actu-ally was. In this sense the principles for political engagement were deliberately left unclear precisely because there was no agreement on their content. Thirdly, the meaning of non-violence and its physical manifestations has changed over the duration of the peace process; decommissioning was only latterly introduced by some parties to the process rather than being a factor at the beginning of it. Fourthly, the process has continued at faster or slower stages against a backdrop of continuing violence; in this sense the pragmatics of politics have ne-cessarily overridden the fact that events on the ground have not matched the moral principles of non-violence. The point is, then, that all of these matters are issues for political negotiation and resolution (or otherwise). They are not free-floating moral principles agreed by the protagonists that have established a firm basis upon which to 'construct' political justice.

Summarising Rawls

In his later work Rawls has presented political liberalism as practical and political rather than metaphysical. However, the values he appeals to as the *a priori* principles of politics reflect Western liberal democratic political culture. Many critics have been keen to note how these very principles of justice are often the source of tensions and disagreements in deeply divided societies. However, even critics such as Bhikhu Parekh share some ground with Rawls' political liberalism:

> The vital need in such a [deeply divided] society, as indeed in every other, is to get people to talk to one another, encourage the spirit of accommodation at all levels, contain their conflicts, avoid contentious issues especially of a moral kind, and in the meantime maintain peace and order by getting them to agree on a minimum structure of authority.   (Parekh 2000: 85)

Thus, whereas Rawls argued for a multiplicity of comprehensive viewpoints held together by commonly accepted political procedures, Parekh argues for a discursive politics where we try to 'avoid' the complex moral issues which divide societies. As we shall see in coming chapters this gives rise to different but equally troublesome problems to those that emanate from Rawls. Ultimately though, Parekh's main criticism of Rawls is that his political liberalism is actually parasitic upon the earlier comprehensive liberalism of *A Theory of Justice*. Parekh's point is that, because there is a multiplicity of comprehensive moral viewpoints, there cannot be an *a priori* 'overlapping consensus'. Rawls was therefore forced to construct one and the principles he used in his political constructivism are the very ones that characterised his original theory of justice – in itself a comprehensive doctrine as Rawls admitted. In this sense Parekh questions the impartiality of Rawls' political liberalism and argues that his later model prioritises liberalism over other comprehensive doctrines: 'political liberalism is ... not a principled and self-limiting moral position but a political device with a large hidden agenda' (Parekh 2000: 88). Ultimately then, Rawls stands accused of giving insufficient attention to social diversity in privileging liberalism over non-liberal ways of life. To further judge this claim it is necessary to examine the ways in which other liberals have grappled with the politics of difference and the extent to which they succeed where Rawls fails in providing a model that could be applicable to politics in Northern Ireland.

The limits of liberalism

Three authors are usually discussed in the context of liberal approaches to the difficulties caused by a multiplicity of groups trying to live together: Chandran Kukathas, Will Kymlicka and Joseph Raz. These authors have in their different ways attempted to grapple with some of the problems that we have identified in Rawlsian theory both in the early or later manifestations. In so doing, they reinterpret some of the key tenets of liberalism and demonstrate the considerable disparities that exist within the contemporary liberal tradition. To clarify these differences, it is worth examining the ideas of these thinkers and the critical responses they have elicited.

Kukathas (1995, 1998) provides us with a libertarian approach to the existence of social and cultural differences and a strong statement in favour of the primacy of state neutrality when dealing with the varying claims of different groups. Effectively, he contends that contemporary multicultural societies contain a range of groups, associations and cultural attachments but, importantly, that these attachments are private and voluntary. As such he believes that they are not in themselves matters for public concern and therefore should not be subject to state intervention or coercion. This theory has been described as 'cultural laissez-faire' (Crowder 2002: 240). Thus, where cultural attachments are voluntary, the primary role for the state is to establish a basic framework of law and order that enables individuals to make free choices about how to pursue their objectives privately. Clearly this is an argument for an impartial and non-interventionist state. However, several critics have noted problems with this perspective. Festenstein, for example, notes how this generates numerous problems when it comes to cultural practices that contradict the premises of liberal society and implies that several of these cannot, in practice, be tolerated. The only condition that Kukathas demands of nonliberal or illiberal groups is the right of exit for their members.[5] For Festenstein however, this notion of voluntarism is ultimately incoherent: 'if we view voluntary associations as subject to legitimate political constraints, then the rationale for insulating illiberal minorities dissolves: for they, like any other voluntary association, may be subject to legislation' (Festenstein 2000: 73).

Therefore, as we noted in the first chapter, we face the problem of neutrality in any liberal democratic political system which, based as it must be on laws and regulations, is likely to intervene in the lives of voluntary groups in one way or another even though this may be inadvertent. Moreover, Kukathas' model is all the more difficult to construct given the practical problems of the whole conception of state neutrality in societies such as Northern Ireland. Indeed the problem in Northern Ireland is often not even one of trying to grapple with the problem of illiberal groups – the problem is one of conflict between groups which are, at least ostensibly, committed to liberal principles. To an extent, Kukathas recognises the difficulties of achieving impartiality because he bases his view of state neutrality on the idea that the state cannot ensure the neutrality of outcomes of its actions. Instead he contends that its *intentions* should always be neutral, that is, he believes in justificatory rather than consequential neutrality (Little 2002a). Thus, Kukathas believes that in establishing a political system on liberal principles which may reflect various majority traditions and so on, the state is not setting out to benefit one way of life over another. This begs the question, however, of why we should present the state as neutral at all. In other words, it would appear to be more honest to recognise that the state represents a particular view of liberalism and that, whilst it will strive not to intervene in voluntary, associational affairs, the state will expect those groups to live according to the law. Ultimately the libertarian tolerance of illiberal groups that Kukathas supports, founders on its own impracticality.

This point is accepted by liberals such as Barry who agree with Kukathas that toleration should be at the heart of liberalism but disagree with the latter's advocacy of a state that does not intervene to protect individuals from whatever practices their culture may try to enforce upon them. Barry asserts that there is nothing in cultural diversity that should trump basic liberal rights, and on this basis he contends that, contrary to his self-perception, Kukathas is not really a liberal (Barry 2001: 133). Barry thinks that the case for maximal toleration is weak and he takes particular issue with the idea that maximal toleration is conducive to peaceful and harmonious relations between different groups:

> If the only rule governing relations between groups is that they shall not intervene in one another's affairs, it may be said, we have a formula for the elimination of conflict between groups. This is true as far as it goes, but it does not go very far. Peace at any price is a curious universal value when the price is measured in terms of the sacrifice of the liberties and even the lives of an oppressive group. (Barry 2001: 135)

There are obvious connotations to be drawn from this exchange between Kukathas and Barry when it comes to the politics of Northern Ireland. Clearly the peace process in Northern Ireland has been driven to some extent by the 'curious universal value' that peace is the ultimate objective. Barry can be accused of being somewhat flippant in his assumption that some people may value peace so highly that they are prepared – on balance – to override some of the misdemeanours carried out in the past or present by others in order to achieve a relatively harmonious existence. Of course, we could take the very strong moral stance that the actions and beliefs of our opponents are so heinous that we cannot countenance any kind of engagement with them and will therefore hold out for our own desired outcome in the face of prevailing public sentiment. This view has advocates across the divide in Northern Ireland (although particularly in the Unionist community) but they are in a minority on the whole. This is not to say that this view should be marginalised, but rather merely to identify how attitudes towards the importance of peace vary more than the binary viewpoints of Kukathas and Barry would suggest. Importantly, Kukathas' view that cultural differences are relegated to the private voluntary domain cannot prevail in politically divided societies such as Northern Ireland; thus Barry is correct to challenge this view. However, he is wrong to believe that liberal universalism provides the foundational elements of resolving conflicts. Rather, these conflicts will tend to be dealt with in a pragmatic, political manner rather than through hard universal principles.

It is also worth noting that Kukathas is troubled by the idea of 'recognising' minorities or cultures because their identities are not fixed entities. This lack of fixity suggests that cultural identities cannot be clearly identified in such a way that they could be publicly 'recognised'. As such Kukathas implies that attempts at recognition are likely to essentialise minorities and obscure the individual diversity within them. Festenstein argues that this is a weak proposition insofar as '[c]laims for recognition do not rest on the presumption of a pristine condition in which cultures exist and which politics ought to preserve. All they need to do ... is to establish that there is some practice or identity which is valuable and which the state may protect or foster (Festenstein 2000: 75). Thus, Festenstein believes that the idea of recognition does not entail the view that the beliefs of groups or cultures are not contested by their members; therefore it does not follow that recognition is a danger to liberal society in the way that Kukathas suggests. However, the latter is on surer ground in suggesting that the process of recognition may – in certain circumstances – undermine the neutrality of the state. As I have argued though, this is not a sound reason for relinquishing recognition unthinkingly; on the contrary, it appears to be a basis for relinquishing the claims of the state to be neutral in either a justificatory or consequential sense. That recognition may generate potential sources of contestation and dispute is undoubtedly true, and indeed such outcomes might be unavoidable in societies such as Northern Ireland. That this provides a *prima facie* case for jettisoning recognition is much more dubious. Put simply, Northern Ireland is too fragile for the politics of 'indifference' that Kukathas (1998) advocates.

What other alternatives exist, then, to enable liberals to cope with cultural diversity? The most important exponent of a liberal theory of group rights for minorities is the Canadian philosopher Will Kymlicka (1995, 2001) who has rejected crucial aspects of Kukathas' thesis. Nonetheless, like Kukathas, he regards cultures and communities as important factors that contribute to identity and provide a context for the exercise of autonomy. Furthermore, Kymlicka believes that the state should be neutral so that there is equal treatment for all. However, in order for that to be the case, he believes that it needs to treat groups in different ways. In Kymlicka's view then, ideally the state should leave people alone to pursue their own vision of the good, but this requires the state to provide a basic framework and appropriate conditions that will allow people to make a free choice. The practical implications of this thesis are evident to Kymlicka as he has modelled his position according to many of the debates in Canada about the appropriate governance of Quebec. In arguing for separate arrangements for Quebec from the rest of Canada, Kymlicka has constructed a liberal nationalist agenda for the protection of special rights for national minorities.

The context of Quebec is important because Kymlicka does not extend the same rights as national minorities to immigrant groups for example, but focuses instead on indigenous groups who have become a minority in their country as a result of historical processes such as colonialism. Thus, Kymlicka views cultures in a narrow sense as communities that occupy certain territories and share language, history and so forth. As such he thinks that they must provide their members with a meaningful way of life and this implies that membership of a national community is fundamental to humans exercising autonomy (Parekh 2000: 101). Kymlicka's position, then, is much narrower than a general theory of minority group rights and focuses instead on specific minority groups with particular claims against their subordination in territory that is 'theirs'. Moreover, for Kymlicka's thesis, this status is bound up with cultural traditions that provide a meaningful way of life for their members and a history of having formerly been self-governing entities. In this sense, whilst his argument might be pertinent to some parts of the world other than Canada, it is more difficult to operationalise in others (of which Northern Ireland is a case in point). The applicability of Kymlicka's perspective depends upon the existence of clear territorial boundaries and coherent minority groups within them to which group rights can be extended. Certainly, in the case of Northern Ireland, the question of territory is highly contested, and consequently, who constitutes the national minority is equally contentious.

Not surprisingly Kymlicka's controversial thesis has generated considerable criticism. Festenstein (2000), for example, criticises him for eliding the case for protecting a cultural network and political self-determination. Where Kymlicka contends that it is through political self-determination that a national minority is able to enjoy cultural autonomy and that culture is able to develop and change according to the wishes of its members, Festenstein argues that it is quite possible for cultures of minorities to be protected without separate political institutions for those groups. However, Kymlicka wants to avoid the reification of cultures by allocating them specific fixed rights because he recognises that cultures are dynamic and do change and develop over the course of time. In this vein he does not believe that it is possible to make a definitive statement of the rights that national minorities should have. Instead he argues that they should have separate political institutions and rights in which the claims of national minorities can be played out. However, the problems of static rights are not solved by Kymlicka's advocacy of political self-determination. Obviously he is aware that the provisions for Quebec have caused much unrest in the rest of Canada. Thus, the fact that national minorities may be granted self-determination does not do away with conflicts both within those new polities and between them and others. Indeed, one might argue that in a bastardised form this is precisely what generated the problems that have blighted Northern Ireland since its inception through the 1920 Government of Ireland Act.

Ultimately Kymlicka wants national majorities to act in a benign fashion when it comes to conflicts with minorities and forgo their choices in order to protect the cultures of minorities. This is where Kymlicka takes a leap of faith. He assumes a reasonableness on the part of majority and minority actors within a given nation and a willingness to relinquish self-interest. This is asking a lot of disputatious groups, especially where their conflict is deep-seated, but for Kymlicka, it is necessary to remedy the structural disadvantage that comes with being part of a minority. In terms of the politics of Northern Ireland, this theory is not capable of dealing with the fact that there is considerable dispute over who is the majority and minority which is bound up with conflict over the very territory which the conflicting groups occupy. Moreover, there is little evidence of either side possessing a disposition to forgo what they want to do in order to protect the culture of the other group (the annual conflict over the Orange Order march at Drumcree is testimony to this inescapable fact).[6] Thus, multiculturalists such as Parekh have argued that Kymlicka is not interested in cultural diversity in the sense that different cultures have to engage with and learn from one another. Instead the latter provides a framework for the separation of conflicting groups. This makes multiculturalist commentators sceptical about whether non-liberal groups will adopt the kind of political approach that Kymlicka advocates:

> He [Kymlicka] shows why human beings need a stable culture but not why they need access to other cultures. His main argument for cultural diversity is that it increases our range of options. This implies that other cultures are important to us only as possible objects of choice and have no value or lose it when no longer options for us ... Even in Kymlicka's own terms, his argument for cultural diversity amounts to little.   (Parekh 2000: 108)

Thus the limitations of Kymlicka's thesis in the context of Northern Ireland become evident. The 'two communities' there are perfectly capable of realising their cultures in relative isolation from one another – the political problem that faces Northern Ireland is how they are to live alongside each other. Kymlicka's approach would only further separate the two major groups that live in Northern Ireland and the nature of political cleavages there make the establishment of distinctive political rights and institutions an unlikely proposition.

There are other implications of Kymlicka's thesis that Festenstein (2000: 77–82) objects to. The latter wants to know why we shouldn't criticise cultural practices of different groups and at least interrogate them to assess whether there are reasonable grounds for separate political institutions. The implication from Kymlicka's argument is that if a group meets his criteria of a national minority, then it deserves self-determination. At the same time, however, it should be noted that he believes that groups which are beneficiaries of multicultural liberal policies should try to be internally liberal as a result. Against this argument, Festenstein rejects the idea that certain activities should be protected by the allocation of rights on the basis that they are cultural practices. Obviously the cultural practices of minority groups might well contradict the ideas and practices of the national majority. This does not mean that those activities should not be protected or even that there should not be rights to engage in those activities. What Festenstein objects to is Kymlicka's assumption that cultural practices of national minorities should automatically be accorded the status of rights; this should be a matter of political dialogue rather than a *fait accompli*. The other key interjection made by Festenstein is that the recognition of rights of minority groups may lead to considerable inconvenience for others in any given society. In such a scenario the adjudication of those rights claims should again be the stuff of politics and it will be the outcome of political negotiations about how con-flicting groups are to deal with the tensions between their conflicting viewpoints. Similarly, Yack contends that cultural minorities 'may be *right* in many circumstances to seek special privileges or even form their own self-governing community. But that does not mean they *have a right* to these things … Every case involves negotiations and compromises that reflect the contingent political conditions within which the case arises' (Yack 2002: 115).

Kymlicka constructs an argument around a very limited notion of a culture, that is, 'an intergenerational community, more or less institu-tionally complete, occupying a given territory or homeland, sharing a distinct language and history' (Kymlicka 1995: 18). As such, the wider applicability of his thesis outside of multinational states (which he dif-ferentiates from polyethnic societies) is severely limited as it is only directed at those with two or more nations, peoples or cultures (as defined above) within them. It certainly does not provide us with a comprehensive liberal theory of group rights that could be applied in Northern Ireland. In the North the very territory at stake is a source of basic disagreement and there is no distinctiveness in terms of language in the sense that he means (where the Irish language may be a source of contention, the vast majority of nationalists conduct their everyday life in English and would continue to do so even if there was radical constitutional change). That said, this kind of theory has been much more influential in the politics of Northern Ireland than the libertarian approach of Kukathas, but both suffer from the burdens imposed upon them by liberal theories of state neutrality.

A third perspective within liberal theories of multiculturalism has been provided by Raz (1986, 1994). The main reason for examining Raz's work in relation to Northern Ireland is that it is predicated upon the idea of value pluralism. In other words, he constructs his position around the basic premise that there are a range of different views as to the nature of the good society. Obviously this corresponds with the lived experience of Northern Ireland. These different perspectives contribute to the nature of any given society and provide the context in which individuals and their viewpoints are shaped. For Raz, the ideal liberal society is one that prioritises autonomy and thus enables the individuals to be the part-authors of their lives (although inevitably the society around us will provide the context in which we exercise our choices). Thus there are two central features of Raz's multicultural liberal argument which I will deal with in turn: the priority of autonomy and the existence of value pluralism.

Many analysts of multiculturalism have criticised Raz's view that autonomy is the ideal objective of liberal societies. Parekh, for example, interprets Raz's view of autonomy as 'a continuous process of self-creation by means of small and large decisions concerning significant areas of one's life ... To be autonomous is to be part-author of one's life and control its direction and development at least to some degree' (Parekh 2000: 92). However, Parekh contends that autonomy is a value that is largely promoted by Western cultures and does not hold such a central position in other parts of the world. Similarly, Festenstein points out that autonomy is not a value that is cherished in some cultures and therefore that it is 'a controversial ethical criterion' (Festenstein 2000: 84). The point raised by Parekh and Festenstein is that the concern and prioritisation of autonomy in Raz's thought is a matter of personal preference (no doubt partially conditioned by the political context in which Raz has formulated his ideas). In other words, they question whether the Western liberal value of autonomy has a wider validity or meaning for other cultures. This is a very serious objection because in many societies the fact of the politics of multiculturalism is concerned with how we construct institutions and relations between liberal and non-liberal groups. The main thrust of Raz's argument in *The Morality of Freedom* (1986) was that we should try to tolerate minority groups, even if they are non-liberal, as long as their values and practices do not throw up serious difficulties for the functioning of the rest of society. However, where their ways of life were not viable in the broader social context, Raz believed that they should be assimilated with the dominant culture (Parekh 2000: 94). Not surprisingly then, these views which remain firmly within the dominant liberal paradigm have been heavily criticised by advocates of multiculturalism, such as Parekh, who reject their assimilationist undertones.

In this early work, Raz's perfectionist liberalism focused on the priority of autonomy. This is problematic because if 'value-pluralism is true, personal autonomy cannot be accorded priority over other values' (Gray 2000: 99). In other words, the acceptance of a multiplicity of views of the good life makes it difficult to establish a foundation upon which autonomy can be prioritised if it is not valued by all cultures. However, Parekh has noted that in *Ethics in the Public Domain* (1994) Raz seems more directly concerned with the issues of a liberal theory of multiculturalism and the idea of value pluralism. Rather than relying on a basic assimilation when conflicts occur, Raz recognises the benefits that are derived by individuals from their cultural membership in the sense that they form the backdrop to our autonomous choices. Nonetheless, this leads him to make strong demands of minority groups insofar as 'nonliberal cultures should allow their members full development and self-expression, give them adequate opportunities for participation in the wider economic and political life, grant them the right of exit, and should not oppress them' (Parekh 2000: 96–7). Ultimately, for Parekh, whilst this is an improvement on Raz's earlier position, it still reflects a desire to impose liberal constraints on the self-organisation of non-liberal groups. Parekh's multiculturalism on the other hand 'requires the dominant culture to curtail its assimilationist zeal, welcome differences, makes space for others to flourish, create a climate in which they do not feel under siege or denigrated, and be willing when necessary to allocate a greater share of public resources to them' (Parekh 2000: 98).

Whilst I will discuss value pluralism in more detail in Chapter Seven, it seems that Parekh is too optimistic here. Even if dominant groups did adopt this benign view towards minority cultures, this does not mean that serious conflicts would not ensue. Importantly, different minority cultures may come into serious conflicts with one another even if a majority is prepared to either overlook or recognise differing cultural practices. Where Raz wants to build upon value pluralism, there is a danger that theorists of multiculturalism fail to recognise the depth of disputes that may emerge from such a pluralistic approach. Certainly Parekh recognises that conflict may occur, but he does not grapple with the possibility that those confrontations may be irreconcilable. His criticism of Raz may have substance: that is, that in such conflicts, dominant cultures and groups with social power often prevail and therefore that Raz's liberalism does not provide us with a way to navigate conflicts (Parekh 2000: 97). However, it is questionable whether Parekh does so either – he acknowledges that cultures may conflict but he only really talks about their relationship with dominant groups rather than with each other. In this sense it is worth returning to Festenstein's analysis for he at least realises that, despite his belief that Raz's thesis ignores the importance of support for particular communities through legislation, Raz does have a stronger argument than procedural liberalism. Raz's later theory develops a deeply political liberalism, whereby instead of resorting to abstract principles of political engagement, we must deal with difficult cases and conflicts on a case by case basis. In other words it argues for pragmatic political engagement over multicultural conflicts, rather than an abstract liberal procedure that is likely to break down when placed in the context of the untidy conflicts of the real world.

What then does Raz's viewpoint have to offer the political analysis of Northern Ireland? Critics like Gray are correct to argue that it is difficult to reconcile value pluralism with the prioritisation of personal autonomy. Likewise, I would agree with Festenstein and Parekh that the prioritisation of autonomy reflects a Western standpoint that may be at odds with the beliefs of non-liberal groupings. In dealing with the politics of Northern Ireland, this has a direct bearing on how a mature polity might deal with the variety of cultures that live there. However, in coupling the concern for individual autonomy with a realisation of the importance of social context and a recognition of value pluralism, Raz's approach may offer more than the libertarian approach of Kukathas or the narrow context in which Kymlicka's thesis might be applicable. Of course, the latter has more to tell us about institutional design but the strength of Raz's approach is in recognising that there are not ideal cross-cultural institutional arrangements that can make a society like Northern Ireland cohere. That objective must be deeply political and will involve a process of (sometimes imperfect) political engagement rather than a pre-determined liberal procedure. Unfortunately, in many respects the bigger challenge of a genuine multiculturalism in Northern Ireland cannot even begin to emerge until a method has been found to manage the immediate conflicts that prevail in the province. Whilst they cannot be 'solved', a process of managing them may allow debates on the issues of multiculturalism to develop in a more meaningful sense.

Conclusion

Before moving on to discuss the recent debate on multiculturalism in the work of Parekh in the next chapter, it is worth summing up the objections that have been raised against the main contemporary liberal approaches to the fact of multiculturalism. These are summed up by Parekh as comprising three main problems (2000: 110–12). Firstly, he argues that they prioritise liberal values at the expense of the values in other cultures and therefore that their perspectives are not neutral. Secondly, he contends that liberals 'absolutize' liberalism because their equation of non-liberalism with illiberalism is not morally or culturally pluralistic. Thirdly, Parekh argues that the treatment of nonliberal ways of life in liberalism is ultimately dealt with by insisting that they will be tolerated as long as they accept the minimal version of liberal principles. In other words, nonliberals must accept liberalism. Parekh rightly recognises that the great fallacy at the root of these presumptions is the idea that liberal principles are (or can be) consensually agreed upon. Moreover, he insists that the idea that there is some kind of universal liberal way of life ignores many of the complexities of modern societies and the fact that most liberal societies are organised around numerous structures and regulations, some of which are liberal and some of which are not. In this sense Parekh is arguing against an essentialisation of liberalism. Thus, to:

> call contemporary western society liberal is not only to homogenize and oversimplify it but also to give liberals a moral and cultural monopoly of it and treat the rest as illegitimate and troublesome intruders. When one then goes on to say that because the society is liberal, it should or should not allow certain practices or be guided by certain principles, one is guilty of bad logic and even bad faith. (Parekh 2000: 112)

Following these assertions it is important to interrogate the arguments put forward by Parekh to assess whether contemporary multiculturalist theory provides us with more useful tools for analysing the development of democratic politics in Northern Ireland than is the case with contemporary liberal theories of multiculturalism.

3
Multiculturalism and the Politics of Difference

One of the primary accusations levelled at the kind of universalism that underpins political liberalism is that it is 'difference-blind'. This criticism takes many different forms but is often associated with feminists (Young 1990) and leftist communitarians (Taylor 1992).[1] However, in recent years it has also been clear that many theorists within the liberal tradition like Kymlicka, Kukathas and Raz have also been concerned with the capacity of liberalism to provide the mechanisms that allow diverse societies to cohere, whilst still remaining true to such values as freedom, equality, toleration and diversity. More recently still, the debate over liberalism and social diversity has been clarified in the literature over the political implications of multiculturalism. The two key contributions to this debate have been the re-working of multicultural politics by Bhikhu Parekh (2000) and the refutation of these arguments from a universalist liberal perspective by Barry (2001). This chapter will examine the applicability of these theories to the political situation in Northern Ireland and assess the value of multiculturalism to the rethinking of democracy there.

At the outset it may be useful to ground our discussion in a working definition of multiculturalism and here the work of Matthew Festenstein is instructive. He describes the politics of multiculturalism as concerned with 'the way in which cultural and ethnic differentiation may be accommodated in social, political and economic arrangements' and, in particular, his focus is on 'the sphere of evaluative or normative inquiry into how the politics of culturally plural societies ought to be conducted' (Festenstein 2000: 70). It is clear how such a model might be seen as relevant to politics in Northern Ireland given the social divisions that prevail there and the way that discussions of those divisions are frequently presented in cultural or ethnic terms.

However, it is worth noting how such an approach also presents dangers in the analysis of politics in Northern Ireland such as the potential for the essentialisation of culture as the primary social division when, in fact, it is only one of many sources of stratification. The problem emerges that, if culture is to be regarded as the major division in contemporary societies, various other types of division may be presented as cultural in order to invest them with a divisive power. Conflicts and divisions in Northern Ireland emanate from a multiplicity of sources including culture, nationality, class, gender and so on, and to view all of these categories as cultural may obfuscate rather than clarify the issues in hand.

Apart from overt discussions of multiculturalism, the pertinent issues are also frequently discussed in terms of the politics of difference or recognition. A key theorist of recognition is Charles Taylor, who contends that identity is a central concern of contemporary politics in diverse societies and that our identities are inherently bound up with the ways in which we are perceived by those within and outside of the groups that we belong to. In this sense, for Taylor, it is not sufficient for our well-being to hold identities as members of groups because the nature of that identity may well be misrecognised or misunderstood by others. In other words, the politics of recognition is concerned with the need to spread understanding between different groups so that there is a greater awareness of what it means to be part of groups of which we are not members. Taylor contends that the reason for this is that misrecognition can be seriously damaging to the social fabric generally and misrepresented individuals in particular: '[n]onrecognition or misrecognition can inflict harm, can be a form of oppression, imprisoning someone in a false, distorted, and reduced mode of being' (Taylor 1992: 25). Again, it should be apparent why this is relevant to Northern Ireland for it implies that not only do the groups there have to learn how to live alongside one another but they also need to strive for greater mutual understanding. This makes much greater demands on people in Northern Ireland than orthodox liberalism because it implies that a future democratic politics is not merely a matter of learning how to rub along with one another, but instead requires a more substantive engagement with those with whom we disagree.

It is debatable how much this moves away from the universalism that normally characterises liberalism. In a sense it is not asking here for differential standards of treatment for divergent individuals or groups, but is instead suggesting a mutual level of engagement with one another that implies rights and burdens for all of us. Thus, Taylor argues that the politics of difference has 'a universal potential ... at its basis, namely, the potential for forming and defining one's own identity, as an individual, and also as a culture. This potentiality must be respected equally in everyone' (Taylor 1992: 42). The difference here then is that the universalism at the heart of the project rests upon a recognition that different groups and individuals will construct their identities in different ways and that it is quite right that they should be able to do so. Taking his previous point on board, not only should groups be able to form their own identities, but those of us who are not members of those groups have a responsibility to recognise the identity that is constructed rather than basing our views on our own partial prejudices about others. In this sense, even if there is a universalism at the heart of the politics of difference it is rather different from that at the heart of Rawlsian liberalism. Advocates of the politics of difference such as Taylor are keen to point to the ways in which 'difference-blind' political liberalism can only countenance diversity in the private sphere and try to 'relegate the contentious differences to a sphere that does not impinge on the political' (Taylor 1992: 62).[2] This is a frequent accusation levelled against Rawls and his followers but one that has fundamental ramifications for our understanding of diversity and the ways in which we construct 'the political'.

Against the precepts of Rawlsian proceduralism, Taylor argues that liberalism cannot claim cultural neutrality and it will always involve drawing the line somewhere with regard to inclusion, participation and so on. Importantly he states that '[s]ubstantive distinctions of this kind are inescapable in politics ...' (Taylor 1992: 62). Of course, this will lead to controversies in contemporary multicultural societies where many members will hold beliefs that emanate from cultures somewhat different from the foundations of liberal democracies. A further problem for this position comes with societies such as Northern Ireland where there may be a fair degree of agreement on the basic premises of liberal democracy, but considerable disagreement on how those principles should manifest themselves in political practice. How then does this scenario fit into the politics of recognition? Taylor says that 'the further demand we are looking at here is that we all *recognize* the equal value of different cultures; that we not only let them survive, but acknowledge their *worth*' (Taylor 1992: 64). Even if we accept this perspective (and as we will see commentators such as Barry disagree with the idea of cultures having equal worth), it does not provide us with a clear programme of action for deeply divided societies. Instead, in common with many advocates of the politics of difference, Taylor is talking about the inability of political structures alone to foster a spirit of recognition and points instead to the need to reform educational curricula to involve cross-cultural education to make us all more aware of the cultures of others. In the context of Northern Ireland this would demand an end to the separate education of Catholic and Protestant children. This is a commonplace view on the problems of Northern Ireland but none the weaker for that. However, such a sentiment frequently founders on the rocks of the powerful role of the major churches in everyday life in Northern Ireland and the intransigence of parents who want to see their children educated in the ways that have been traditional there.

Having noted this difficulty, however, it is worth exploring what Taylor believes can be achieved by educational reform and cross-cultural curricula. He articulates a desire for us to see recognition in terms of an engagement of different cultures. This he sees as a means of enabling us to interrogate our beliefs in comparison with those of others. Even if we end up reinforcing our already held views, Taylor believes that benefits accrue from a process in which we have encountered the views of others and been forced to evaluate our own beliefs. In this sense Taylor does not want to see different groups pragmatically agreeing not to bother with each other; instead, he believes that genuine recognition only comes with a substantive engagement between conflicting groups. Thus, he is deeply sceptical of patronising and condescending awards of value to cultures different from our own because they will frequently be based upon misunderstandings or misrepresentations of what those groups stand for. Indeed they are likely to homogenise different cultures and the diversity within them due to preconceived misconceptions. Taylor's conclusion is that we must engage with people on the basis of the *presumption* of equal worth, even though when we come to interrogate the views of others, there may be much with which we disagree:

> merely on the human level, one could argue that it is reasonable to suppose that cultures that have provided the horizon of meaning for large numbers of human beings, of diverse characters and temperaments, over a long period of time ... are almost certain to have something that deserves our admiration and respect, even if it is accompanied by much that we have to abhor and reject. Perhaps one could put it another way: it would take a supreme arrogance to discount this possibility *a priori*.   (Taylor 1992: 73)

Ostensibly Taylor's thesis on recognition does not ask too much of cultures in suggesting that they must engage with others in such a way as to presume that each culture will contain something of worth. Recognition in this sense is not too strenuous a demand and seems a reasonable basis on which to enter cross-cultural dialogue. However, many societies are clearly permeated by conflicts which make this demand for recognition more problematic. Northern Ireland is one such society insofar as the political divisions and conflicts are often closely bound up with cultural practices and this makes the normative position where different cultures recognise the worth of each other difficult to achieve. Moreover, the extent of recognition is difficult to measure and recognition in itself does not provide us with a model of how political institutions that guarantee such recognition are to be organised. As such, the implications of recognition for institutional design remain open, but as we shall see later in the book, this kind of thinking has been reflected in recent Northern Irish politics, particularly in the Belfast Agreement. Nonetheless, it is in trying to put demands for recognition into practice that we encounter some of the problems of such a model when it comes to institutional design in deeply divided societies such as Northern Ireland. One such attempt to reconcile a theory of recognition with the practicalities of diverse societies has been the emergence of the politics of multiculturalism.

Bhikhu Parekh's theory of multiculturalism: human beings and culture

The debate over multiculturalism has been most notably advanced in the recent exchange between Bhikhu Parekh and Brian Barry. In this section I will examine the ideas put forward by Parekh in *Rethinking Multiculturalism* (2000). This should clarify contemporary arguments on cultural diversity and explain the critique of the liberal positions outlined above. Parekh's thesis is wide-ranging, but essentially sets out a new multicultural theory that is founded upon liberalism but rejects the dominant ways in which liberalism has tried to deal with issues of cultural diversity. He begins his contribution by rejecting different forms of monism that have merged in the history of political thought from the rationalist monism of classical Greek theories of democracy (Plato and Aristotle), through the theological monism of Christian philosophy (Augustine and Aquinas), and the 'regulative monism' of classical liberalism (Locke and Mill). Parekh argues that monism of whatever variant is problematic because it makes assumptions about human nature and implies that this can be realised only through following the course of one way of life. Here we see a tension in Parekh's thought because, whilst he is right to be sceptical about universalist theories of human nature, he runs the risk of lapsing into cultural determinism when he contends that since 'cultures mediate and reconstitute human nature in their own different ways, no vision of the good life can be based on an abstract conception of human nature alone' (Parekh 2000: 47). Nonetheless, in his rejection of moral monism he makes a case for recognising that the idea of a universal human nature is likely to generate considerable opposition from different cultures (and indeed other groups that he would not deem to be 'cultures').

Parekh is also critical of the development of pluralist political thought especially as it emerged in the work of Vico, Montesquieu and Herder. Here he accuses Vico of understanding cultural diversity but wrongly seeing societies as integrated and harmonious; Montesquieu is criticised for Eurocentrism; Herder is chastised for identifying diversity between nations but for seeing those nations as cohesive and prescriptive of identity. Parekh's critique of the latter is particularly pertinent to our considerations here because Herder constructs a romantic cultural nationalism that clearly resonates with some commentators on Northern Ireland today. The problem for Parekh with Herder is that '[w]hile appreciating the diversity *of* cultures, Herder is antipathetic to that *within* it ... He cherishes a culturally plural *world* but not a culturally plural *society*' (Parekh 2000: 73). Thus, Parekh values pluralist accounts for their challenge to moral monism but notes the existence of a number of fallacies in the pluralist position. These include the view of cultures as holistic, the assumption that cultures are distinct and self-contained, the rather static understanding of cultures, and the tendency to ethnicise cultures by seeing culture and community as homogeneous. Moreover, Parekh accuses pluralists of adopting a conservative, closed attitude to the development of cultures, of being deterministic in seeing cultures as collective actors, and of failing to establish the important links between culture and other social, political and economic structures. Thus, he contends that the 'task facing a theorist of cultural diversity is how to account for the importance, power and coherence of culture without committing these and related errors' (Parekh 2000: 79). When we add these criticisms to Parekh's rejection of Rawlsian political liberalism and the multicultural liberals in the previous chapter, it is clear that he constructs a distinctive position on cultural diversity and political liberalism.

Before setting out the political implications of Parekh's multiculturalism, it is worth examining his conceptualisations of human beings and culture as they provide the foundation of his political position. Parekh's theory of human beings is constructed around a minimalist theory of human nature which he describes as 'a complex whole composed of related but often dissonant capacities and dispositions which cannot all be reduced to a single master or foundational capacity, desire or disposition' (Parekh 2000: 116). Thus, he rejects internal and ahistorical naturalist views and argues that a number of external and environmental features impact on humans. This is not a constraining view of human nature whereby we are imprisoned within a preordained condition, but one that recognises that human nature is not 'natural' as it is traditionally conceived in naturalist theory but is instead a product of human struggle: 'It is natural in the sense that it is acquired by virtue of belonging to the human species, but it is not natural in the sense that it is a result of the efforts of the species itself and forms part of its process of self-creation' (Parekh 2000: 119). This begs the question of why Parekh bothers to use the terminology of human nature at all for he is clearly deviating from the common understanding of human nature. He is aware of this as he refers to the way in which appeals to human nature are assumed to have normative advantages because of their grounding in 'nature' which sometimes gives them a moral finality. However, what seems more important than this point is the frustrating absence of real justification by theorists of human nature as to why, even if such a thing is identifiable, that it should form the basis of politics. Moreover, such apolitical posturing is positively dangerous when it comes to societies such as Northern Ireland where uncritical assumptions about human nature could be used to provide justification of violent political activities.

The reason that Parekh employs a discourse of human nature is instead deeply political. He is concerned that attempts to construct a multicultural society are hindered by appeals to human nature in which dominant Western values are cherished as those that are 'natural'. In political theory this has been manifest in the way the values of the West have been universalised at the expense of behaviours, practices and ways of life elsewhere in the world. To challenge this reification of Western conceptions, Parekh advocates a cross-cultural dialogue to enable broader understanding and respect between different cultures. However, he does not explain how we should act when these cross-cultural dialogues generate further conflict and dispute and he cannot tell us how to decide if people are behaving reasonably in these dialogues. Instead, his arguments about cross-cultural dialogue and its potential for the rethinking of human nature seem somewhat optimistic and impractical as a means of solving deep-rooted conflicts. A more substantive approach to these debates may well be to reject theories of human nature altogether on the grounds that they fail to understand human differences and do not provide any adequate reasoning as to why politics should be constructed around naturalism. In other words, political judgements about respect, worth and value should be based upon the grounds of moral principles. Parekh seems to realise this much in arguing that human beings 'have worth because we have good reasons to value their capacities and achievements. Human worth is not a natural property like eyes and ears but something we confer upon ourselves, and hence a moral practice' (Parekh 2000: 130). The reasons why Parekh chooses to adopt a minimalist theory of human nature as a political implement remains unclear unless his own charge against naturalists can also be levelled at him: that is, that he maintains the concept of human nature because it is regarded as a powerful normative weapon to vindicate values and practices that are anything but universal.

The second foundation of Parekh's multiculturalism is his perspective on the meaning and importance of culture, and this appears to be considerably more substantive than that on human nature. For this reason it is worth citing Parekh's definition of culture:

> Culture is a historically created system of meaning and significance or, what comes to the same thing, a system of beliefs and practices in terms of which a group of human beings understand, regulate and structure their individual and collective lives. It is a way of both understanding and organizing human life. (Parekh 2000: 143)

From this baseline he contends that we must recognise the internal variations within cultures and the ways in which different cultures will construct moral positions. Thus, morality is culturally embedded but, using Parekh's own logic, we should also say that the variations within a culture will lead to different moral positions *within* as well as *between* cultures. What this point should demonstrate is that, whilst Parekh expresses numerous caveats about understanding variations within communities, he also lapses at times into rather holistic interpretations of cultures. Indeed, the underlying problem in Parekh's argument is the tendency to essentialise cultures as the primary form of social difference and to overlook the importance of other forms of social stratification.

Thus, whilst Parekh's recognition of diversity within communities is welcome, it is not necessarily consistent. Take the following statements: '[b]elonging to a cultural community, then, admits of much variation and is not homogeneous in nature. Some members might share all of its beliefs and others only a few, and the former might differ in their interpretations of or degrees of allegiance to these' (Parekh 2000: 148) and '[s]ince a culture's system of beliefs and practices, the locus of its identity, is constantly contested, subject to change, and does not form a coherent whole, its identity is never settled, static and free of ambiguity' (Parekh 2000: 148). From this he would appear to have a clear position on this issue. However, he goes on to state that disagreements within a culture are manageable because their members actually agree on most things. There is then a broad consensus and change is slow. This presents cultures as more cohesive than the earlier statements and neglects much of the dynamism in cultures. Thus, whilst he understands that we can be critical towards the cultures we belong to, the understanding that we may belong to a multiplicity of different cultures or sub-cultures appears to be lacking. Evidence of this appears in his statement that people who are 'culturally footloose' run the risk of becoming 'shallow and fragile'. At this point his argument looks suspiciously conservative, especially when he argues that because such a lifestyle lacks 'historical depth and traditions, it cannot inspire and guide choices, fails to provide a moral compass and stability, and encourages the habit of hopping from culture to culture to avoid the rigour and discipline of any one of them (Parekh 2000: 150). This is a rather wholesome interpretation of culture which ignores the problematic attitudes and beliefs which might also develop in the name of culture. Moreover, it appears to be a rather blasé dismissal of eclectic, critical individuals who do not want their beliefs and practices to be defined by a single culture. Not surprisingly, then, Parekh is equally critical of postmodern approaches, especially those that stress that individuals are members of several cultures and indeed that their personal values may be internally contradictory:

> there is a tendency to romanticize this approach to culture, based on the mistaken belief that all boundaries are reactionary and crippling and their transgressions a symbol of creativity and freedom. Boundaries structure our lives, give us a sense of rootedness and identity, and provide a point of reference.   (Parekh 2000: 150)

The essentialisation of culture at the root of Parekh's argument becomes clearer when he talks about culture in relation to community. In recognising that all cultural communities are characterised by contestation and change, he asserts that:

> since every culture is the culture of a particular group of people, its creator and historical bearer, all cultures tend to have an ethnic basis ... When we talk of a cultural community, we ... refer to a community based on a shared culture irrespective of how the latter is derived and what else it shares in common.   (Parekh 2000: 154)

Parekh appears to replicate the problems of theorists of human nature. He assumes the importance of culture and then goes on to construct the cultural community as the basic building block of diverse contemporary societies.[3] But, like any community, cultures are riven by conflict and dispute. Whilst Parekh recognises internal differences, he is still able to assert that our culture is what provides meaning in the world. But he never satisfactorily explains why culture is going to provide greater meaning or stability than a sexual, sporting, local or religious community for a particular individual. If it were the case that cultural communities were superior to other forms of community, then why would people leave them and live their lives quite happily without joining a different cultural community? Or perhaps, following Parekh, they are footloose, shallow and fragile?

There is then an uncomfortable tension in Parekh's theory between his rejection of homogeneity and cultural determinism on one hand, and the wholesome view of culture that he presents on the other. He rightly recognises that cultures are not cohesive and that their members are not 'passive and pliant'. As such, we are capable of adopting a critical stance towards our culture (although Parekh believes this varies between cultures) and indeed it is possible that we might reject our culture if we have been ill-served by it. This appears to be a coherent rejection of cultural determinism, but Parekh goes on to construct a somewhat dubious argument about the benefits of loyalty to culture because of 'its profound contribution to our lives and also perhaps because of its universal value'. Thus, whilst he allows us to challenge the values and practices of the cultures we belong to, he simultaneously contends that our culture has 'at least some claim on our loyalty...' (Parekh 2000: 160). The problem with this hypothesis comes when we try to operationalise this conception in practice. Although cultures can and do change, the idea of loyalty to culture is a powerful weapon for cultural conservatives who can defend the orthodoxy on the basis of loyalism and tradition. Those who may seek to change the values or practices of a culture can face intractable obstacles constructed by those who oppose any kind of change. Parekh tries to circumvent this criticism by stating that '[l]oyalty to a culture also involves a duty to explore, deepen and enrich its resources and remove its defects ... To love one's culture is to wish it well, and that involves criticizing and removing its blemishes' (Parekh 2000: 160), and argues that conservatives should not override reformers in matters of culture because cultures have no essence to conserve (Parekh 2000: 175). But, of course, this is precisely what tends not to happen in the real world, especially when matters of cultural practice are a source of conflict with other communities. The various marching controversies in Northern Ireland are an example of how tradition is used to reinforce those cultural practices which are most resisted by opposing cultural groups. The common history that Parekh lauds as having a claim on our loyalty is precisely that which is appealed to in order to let one community have its way over the other.

A further danger in Parekh's thesis about culture and community is that different members of the same cultural community may be treated inequitably. Parekh differentiates between membership of a cultural community and voluntary associations such as clubs and pressure groups because the latter are frequently instrumental in nature. Thus, he argues that where associations and groups are joined on an elective basis, cultural identity is 'an inheritance which we may either accept or reject. Unlike voluntary associations we are deeply shaped by our cultural communities and derive our values and ideals from them' (Parekh 2000: 162). Under this understanding of cultural community, the question arises as to what will happen to those who choose to join cultural communities. For Parekh, it appears to be accident of birth that provides this inheritance. This implies that those who choose to become Muslims, for example, will not have this 'inheritance' to 'shape' their 'values and ideals'. The context of choice is fundamental here. Parekh is correct to view the membership of voluntary associations as sometimes instrumental; however, some people are also part of cultural communities for instrumental reasons. They may decide not to leave a cultural community because it would aggravate their family or might harm their economic prospects. Similarly, they can join groups for instrumental reasons as well. In this sense, Parekh's understanding of cultural community is problematic because it seems to speak only of those who have been born into a particular culture and ignores those who have joined communities on an elective basis.

The dangers of Parekh's argument emerge more clearly when he goes on to argue that '[i]f others continue to see and despise me as a Jew or a black man even when I no longer define myself in this way, both my sanity and self-interest require me to find a way of strategically aligning myself with the community while retaining a critical distance from it' (Parekh 2000: 162). The implications of this are dangerously insensitive to the beliefs that people hold. People who choose to become members of a cultural community do not do so at the drop of a hat. If an individual chooses to follow the path of Islam and as a result faces bigotry, presumably they are not encouraged to return to their former cultural community as a response. If another person chooses to leave behind their Muslim upbringing but still faces bigots, Parekh tells them not to be true to their beliefs but instead to 'strategically align' themselves with that which they have rejected. This is deeply troubling not least for the fact that it would appear to suggest that we tackle bigotry and racism in some way by renouncing what we actually believe in and by returning to the categories that the bigot or racist denounces. It is worth applying Parekh's logic in the context of Northern Ireland. To locate his example there, an individual could face discrimination or the threat of violence because they supposedly belong to a particular religion. The bigot may assume this to be the case because of the individual's name, for example, and yet, this individual may well have rejected the religion and accompanying culture that they were inducted into. However, faced with this threat, rather than stating their rejection of the category of the bigot, Parekh implies that the individual should 'strategically align' themselves with the cultural community they were previously part of. The irony in Northern Ireland, of course, is that the individual weighing up this scenario may decide to 'strategically align' themselves with the community they are not part of in order to avoid the threat of violence. This is a matter of judgement that can have the most serious consequences if the individual miscalls their strategic alignment.

The political implications of Parekh's thesis are undermined by the muddled thinking in the section on culture and the thin line he often treads between essentialising culture and stating the strengths of cultural diversity. This is evident when he points out that:

> [c]ultural diversity is also an important constituent and condition of
> human freedom. Unless human beings are able to step out of their

culture, they remain imprisoned within it and tend to absolutize it, imagining it to be the only natural or self-evident way to understand and organize human life. And they cannot step out of their culture unless they have access to others ...   (Parekh 2000: 168)

Parekh argues that the existence of cultural diversity makes us better able to interrogate our own cultures and understand the differences that exist within them, such that it helps to prevent us from absolutising or homogenising our own culture at the same time as discouraging us from suppressing others. However, the mixture of liberalism and conservatism remains part of Parekh's argument on culture. For example, he openly agrees with cultural conservatives (against 'postmodernist adventurism'!) that traditional cultures are easily destroyed but are much more difficult to create. So he supports different cultures and their historical inheritance, but he does so in the sense that culturally diverse societies can forge the same values as homogeneous societies. Thus, he contends that 'a culturally diverse society can reproduce most of the desirable qualities of the homogenous society, but the reverse is not the case. There is no obvious reason why a culturally plural society should not develop a sense of community, solidarity, common loyalties and a broad moral and political consensus ...' (Parekh 2000: 171). Here we get multiculturalism defended on the basis that it is not that different from traditional organic views of society when for much of the book he is concerned with the problems associated with those kinds of theories.

Parekh's standpoint on culture is something of a curate's egg. There is much to commend in it but also several points of slippage into a more conservative position that essentialises culture as the basic building block of contemporary societies. Indeed commentators such as Yack (2002: 112) have argued that Parekh 'vastly exaggerates the closed character of cultural boundaries'. Importantly, though, Parekh concludes this section with an argument that we do not have to engage in arguments about having respect for all cultures or allocating them equal worth. Rather, he says that we need to respect people rather than their cultural beliefs. Whilst this seems a reasonable position, obviously it does not provide guidance in many conflictual situations. In Northern Ireland the problem has been one of trying to achieve this basic respect for people to follow their own beliefs, as is evident in the discourses of 'parity of esteem' that have permeated the recent peace process. It is important that, ultimately, Parekh is not asking us to take on board or even agree with the cultural beliefs and practices of others, he merely wants us to respect their rights as individuals to hold these alternative views. He states this very bluntly:

'[a]lthough all cultures have worth and deserve basic respect, they are not all equally worthy and do not merit equal respect' (Parekh 2000: 177). However, part of the criteria that he establishes for a culture to receive this basic respect is that it 'poses no threat to outsiders', but this is clearly a highly subjective criterion. In Northern Ireland the threat from others is often real, but at the same time, the threat from others can be just as damaging in political terms when it is perceived to exist whether real or not. Again, the point is that there are a number of practical obstacles in the context of Northern Ireland to the kind of multicultural approach that Parekh advocates. This point not withstanding however, Parekh importantly stresses that 'we should respect the community's right to its culture but should also feel free to criticize its beliefs and practices' (Parekh 2000: 177). This is a fundamental statement and a baseline upon which we can try to explore the implications of multiculturalism in Northern Ireland.

The political implications of Parekh's multiculturalism

The second half of Parekh's *Rethinking Multiculturalism* is more focused on the ramifications of his perspective for political structures. The section on the implications for the role of the state are particularly relevant in the context of Northern Ireland given the controversial status of state institutions and challenges to their impartiality. As much as policy makers may try, it is difficult to envisage any set of institutional arrangements that will meet criteria of impartiality to all sections of the community in Northern Ireland. Parekh criticises the homogeneity at the root of most theories of the liberal democratic state and notes that this shared political self-understanding is the 'constitutive principle and necessary presupposition' of the state (Parekh 2000: 184). Thus, he makes the valid point that liberal states have generally been hostile to ethnic forms of nationalism but tend to base their own homogeneity around civic nationalism. Not surprisingly, Parekh sees this as a case of double standards. Moreover, a civic nationalist approach to Northern Ireland is much more difficult to articulate than in other less divided liberal democracies due to the contested nationhood at the root of political cleavages there.

One political development that Parekh supports is the potential of a bill of rights to further multicultural aspirations:

> although it is not always necessary for a country to have a constitutionally enshrined bill of rights, a good case can be made out for it

in a multicultural society provided that the rights enjoy broad support among its constituent communities, do not enshrine the domination of one culture, and, subject to certain constraints, allow the communities to interpret and prioritize them to suit their culture, traditions and aspirations'   (Parekh 2000: 88).

Although a bill of rights was not officially enshrined in the Belfast Agreement, the discourse of rights permeates the Agreement and, if it was to provide the basis for a future politics in Northern Ireland, it is likely that a bill of rights would eventually emerge. However, it is worth sounding a note of scepticism about the extent to which a bill of rights could provide substantive arrangements that would guarantee genuine equality in Northern Ireland. Of course, the formal equality that emanates from documents such as bills of rights may enshrine some real benefits that would protect individuals from both minorities and majorities. At the same time, however, the problems in Northern Ireland are deeply rooted in social and economic structures and it is difficult for legal documents to undermine ingrained prejudice and discrimination of this kind.

Unsurprisingly, Parekh bases his discussion of the state on the changing nature of the world (for example, globalisation) and argues that this has fundamental ramifications for the state in deeply diverse societies. In this vein he maintains that it is incumbent on the state to continue to carry out some of its traditional roles such as the establishment of the rule of law, the maintenance of order, the management of conflict and the provision of social justice (Parekh 2000: 193–4). However, this does not mean that the state should stay as it is; rather Parekh contends that a new range of external pressures and tensions will challenge the kinds of moral consensus that has been articulated as the foundation of Western states. Thus, the state 'is no longer a cohesive cultural unit and cannot base its unity on the cultural homogeneity of its citizens' (Parekh 2000: 194).

This has ramifications for how a multiculturalist might view the state in Northern Ireland. Clearly, the traditional roles that Parekh outlines above are controversial in Northern Ireland and it is unlikely that whatever form of political authority was established there would mollify all of the population. The accepted fact that there is no moral consensus on the location of state authority is likely to lead, in the short-term at least, to a mixed, shared authority between devolved institutions in Northern Ireland, elements of the British state and new forms of governance in unison with the Republic of Ireland. By its very nature then, Northern Ireland is proceeding towards innovative forms of governance that will lead to a unique state. It is interesting that in this discussion Parekh makes one of the few mentions of Northern Ireland in his book. He notes how the ideal shape of the multicultural state might enjoy varying, possibly federal, structures for different parts or cultures of a country 'but all held together by shared legal and political bonds' (Parekh 2000: 194). Interestingly, he sees the new structures in Northern Ireland as an example of these kinds of measures; for example, in the sharing of sovereignty and cross-border institutions (Parekh 2000: 195). He concludes that:

> There is no reason to believe that the state should represent a homogeneous legal space, for territorially concentrated communities with different histories and needs might justly ask for different powers within an asymmetrical political structure; or that every state should have a uniform system of laws, for its different communities might either not be able to agree on them or might legitimately demand the right to adapt them to their circumstances and needs. The state should obviously treat all its communities equally but that need not entail identical treatment. Some communities might trust and authorize it to play an active reformist role in their internal affairs, whereas others might take the opposite view, making state neutrality desirable in one case but not in another.   (Parekh 2000: 195)

It is clear that the situation in Northern Ireland is interesting for multicultural theorists but the passage above also demonstrates the difficulties that such an approach would encounter in Northern Ireland. Given the dominance of zero-sum game thinking in Northern Ireland, it would take a lot of effort to try and persuade the main communities there that equality might necessitate differential treatment. Indeed, the legislation coming out of the peace process thus far has been characterised by an 'equality as sameness' agenda. Thus, whilst there is a recognition that people are different in the Belfast Agreement, the underlying discourse is one of treating people the same way to ensure their equality. In this sense, whilst the sentiment of Parekh's statement is useful, the difficulties of its practical realisation in Northern Ireland should not be underestimated.

The rationale underpinning Parekh's argument is that there has been a long tradition in liberal thinking and Western democracies of trying to assimilate minorities within the dominant values and practices. It is worth noting that in Northern Ireland the pressure for minorities to assimilate in society has been less apparent because of the nature of the prevailing political difficulties. Thus, there has been a tendency to simply ignore minority cultures in Northern Ireland given that they do not fit comfortably in the main social and political divisions in the province. In Parekh's thesis the idea of assimilation is deeply problematic if it is a precondition of equal citizenship (although he does not have a difficulty with it if it is voluntary). However, he would be equally opposed to the kind of packaging of cultural minorities into the private sphere. As such Parekh maintains the rights of minorities to preserve their cultural differences and he questions the whole idea of what they are supposed to assimilate to given that Western societies do not tend to have 'a coherent and unified cultural and moral structure'. Thus, although 'the moral and cultural structure of a society has some internal coherence, it is not a homogeneous and unified whole' (Parekh 2000: 197). The implications of this for societies such as Northern Ireland that have to establish political institutions on contested ground is that they should be careful to provide recognition for cultural minorities that do not subscribe to the dominant cultural paradigm.

In dealing with these issues Parekh contends that there are three main views on political structures in diverse societies: the proceduralist view, the civic assimilationist view and the millet system. The proceduralist position (an example of which is Kukathas' thesis) is to construct a minimal, neutral state that enables individuals to freely follow conflicting ways of life. Parekh rejects this view on the grounds that the procedural state will tend to reflect the concerns of the dominant culture and will therefore discriminate against minority cultures. From this perspective it is impossible to achieve the degree of impartiality required by proceduralists. The civic assimilationist perspective (which Parekh associates with the later Rawls and Habermas) focuses on the need for a shared, universal political culture, whilst the private domain and civil society are more diverse and particularistic. For Parekh, this view is problematic because he sees no clear cut distinction between public and private, especially in areas such as religion and education. He also points out that the political culture will often become dominant over the other parts of society and that the former will be based upon the historical background, development and values of the cultural majority. Lastly, he points to the millet model in which the state has no moral status and cultural communities are all that matter to humans. Parekh notes some strengths of this model and examples of where it is or has been influential, but sees it as a recipe for minimal social interaction. Thus, he argues that 'it militates against the development of common social and political bonds without which no political community can act effectively and maintain its unity and cohesion' (Parekh 2000: 205). Therefore, all of these models of political structure are deemed defective:

> The assimilationist theory more or less ignores the claims of diversity, and the millet theory those of unity. The proceduralist and civic assimilationist theories respect both, but fail to appreciate their dialectical interplay and strike a right balance between them. They confine unity and diversity to separate realms and draw too neat a distinction between the private and public spheres with all the difficulties that these create.   (Parekh 2000: 206)

These reflections extend equally to Northern Ireland insofar as proceduralist claims of state neutrality are usually rejected by nationalists, civic assimilationist ideas underestimate the ways in which religion and claims of nationality permeate political life in the province, and the millet system is unworkable in a society where the conflicting communities are in many ways closely intertwined, live alongside one another, and share political institutions.

What then does Parekh envisage as the key principles of political organisation in a multicultural society? He identifies six interdependent structural features for multicultural societies (that is, none of them can guarantee multicultural citizenship by themselves). Firstly, there needs to be a structure of authority establishing a minimal constitution to provide baseline standards. For Parekh, this structure of authority must be subject to change. Secondly, there needs to be an agreed system of justice and policing to ensure equality for all cultures. This should be a decentralised system which would reduce conflict and reinforce social capital through cross-communal linkages. Third, he argues for the establishment of collective rights which may differ in practice between groups. However, he does recognise it might be 'better not to grant rights with all their legal and other complications, and settle the matter by accommodation or by imposing duties on others' (Parekh 2000: 218). Fourthly, Parekh argues for a common culture, although it will be comprised of a variety of different components in a multicultural society. He believes that this common culture must be open-ended and subject to dispute and that it should be prepared for affirmative action. The fifth dimension of Parekh's multiculturalism is the need for multicultural education in which we address both the curriculum and the methods of teaching. Lastly, he argues for a need for national identity to be articulated through public institutions and discourses. Not surprisingly, Parekh argues that this must accommodate all cultural identities, include all minorities and provide equal value to all citizens. A strong national identity will be one in which conflicting demands and interests can be reconciled.

All of these proposals have their merits but it is highly debatable whether some of them are feasible options for a future politics in Northern Ireland. Clearly the call for a stable system of authority is not particularly contentious but there will be considerable difference in Northern Ireland as to what that authority should be. Again, a unified and equally respected system of justice and policing is desirable but it meets all kinds of obstacles in Northern Ireland because of the historical background to the conflict and the disagreement on the source of authority. I have already noted that collective rights which are differentiated between groups in Northern Ireland are contentious because of the prevalence of the zero-sum game mentality. Parekh's fourth requirement for a common culture is another controversial issue in the Northern Irish context because the two traditions tend to define themselves as much in terms of their opposition to each other as in the terms of what they actually are. Although the call for affirmative action would be highly divisive, it is fair to say that some aspects of common culture do exist in Northern Ireland. The fifth factor of multicultural education is a common panacea put forward to resolve the difficulties of Northern Ireland. Whilst it seems reasonable to support mixed education in Northern Ireland, it is wise not to underestimate the extent to which the churches want to retain their power in the field of education. Moreover, many of the divisive views in Northern Ireland are being imbued in children long before they reach formal education so it would be sensible not to place all of our hopes in mixed or multicultural education. Parekh's last claim is for a sense of national identity and, of course, this arouses considerable conflict in Northern Ireland. Nonetheless, this is not to say that such an identity could not be constructed around ideas of binationalism whereby public institutions and discourses recognise that people in Northern Ireland direct their affinity to different nations. However we should be careful not to underestimate the difficulties of enacting any of this and, as Parekh reminds us, these factors are inter-dependent and cannot achieve multiculturalism on their own. The likelihood of them all developing in the context of Northern Ireland is distant, although that is not to suggest that they are not worthwhile political objectives.

One final section of Parekh's book that should be analysed in the light of Northern Ireland is the section on religion and public life. Here Parekh makes the point strongly that the dominant trend in liberal theory is to regard religion as a private matter that should be separated from the political domain. This trend takes two main forms. Firstly, there is a weak form of secularism which stresses the need to separate religion and the institutions of the state. Secondly, there is a stronger type of secularism that focuses on the need to separate religion from politics *per se*. Obviously, given the preceding arguments, Parekh is sceptical about this and questions whether the contribution of religion to moral principles can ever be disassociated from the political realm. Clearly a similar problem emerges in the Northern Irish context where it is nigh on impossible to imagine a situation in which religion did not impact upon political relations. The problem in Northern Ireland then is the opposite of that which Parekh identifies. For Parekh, liberal society has tried to marginalise religion, whereas in Northern Ireland it is an accepted and sometimes over-powering agent. Because religion is a divisive aspect of Northern Irish society, it may be argued that a future separation of state and religion is a laudable objective. In this sense, there is no need in Northern Ireland to encourage further church influence on public life that Parekh advocates for less complicated societies. However, there may be a case for trying to balance the Protestant and Catholic influence in Northern Ireland by giving a greater public prominence to other com-munities based on non-Christian perspectives. Ultimately Parekh argues for 'an inclusive and religiously sensitive secularism [that] offers the best basis for a creative and mutually beneficial engagement between religion and political life' (Parekh 2000: 335). Unfortunately in Northern Ireland such a sensitive atmosphere is almost impossible to achieve.

To conclude this section then, it is worth briefly summarising Parekh's argument for multiculturalism. He accepts that multicultural-ism refers as much to a way of life as a coherent political philosophy. This is based upon three basic principles:

- Humans are culturally embedded in their cultures but their identity or potential for criticism is not prescribed by them.
- Cultures are different and partial and have limited horizons but they can achieve a wider view by engaging with other cultures. No culture is worthless although we can judge some as more substantial than others.

- Nearly all cultures are internally diverse – their identity is plural and fluid. Cultures need to understand this diversity and the ways differences may be opened up when they enter into open dialogues with other cultures.

In this vein Parekh argues that '[n]o multicultural society can be stable and vibrant unless it ensures that its constituent communities receive both just recognition and a just share of economic and political power. It requires a robust form of social, economic and political democracy to underpin its commitment to multiculturalism' (Parekh 2000: 343). As we have seen, whilst there is much to cherish in these sentiments, their practical implications in Northern Ireland are sometimes problematic.

Beyond multiculturalism: Brian Barry and the liberal backlash

The liberal backlash against multiculturalism is most notably expressed by Brian Barry in his argumentative and entertaining book *Culture and Equality* (2001). Effectively this book provides a rebuttal of the growing prevalence within liberal theory of the politics of difference. As such, Barry draws on Millian liberalism and the work of the early Rawls to construct a universal liberal theory of justice that focuses specifically on issues of equality. His main concern, then, is to show how universal liberal rights are much more capable of generating equality than the kind of group differentiated rights demanded by some multiculturalists and advocates of the politics of difference. He is particularly concerned with their focus on culture and wants to challenge 'views that support the politicization of group identities, where the basis of the common identity is claimed to be cultural' (Barry 2001: 5). This takes the form of a basic objection to the special claims put forward for groups, particularly when those groups are thought to be internally differentiated. Thus, he criticises Iris Marion Young's idea of representation of group difference on the grounds that if, as she says, groups are not internally homogeneous, then why and how can they be represented *qua* groups? The point he makes is that universal rights are better equipped to provide basic freedoms on an equal basis than establishing specific rights for groups that contain differences within them. At the heart of Barry's arguments is the view that the struggles of the under-privileged are undermined by political strategies that weaken universalism. Thus, the politics of difference tends to result in a situation that benefits powerful groups at the expense of the poor or weak. These are important points that deserve serious consideration despite the rhetorical flourish and polemical vigour that sometimes detract from the highly relevant points that Barry wants to make.

The most pertinent parts of Barry's *Culture and Equality* for our consideration are the first and third sections of the book. The first focuses on issues of culture and equal treatment and the third on debates about universalism and egalitarianism. To take the first of these arguments in hand then, Barry argues that the historical experience of liberal systems have shown that there are relatively few problems generated by uniformity of rights. Certainly he sees such uniformity as a more effective strategy for providing rights than the politics of difference which he regards as 'a formula for manufacturing conflict' (Barry 2001: 21). This is an important statement because it proposes that the existence of different groups in society does not mean that conflict is inevitable. Rather, the history of liberal societies shows how such differences have traditionally been managed successfully by the liberal rule of law. The salience of this is that Barry is clearly welcoming of social diversity whilst constructing a 'difference-blind' liberalism: '[r]ecognition of the fact of multiculturalism can easily be taken to entail a commitment to the multiculturalist programme; conversely, anybody who dissents from normative multiculturalism automatically stands accused of blindness to the fact of multiculturalism' (Barry 2001: 22). It is vital to recognise, then, that opposition to multicultural theory does not entail opposition to the fact of multiculturalism.

The implications of social diversity for political conflict also emerge in Barry's theory. He contends that difference in itself does not inevitably lead to conflict but it does tend to do so when the difference leads to incompatible demands. This is particularly the case where religion is involved: 'where members of different religious faiths have incompatible ideas about the way in which a polity and a society should be organized, and at least one group seeks to impose its ideas on a territory containing other groups, that is bound to result in conflict' (Barry 2001: 24). This is an interesting point with regard to Northern Ireland because, whilst there is a clear incompatibility in the organisation of the Catholic and Protestant churches in Northern Ireland, the extent to which they try to 'impose' their ideas on the territory of the province is perhaps more limited in the contemporary era than was the case in earlier historical periods. However, conflict remains and this is testimony to the basic incommensurability of Catholicism and Protestantism in the way they manifest themselves in

Northern Ireland (although clearly in other societies they can cohabit social, public spaces without difficulty). Therefore it is not just in the pursuit of power that religions conflict in Northern Ireland; dispute is also evident in basic cultural practices given the intertwined nature of religion and conflict in Irish history. For Barry, the way around this is not to grant special rights for such cultural groups but to ensure that they are treated fairly and equally. Importantly, though, he thinks the best way to achieve this is to try where possible to depoliticise religion through treating it, at least to some extent, as a private matter (Barry 2001: 29). In the context of Northern Ireland, Barry's thesis is persuasive insofar as he notes the dangers of special rights for religious groups. It is fair to say that the progress made in the Northern Ireland peace process has been based upon establishing structures where the divisions are understood as political rather than religious. That is not to say, however, that Northern Irish politics has become secular – the churches played a major role in the facilitation and execution of the Belfast Agreement. On the whole then, Barry's desire to separate politics and religion is not plausible in Northern Ireland.

Barry's claims for justice are that it should be understood in terms of providing equal opportunities for all individuals. In this sense, he thinks there should be universal rights that provide people with opportunities to follow their own objectives. Therefore, he opposes the multiculturalist view that justice may require the differential treatment of groups – he thereby rejects what he calls the 'rule-and-exemption approach' (Barry 2001: 33). By 'rule and exemption', Barry means the view that we establish various laws and regulations but provide a variety of dispensations from those provisions for certain groups in society that disagree with them for cultural reasons. He justifies this position by arguing that procedural theories of justice are not unfair or partial just because their laws or institutions impact upon people in different ways. This is a justificatory theory of state neutrality.[4] Barry contends that all kinds of fair and just laws exist which preclude people from doing certain things. Thus, the right of people not to be raped overrides the freedoms of the rapist and the same goes for the rights of children in relation to paedophiles. Nonetheless, there is a problem with Barry's examples – whilst they clearly sustain his argument, he is not talking about *cultural* practice here. Within the multiculturalist literature, no-one is suggesting that a culture that believed in paedophilia should be accorded exemption from the rule of law. To some extent, the extremity of Barry's examples draw attention away from the less contentious exemptions that groups may want.

What I am suggesting is that these are often pragmatic political decisions rather than serious debates about vindicating measures that would violate basic human rights. That said, Barry is right that the ways that laws and policies affect people is effectively a political decision. Another example he introduces is the exemption of Sikhs from laws on offensive weapons to enable them to carry *kirpans* because of their religious significance. For Barry, this is not fair because the rest of us are not allowed to carry daggers around. This misses the point that these demands require contextualisation. The exemption would only be unfair to the rest of us if we were precluded from carrying knives against our cultural practice or if we intended using knives. The former would not be defensible in the light of exemption for Sikhs, whilst the latter falls foul of Barry's own dictum that we make political decisions about what we do or do not want people to be able to do. Ultimately, Barry comes down to the point that it is an 'absurd' exemption because it 'reduces the personal security of all the rest of the population' (Barry 2001: 38). However, quite frequently Sikhs have been able to follow their cultural practices without requiring a major exemption from law. Indeed it has been through pragmatic engagement with employers that Sikh health workers, for example, have been able to negotiate the wearing of cultural symbols without undermining safety in hospitals through carrying *kirpans*.

Sikhism also provides another example that Barry sees as a way to demonstrate the problems with the rule and exemption approach. In terms of equal opportunities he argues that Sikhs should not be exempt from wearing motorcycle helmets. The reason for this is that Sikhs have the opportunity to ride motorcycles like the rest of the population as long as they follow the regulations of the road. Thus, what would be unjust to Barry would be a law that said Sikhs cannot ride motorcycles. If they choose not to, for whatever reason, then that is their affair. Philosophically he may be justified here, but there are also political practicalities to deal with. He underestimates the depth of cultural identities and their importance to people. One way around this could be to say that rather than there being a special right for Sikhs, the law could merely be framed to say that everyone riding a motorcycle must wear a helmet or other agreed forms of headgear (including turbans). There is a resonance here with some of the debates that took place around the Belfast Agreement in Northern Ireland, such as the provisions for the use of languages other than English. This was effectively a provision that would justify and legitimise those nationalists who do or want to communicate in Irish. However, as it appeared in the legislation, the right was for anyone to communicate in a language other than English including Ulster-Scots which is a little used language but one that is associated with the unionist community. The point was that rather than provide an exemption for nationalists to use Irish and therefore potentially irritate the unionist community, the law was framed in such a way as to justify the use of alternative languages for everyone. In this sense, we can see how the Belfast Agreement dealt with an issue that could have been seen as an exemption for one group by providing a universal right that applied to all. Again this would appear to be a matter of pragmatic decision rather than a general principle that provides guidance for all matters of contention.

Barry is very clear that he rejects discrimination on any basis linked with ascriptive characteristics such as ethnicity. Interestingly, in terms of locating discussions about multiculturalism and Northern Ireland, he notes how job discrimination on the basis of religion is not illegal in mainland Britain but is in Northern Ireland:

> There is a certain rationale for treating religion in Northern Ireland as the equivalent of ethnicity because it is a place in which 'Protestant' and 'Catholic' are the names of communities ... In this context, discrimination on the basis of religion is the equivalent of discrimination on the basis of any other ascriptive characteristic. What needs to be emphasized ... is that religion here has nothing to do with any kind of behaviour related to ability to do the job. (Barry 2001: 56)

Here he tones down his criticism of 'rule and exemption' where he thinks that there are special circumstances and the situation in Northern Ireland is clearly different from elsewhere in the United Kingdom. Therefore, he makes the concession that 'rule and exemption' can help with the process of accommodating minorities but he rejects the multiculturalist view that it should be a widely used tool within the law. The expansion of numerous exemptions to a wide variety of minorities would make laws and regulations increasingly ridiculous and would make their legitimacy for anyone questionable. Thus he argues that '[i]t must be important to have a rule generally prohibiting conduct of a certain kind because, if this is not so, the way in which to accommodate minorities is simply not to have a rule at all' (Barry 2001: 62). In other words, for Barry, the 'rule and exemption' approach becomes increasingly detrimental to the jurisdiction of the law the more it is employed to the benefit of minorities. This, of course, does not mean that the law should not help minorities but that it should do so through applying laws universally.

As we have seen in Northern Ireland this kind of approach has been employed during the peace process since the 1990s. The provisions of the Belfast Agreement focus steadily on providing equal rights and there is little mention of the issues such as assimilation and acculturation that energise the debate between liberals and multiculturalists. Indeed it is worth noting that the Belfast Agreement is framed in terms of justifying and legitimising the differences in Northern Ireland. It abounds with references to the value of the different aspirations that people there hold and the equality that should allow those values to prevail. Here, of course, we run into the dangers of essentialising culture, of viewing it as fixed and unchanging. It is worth pointing out, as Barry does, that cultures cannot have rights, only the individuals are who are part of cultures can.[5] For Barry, rather than thinking of rights as attributable to groups, it is better that we think of them as individual and that we support the rights of individuals to be part of the cultures they choose. This is an important argument in terms of Northern Ireland and it provides a dividing line that the Belfast Agreement falls both sides of.

A crucial and perhaps under-developed part of these debates relates to the timescale of cultural difference. Thus, Barry argues that what multiculturalists propose are 'group-based policies deliberately intended to perpetuate cultural differences indefinitely' (Barry 2001: 117). He sees this as problematic both in terms of the fact that individuals should be the holders of rights and also that cultures change and mean different things to different people. However, the idea of perpetuating cultural difference is an interesting one insofar as the decision making processes of the Northern Ireland Assembly are established on the necessity of achieving cross-community support for legislation. To this end, as we have seen, members of the Northern Ireland Assembly have to designate themselves as 'unionists', 'nationalists' or 'other'. Clearly this can perpetuate the differences that have been constructed around those labels, but it is difficult to see how else those who framed the Belfast Agreement could manage to ascertain cross-community agreement without differentiating the groups. Thus, whilst Barry is right that it is difficult to ascribe rights to groups, this is not to say that there are not circumstances where group differences may need to be perpetuated over time. Barry also believes that the underpinning presumption of multiculturalism is that we should tolerate uncritically illiberal cultures and accord them respect and equal worth. As noted above, Parekh can be partially exonerated from Barry's criticism because the former explicitly does not believe that all cultures have the same value. Nonetheless, Parekh does want us to tolerate some non-liberal practices that Barry regards as problematic. For the latter, this is asking us to respect illiberal cultures which do not, by definition, extend that respect back to dominant liberal mores. Instead 'the value underwriting the freedom of groups to operate in illiberal ways is not respect for their culture but rather an acknowledgement of the significance in people's lives of free association' (Barry 2001: 128). In this sense, Barry does not have a problem with people who choose to be part of illiberal cultures. Following Mill, Barry contends that we should value diversity but for the reason that it is an expression of individuality rather than reifying illiberal cultural practices by allocating rights to groups (Barry 2001: 129).[6]

In the third section of *Culture and Equality*, Barry goes on to make some more general comments regarding universalism and egalitarianism. He begins by outlining the ways in which multiculturalists adopt the view that cultures are incommensurable and therefore it is impossible to judge them against each other by any neutral criteria. Barry feels that this is logically incompatible with the third multiculturalist view that all cultures have equal value, presumably on the basis that we cannot know this unless there is some objective criterion on which to establish their equality.[7] This type of multicultural thought closes cultures to interrogations from others and reifies views and practices that members of those cultures might choose to change if they were opened up to greater dialogue with other cultures (although, of course, they might not choose to do so). Of note here is Barry's example of the parading tradition in Northern Ireland as one where traditional practices get bound up with culture to form a formidable barrier to critical interrogation from others. He contends that his slogan would be:

> '*culture is no excuse*'. If there are sound reasons against doing something, these cannot be trumped by saying – even if it is true – that doing it is a part of your culture. The fact that you (or your ancestors) have been doing something for a long time does nothing in itself to justify your continuing to do it.   (Barry 2001: 258)

In other words, for Barry, individual rights cannot be trumped by conservative claims of cultural practice or tradition. Many of these conservative ideas about cultural renewal are in fact distinctly modern and often manifest themselves in a romantic cultural nationalism that tries to establish firm horizons on the principles of the culture. Arguably forms of this romantic cultural nationalism are identifiable in both of the 'two traditions' in Northern Ireland.

In the final chapter, 'The Politics of Multiculturalism', Barry's liberal universalism is applied to the political structures that have to be built and the decisions that have to be taken in the context of diverse societies. In arguing against the politics of difference, Barry posits a politics of solidarity which he clearly establishes as a majoritarian doctrine. Thus, he argues that where there are political disagreements that turn out to be irresolvable 'we have a clear prima facie case for resolving disputes by adopting the policy favoured by the majority' (Barry 2001: 300). He continues that, in this context, '[i]t would surely be absurd to say that a minority ... should have a veto on the policy favoured by a majority, or that its members should be able to demand that the policy with which they disagree should not apply to them' (Barry 2001: 300). This passage clarifies the reasons why Barry's liberal universalism is inapplicable in deeply divided societies such as Northern Ireland. It was noted above how designation works to ensure cross-community support for legislation in the Northern Ireland Assembly. It does this precisely to avoid the resort to the simple majoritarianism that Barry advocates. Obviously this would be disastrous in Northern Ireland where the exercise of majority rule in the fifty years after the Government of Ireland Act led to considerable discrimination and social unrest. Moreover, it is also the case that the majority-minority distinction in Northern Ireland is contested; that is, that the minority in Northern Ireland is in the majority in Ireland as a whole. Whilst this distinction is not one of much value to those who want to defend the status quo in Northern Ireland, it does nevertheless undermine the sweeping support for majoritarianism in Barry's argument. Indeed, we might add that a simple majoritarianism would be no more effective a strategy at managing conflict if the position were to arise where there was a nationalist majority in Northern Ireland due to demographic changes. Ultimately the management of conflict in Northern Ireland is a gradual and pragmatic process that cannot be furthered through the use of blunt instruments such as majoritarianism. This is the sense in which Barry's argument is not a plausible option for Northern Irish politics.

In summary then, there is much in Barry's critique of multiculturalism that clarifies the difficulties of a multiculturalist solution to Northern Ireland's problems. At the end of the book he returns to Iris Marion Young and points out how a group-differentiated politics may make the achievement of broad universal social objectives more difficult to achieve. Whilst there may be some currency in this argument, it is clear that group differentiation is of fundamental importance to Northern Irish politics. Barry is correct in arguing that group differentiation can reinforce group differences and this is a real risk in the context of the Northern Ireland Assembly. Whilst cross-community support for legislation is necessary, it can also concretise the dominant ethno-national allegiances in Northern Ireland. As such, these measures can reinforce the perception of the zero-sum game; that is, that any legislation that is favoured or driven by one's political opponents must favour their constituency and therefore as a result militate against your own. This is a perennial danger and one that will have to be revisited in the future politics of Northern Ireland. Nonetheless, without such a measure we would be left with Barry's majoritarianism. Barry is aware of these issues and recognises that the 'more severe form of the conflict between group-based and universalistic policies arises where group-based policies split the potential coalition for broad-based egalitarian reform down the middle' (Barry 2001: 325–6). He is magnanimous enough to accept that much of the inspiration of group-differentiated politics has been the failure of liberal egalitarianism to deliver the goods for certain minority groups. That said, he thinks the capacity of the politics of difference to do anything about this is a fallacy.

What Barry's book demonstrates is the difficulties of group differentiation as a strategy for already divided societies. However, his individualistic approach to liberal universalism also looks unworkable in societies where the problems are not just inequalities between individuals but deep ruptures between group actors. Thus, neither the group differentiated nor the individualist approach to politics is a feasible option for the future politics of Northern Ireland.

Conclusion: applying multiculturalism in Northern Ireland

To conclude this chapter I will reiterate some of the difficulties in applying multiculturalism to the context of Northern Ireland. It is clear that, whilst multiculturalist theory may focus on the kinds of difficulties that have emerged in Northern Ireland, the situation there provides a range of dilemmas and problems that are difficult for any theory to resolve. It is no mistake that the two theorists who have applied their theories most directly to real world problems, Kymlicka and Parekh, have relatively little to say about Northern Ireland (except for the odd brief reference). Both would deny that Northern Ireland fits their criteria in the sense that the two traditions there are different from Kymlicka's idea of a multinational society or the definition of culture that Parekh employs. Similarly, many contemporary analysts of Northern Irish politics reject the attempts of some commentators who want to view the conflict through the lens of culture (Rolston 1998). This stance is encapsulated in the words of Eagleton:

> Whatever the conflict in Northern Ireland is about, it most certainly is not in the first place about 'culture', and to assert that it is an instantly recognisable ideological stance in Ireland today, one intimately allied with liberal unionism in the North or some left postmodernism in the republic. What is in train in the North is an ethno-political contention, not chiefly a cultural or religious or economic one; and here the customary culturalism of postcolonial theory simply will not serve. Neither, for that matter, will its occasional dogmatic opposition of nationalism (homogenising, essentialist, spiritualist, chauvinist) to radical pluralism, hybridity or multiculturalism.   (Eagleton 1998: 130)

Eagleton is sceptical of those theoretical approaches that warn of the dangers of essentialism. He states that some essentialisms are 'excellent doctrines' that are more radical than most anti-essentialist doctrines and rejects the well-worn view that all Irish nationalism is essentialist anyway. This is an important reminder that nationalism, like all political traditions, contains considerable variations. Nonetheless, the knee-jerk rejection of 'postmodernism' as emaciated lifestyle politics as opposed to the real politics that have traditionally characterised Northern Ireland runs the risk of underestimating the importance of issues of culture and identity. Whilst these might not be the fundamental issues behind the conflict in Northern Ireland, they are undoubtedly important and arguably increasingly so. Thus, I would contend against Eagleton that the analysis of identity politics need not take the form of 'doctrinal postmodernism' that he rejects because as long as 'nationalists and Unionists continue to lock one another into quasi-pathological forms of identity, all the brave postmodern talk of decentred subjects, multiple selfhoods and the rest will remain so much academicist rhetoric' (Eagleton 1998: 132–3). The point I want to argue is that identity politics can regenerate and indeed radicalise the analysis of democracy in Northern Ireland. Thus, identity politics need not lapse into the vagueness and relativism which Eagleton accuses it of, although we should also remember at the same time that it is necessary to build a radical democratic politics around more than issues of identity.[8] The need, then, is to couple identity politics with analysis of the socio-economic conditions that prevail in Northern Ireland.

In conclusion, multiculturalism offers a number of desirable objectives for Northern Irish politics but it is always too grand a vision to be practically applicable to conditions in Northern Ireland. The danger of multiculturalism (and it is one that is recognised by some of its advocates) is that it essentialises culture by placing it at the centre of social and political stratification. Culture may be more or less significant a factor in the structures of different societies. However, as we will see later in the book, the problem in the contemporary politics of Northern Ireland has been the closure of the political system to many groups there. It has been an élite driven system that is largely white, male and middle class. In this sense, theoretical analysis of Northern Ireland has to take into account not only ethno-national divisions but also the way they are bound up with stratification along lines such as gender, class, sexuality and so on. From this perspective the analysis of culture is important because it remains a source of stratification within and between the two traditions, and between them both and the minority cultures in the province. However, ultimately, this is only part of the political conflict in Northern Ireland and, as such, the theory of multiculturalism offers a partial resolution at best to the problems there. When we add to this the implausibility of the demands made by some multiculturalists such as Parekh in the context of Northern Ireland, it becomes clear that the focus on culture in those theories needs to be broadened if they are to be applicable there.

4
Deliberative Democracy and Democratic Communication

Since the 1980s there has been a 'deliberative turn' in the theorisation of both liberalism and democracy. As we saw earlier, Rawls has introduced a clear deliberative dimension to his liberal thought and this has been complemented in recent years by Jürgen Habermas who has developed his theory of communicative action to construct a distinctive discursive model of politics. In democratic theory more generally, we have also witnessed the growth of deliberative theories from, amongst others, feminist theorists of difference such as Iris Marion Young, ecologists such as John Dryzek and those associated with the concept of civil society such as Joshua Cohen.[1] This chapter evaluates the growth of deliberative models of democracy and their potential implications for Northern Ireland. Northern Ireland is a particularly interesting context in which to analyse deliberative democracy because there has been considerable dialogue there in recent years and there are continuing debates about where, when and with whom dialogue is appropriate. This demonstrates some of the difficulties of deliberative models of democracy and suggests that the practical implementation of these theories faces many obstacles. Nonetheless, it is clear that deliberative thinking has made a key contribution to contemporary politics in Northern Ireland especially in the build up to and aftermath of the Belfast Agreement.

Before examining some of these theories in more depth, it is worth considering the 'deliberative turn' in more general terms. At the outset it is pertinent to remember that the emphasis on communication is not a new feature of political thought. In terms of human life, Charles Taylor reminds us that language and communication are central to existence. Thus, we become 'full human agents, capable of understanding ourselves, and hence of defining our identity, through our acquisition of rich human languages of expression ... The genesis of the human mind is in this sense not monological, not something each person accomplishes on his or her own, but dialogical' (Taylor 1992: 32). For this reason, language and communication provide a basic function in the construction of human identity and, thus, are major components of the foundations of contemporary societies. According to Taylor, individual identity is constructed through a dialogic relationship with others and this dialogue is all the more notable in the complex differentiated societies which characterise so much of the world today. In this sense, it would seem that dialogic or deliberative processes and relationships are of central importance to identity formation and mutual self-understanding. However, this notion has been developed during the 'deliberative turn' so that the process of deliberation is not merely to achieve self-understanding but has also become the cornerstone of democratic organisation.

According to deliberative theorists, democratic institutions are legitimate insofar as they embrace dialogue between relevant actors on a wide range of issues and that those discussions have a direct bearing on decisions made and the policies which emanate from them. Thus, deliberative democracy is a perspective that tries to encourage interaction between different groups in order to deal with the differences which exist in complex, differentiated societies. Deliberative democratic theories take many different forms but the most important of these have been procedural theories such as that of Habermas (1996a). Habermas attempts to circumvent the variety of discourses and conflicts that permeate civil society by separating a legal and political sphere where discourse operates according to strict regulatory procedures. It is because of the influence of this model that I will devote considerable attention to it here, but it will also be important to highlight a more disputatious and contentious theory of democratic engagement which emanates from Dryzek's (2000) theory of discursive democracy as possibly a more pertinent model for deeply divided societies such as Northern Ireland.

Before going on to discuss these perspectives, it is worth taking time to sound a cautionary note about the potential of deliberative democratic procedures to resolve conflicts where substantial social divisions reside. An instructive warning here is provided by Fred Dallmayr (1996). Dallmayr examines the Spanish conquest of America and the way in which the native Indians and Spanish colonisers used different forms of communication. After the war had been won, the human communication between the two groups was inevitably weighted towards the Europeans as interhuman discourse was their preferred form of communication. Thus, in the process of winning the war and establishing their mode of communication as dominant, the Spanish subverted the native form of communication ('between man and the world'). In this sense the establishment of superiority by one group led to the denigration of the way of life of those who were defeated. Dallmayr states that the Spanish victory was tinged with defeat as the maintenance of their superiority led to the loss of the native forms of communication. For Dallmayr, this is a metaphor for contemporary developments whereby 'Western culture ... is in the process of imprinting its mark upon the entire world' (Dallmayr 1996: 279).

However, Dallmayr's tale perhaps has an even greater resonance in Northern Ireland where the process of communication has often been at cross-purposes. The dialogic process of Northern Ireland has often been a mixture of the pursuit of strategic interest, the desire to end violence, the attempt to change the behaviour of one of the two governments, the desire to defeat one's opponents and so on. These different practices have cross-cut the ethno-national divide in Northern Ireland and this added complexity has been further complicated by the unwillingness of some to engage in full and frank discussion. When there is no clear agreement about what dialogue is for, then the perception of gains by the other side become deeply important. Thus, whether one side is winning or not (and it is possible to argue that, given the complexity of the situation, 'winning' is not really possible in absolute terms), the perception of the process is all that counts. Clearly, in Northern Ireland there is a substantial perception within the unionist community that the peace process has been one of granting wishes and concessions to the nationalist community. In light of the fact that many unionist demands have also been met, we might argue that such a point is wrong and that unionists should continue dialogue. However, my point is a different one: following Dallmayr, we can see how unionists may *perceive* that they are losing out in the dialogic process and therefore it is understandable that some may view it as loaded in nationalist favour. The sense of loss may undermine unionist faith in the process of dialogue *per se* and, if nationalists continue to support the process as it stands, then unionists are likely to become even more suspicious of their reasons for doing so. Therefore, even if we can imagine deliberative democratic procedures, we must remember that not everyone will view those procedures in the same light.

All of this suggests that there may well be problems when it comes to the practical enactment of deliberative theories of democracy. Moreover, the lesson of Dallmayr implies that there may be problematic aspects of communication when it is combined with the existence of social power. When we add to this mix the specific difficulties of political engagement in Northern Ireland, then inevitably the obstacles to deliberative democracy look hard to surmount. Nonetheless, deliberative democracy is not uniform and it is important to assess some of the key variants to understand whether some dimensions are more applicable to Northern Ireland than others. To this end, we turn first to the ideas of Jürgen Habermas who is the most notable author on deliberative democracy in contemporary political thought.

Habermas and the discursive conception of politics

Habermas' perspective on deliberative relations emerged with his theory of communicative action (Habermas 1984, 1987).[2] In his later work, however, Habermas has constructed his position around a boundary drawn between civil society or the public sphere where a wide range of discursive interactions take place on an informal basis on the one hand, and on the other a sphere of politics which is governed by legally constructed rules and procedures for engagement. Habermas is aware of the practical problems that such a position encounters. For example, he knows that questions will be raised over how his procedural mechanism and idealised vision of communication can be put into practice: 'it is unclear how this procedural concept, so freighted with idealizations, can link up with empirical investigations that conceive politics primarily as an arena of power processes' (Habermas 1996a: 287). Nonetheless, he is clear that this does not imply an opposition between the ideal and the real. Moreover, it would be within reason to suggest that, whilst politics is permeated by variations of power, this does not mean that politics can merely be reduced to the strategic pursuit of gain and power as is suggested by some empiricist approaches. However, what is more problematic for Habermas is that he does not adopt a pragmatic approach to the realisation of his thesis. On the contrary, he employs his view of communication as the foundation of a fair procedure as a *normative* model. Whilst this is justifiable in terms of the validity of utopian approaches to political theory, such an approach does not inform the kind of project which Habermas wants to construct. Instead, he wants to build a model whereby the proper operation of rational procedures for political engagement will confer legitimacy on the decisions made by constitutional bodies. Thus he contends that:

> bargaining partners need not accept the outcome of successful bargaining for the *same* reasons. But the prudential considerations that each side weighs from its point of view tacitly presuppose the common recognition of normative reasons. These reasons justify the procedure itself as impartial by explaining why outcomes reached in conformity with the procedure may count as fair. (Habermas 1996a: 295)

The point of the Habermasian approach is not to promote some kind of advertisement for his favoured liberal perspective, but rather he wants to *justify* a deliberative form of liberal constitutionalism. From this angle he does not want to persuade us that liberalism is the most appropriate ideological system for political deliberation to take place, but rather he assumes that liberalism is the most appropriate vehicle for the furtherance of rationally grounded decisions formed through democratic deliberation. That said, Habermas is clear that the proceduralist theory of democracy he wants to promote must be differentiated from the liberal and republican paradigms which have characterised traditional debates about democracy. He is more sympathetic to the republican understanding of democracy because the 'republican trust in the force of political discourses stands in contrast to the liberal skepticism about reason' (Habermas 1996b: 23). However he rejects the way that in recent times, this republican perspective has tended to be couched in communitarian terms. The problem here is that this approach leads to 'an *ethical constriction* of *political discourse*' (Habermas 1996b: 23) in which the form of politics is decided *a priori* by an ethical consensus:

> In contrast, a discourse-theoretic interpretation insists on the fact that democratic will-formation draws its legitimating force not from a previous convergence of settled ethical convictions but both from the communicative presuppositions that allow the better arguments to come into play in various forms of deliberation and from the procedures that secure fair bargaining processes. Discourse theory breaks with a purely ethical conception of civic autonomy. (Habermas 1996b: 24)

From this basis, he criticises the communitarian view that there needs to be a shared ethical understanding of sameness and difference to enable political dialogue. Whilst Habermas accepts that discussions about identity and the type of society we want to live in are indeed part of politics ('discourses aimed at achieving self-understanding'), he contends that these are the questions which can be adequately dealt with in the political debate which takes place in civil society.

For Habermas, it is essential to deal with moral questions about justice and *'legislative politics'* which will enable us to grapple successfully with the views that emanate from civil society. For this reason, norms of equality must be constructed to enshrine an appropriate system of justice: '[t]he politically enacted law of a concrete legal community must, if it is to be legitimate, at least be compatible with moral tenets that claim universal validity going beyond the legal community' (Habermas 1996b: 25). In this sense, for the Habermasian, ethical considerations must be overridden in the sphere of politics; in plural societies there are numerous ethical positions and a broader universal paradigm is required to enable politics to function. So what Habermas requires is an agreed system of engagement that we can agree upon from our separate perspectives. The common objection to Habermas here is that, whilst he opposes an ethically informed structure for political engagement, surely he must recognise that certain values and principles will inform those structures. The problem, as noted in relation to Dallmayr's argument above, is that even if structures could be agreed between all, the perception of them would be that they favoured particular ethical approaches or standpoints in practice. Once procedures have been put in place then our acquiescence to them is unlikely to be uniform. Therefore we should not be surprised that theorists of multiculturalism like Parekh argue that liberal constitutional procedures tend to reflect the dominant liberal lifestyles in Western liberal democracies rather than ethical positions which may be derived from alternative cultures. Similarly in Northern Ireland, even if procedures were fair and agreed as such by all (which is not the case), we should not be surprised that over the course of time the legitimacy of these procedures may be called into question by groups which feel that they are treated unfairly by the procedures.

Habermas regards his theory as placed between liberal and republican views on democracy but he criticises both of these earlier democratic theories for being too heavily focused on the state. This state-centred stance is evident in the liberal view that individuals had negative freedoms and formal rights guaranteed by the state which enabled their freedom. In the republican view the state embodied the national community and the preordained consensus. However, for

Habermas, in proceduralist discourse theory we can see that '[w]eaving together pragmatic considerations, compromises, discourses of self-understanding, and justice, this democratic procedure grounds the presumption that reasonable or fair results are obtained ... In the final analysis, the normative content arises from the very structure of communicative actions' (1996b: 26). Habermas regards this normative basis as stronger than the liberal view but weaker than the republican perspective. The important point here is that the differences of civil society are informal and indeed disputatious in many cases. Where liberals seek a state which merely enables the pursuit of individual objectives, republicans try to subvert these differences in the construction of an over-arching communal identity. Where Habermas differs is in arguing that the conflict of perspectives in civil society is the ground upon which the public will is articulated and transmitted to political institutions:

> Informal public opinion-formation generates 'influence'; influence is transformed into 'communicative power' through the channels of political elections; and communicative power is again transformed into 'administrative power' through legislation. As in the liberal model, the boundaries between 'state' and 'society' are respected; but in this case, civil society provides the social basis of autonomous public spheres that remain as distinct from the economic system as from the administration.   (Habermas 1996b: 28)

According to this view, discourse theory advances the earlier presuppositions. Liberals use democracy to legitimise the exercise of power by governments. Republicans believe democratic practices to constitute the political community. Habermas introduces a discursive rationalisation to the understanding of democracy: 'The public opinion that is worked up via democratic procedures into communicative power cannot "rule" of itself, but can only point the use of administrative power in specific directions' (Habermas 1996b: 29). But the presupposition here is that such a unitary thing as 'influence' or 'communicative power' is in any sense achievable. It is welcome that Habermas understands the differences of civil society, but like Benjamin Barber he appears to think that these differences can be moulded into something tangible which can be a source of political action.[3] Why those who disagreed with whatever 'voice' came out of civil society should accept the transformation of opinions into 'communicative power' and thenceforth 'administrative power' is not immediately clear unless we adopt a simple majoritarian approach and, as we shall see, that is what a Habermasian approach to deliberation offers us. Whilst majoritarianism might be an unavoidable feature of liberal democratic politics, there is no adequate reason given as to why those who disagree with the majority position should acquiesce with the dominant view.

It is in this sense important to note that Habermas recognises that in 'democratic procedure, the ideal content of practical reason takes a pragmatic shape; the realization of the system of rights is measured by the forms in which this content is institutionalised' (Habermas 1996a: 303). The significance of this statement is that the normative basis of the state must not be set at too high or too low a level. This leads Habermas into a discussion of Bobbio whom he feels constructs a somewhat minimalist model which is based upon the prevailing forms of Western liberal democracy. Using Dewey, Habermas argues that it is not mere majority rule that should be supported in democratic decision-making, but rather we should focus our attention on the ways in which majorities are constructed. Thus, he contends that deliberative politics attains its 'legitimating force from the discursive structure of an opinion- and will-formation that can fulfill its socially integrative function only because citizens expect its results to have a reasonable *quality*. Hence the *discursive level* of public debate constitutes the most important variable' (Habermas 1996a: 304). Here we get to the crux of why Habermas believes we might acquiesce with majorities with whom we disagree. If we have faith in the outcomes of the deliberative process in terms of their quality whether we agree with them or not, then Habermas is probably right that there may be a pragmatic acquiescence and a reluctant acceptance of the decisions which are made. However, the existence of such magnanimity in those who lose out in such decisions in real life is more difficult to identify.

In societies like Northern Ireland it is even less likely that those who find themselves in a minority position on a given issue will merely accept the decision on the grounds that it has sufficient quality. Those who voted 'No' in the Belfast Agreement referendum have not faded into the background content with the fact that they fought a fair fight and lost. As with many who find themselves in a minority on a given issue, they have tended to reject the procedures which were used (e.g. the rectitude of the participation of republicans) and subsequently have resisted the provisions of the Agreement (e.g. the Democratic Unionist Party have refused cooperation with elected Republicans in the Northern Ireland Assembly and have undertaken a limited participation in the work of the Executive). The rights and wrongs of these approaches are not the point here; rather the idea that people will merely acquiesce with majority decisions on the grounds that the quality of the decision will be high is a fallacy. Habermasians might argue that the examples I use are evidence of groups of people who do not have sufficient faith in the procedural mechanisms which have been established and therefore that it is a moot point. They would have a case if they could find evidence of a complex, diverse society where everyone supports the existing procedural mechanisms. But we need to recognise that political procedures will always be the source of contention as is evident from the dimpled chads of Florida during the 2000 US Presidential Election to the campaigns of electoral reformers in Britain. The dubious election of Presidents or unrepresentative governments are not quietly accepted by those who disagree with these procedures and there is absolutely no reason why we should just go along with these decisions on the subjective grounds of 'quality'. Those who purport to support majorities on these issues should remind themselves of the transience of majorities and the fact that groups who find themselves in majorities over the passage of time may well end up as minorities. Nowhere is this warning more pertinent than in Northern Ireland.

Habermas is keen to differentiate his ideas from those of deliberative democrats such as Joshua Cohen who argue that the associative, deliberative ethos of civil society should be extended throughout society as a whole including the legal system and political institutions. Habermas argues that this is problematic because of the complexity of wider society and the difficulty of allowing all of the differing perspectives to engage in the key political decisions without formal procedures to guide political conduct. Instead, his view of deliberative democracy is built upon the idea of a 'core structure in a separate, constitutionally organized political system, but not as a model for all social institutions (and not even for all government institutions)' (Habermas 1996a: 305). Thus, whilst he agrees with Cohen's description of deliberative engagement in the civic sphere, Habermas adds further procedural postulates of his own that apply specifically to the political system. These are what differentiates the political community from the realm of more partial associations. Habermas argues that communication is more diverse and open in a public sphere in which numerous associations exist, whereas it needs to be more strictly controlled in the sphere of law and politics. That people can develop different perspectives in civil society is as a result of equal rights of citizenship which are only sustained through the universal constitutional mechanisms of the law.

The key to understanding where Habermas stands then, is in the drawing of boundaries between law and politics on the one hand and informal social communication on the other. Deliberative politics as a whole is comprised of both 'democratically institutionalised will-formation' and 'informal opinion-formation' (Habermas 1996a: 308). Habermas understands that liberal theories of neutrality (such as that of Ackerman and some of the theorists discussed in Chapter Two) which try to bracket ethical questions out of political discourse are problematic because they suggest that only matters with a tradition of agreement will be accepted as items conducive to political discourse. Therefore, Habermas wants to avoid 'rules of avoidance' (such as those in Rawlsian theory) or 'gag rules'. Instead, he wants us to engage in dialogues with each other regarding our political differences and transmit the resulting decisions through agreed procedures such as elections. Thus, when we are faced with 'questions of conflict resolution or concerning the choice of collective goals and we want to avoid the alternative of violent clashes, then we must engage in a practice of reaching understanding, whose procedures and communicative presuppositions are not at our disposition' (Habermas 1996a: 310). Habermas is aware of communitarian objections that these presuppositions will always be partial, reflecting certain values and principles. However, he contends that these procedures will be neutral if everyone involved in the political engagement agrees upon their rectitude and abides by the outcomes of those procedures.

This position has interesting bearing in the context of Northern Ireland. It assumes that we can reach agreement on the appropriate mechanisms for dealing with disputes when there is little evidence that this is the case. Traditionally, some nationalists have refused to participate in or cooperate with the institutions or procedures of Northern Ireland on the basis that they represented unionist hegemony or the British state. In the contemporary era some unionists have not cooperated fully in the devolved institutions of Northern Ireland because they see the procedures as they stand as a sop to nationalism. In terms of reaching compromises, we need to recognise internal differences within the 'two communities' and therefore the likelihood that people will take different perspectives on where appropriate compromises lie. This much is evident in contemporary unionism in Northern Ireland. Moreover, the appropriateness of the compromise is subject to change over time and this suggests that our political agreements and the institutions they establish will be transient and contingent. Habermas is at least partially aware of these problems when he notes that 'how private and public powers and responsibilities must be divided up in particular cases in order to adequately realize civil rights depends on the historical circumstances and, as we will see, on *perceived* social contexts' (Habermas 1996a: 314). This is an important statement especially in the light of the issue of perception in Northern Irish politics which I have been keen to emphasise. Habermas seems attuned to the difficulties in stating that 'boundary drawing ... must be a legitimate object of political debate' (Habermas 1996a: 314). All of this would be reassuring except that Habermas does not want to construct a contingent politics which is open to substantial reform and alteration where necessary. The Habermasian model is focused on *fairness and rationality*. But what is fair and rational will change over the course of time as a result of the changing social context and historical events. The willingness of Habermas to countenance such change is dubious given the way he wants to protect political and legal discourse from the vagaries of open contestation and informal engagement. Ultimately, the validity of his approach depends on the capacity of the procedures he values to change, and as we shall see there is insufficient evidence that such development is an integral part of his philosophy.

It is worth remembering the extent to which Habermas wants to separate the sphere of legal-political discourse from the informal communication of civil society. He argues very clearly that it would be an error to 'misunderstand the discursive character of public opinion- and will-formation if we thought we could hypostatize the normative content of general presuppositions of rational discourse into an ideal model of purely communicative social relations' (Habermas 1996a: 322). He admits that even his 'ideal speech situation' has been misinterpreted as a model for political discourse in just this way. For Habermas, the only legitimate use for the ideal speech situation in this area is as a 'thought experiment' (Habermas 1996a: 323). However, it is the strong boundary that Habermas establishes between the political and the social or cultural sphere which enrages many of his critics. After all, in a society like Northern Ireland political discourses are permeated by dispute and conflict not only over matters of substance but also over matters of procedure. Many of these views are not presented in the communicative fashion that Habermas promotes:

> Reaching mutual understanding through discourse indeed guarantees that issues, reasons, and information are handled reasonably, but such understanding still depends on contexts characterized by a capacity for learning, both at the cultural and the personal level. In

this respect, dogmatic worldviews and rigid patterns of socialization can block a discursive mode of sociation. (Habermas 1996a: 324–5)

What Habermas fails to deal with here is the pragmatic nature of many of the agreements which people make. In Northern Ireland there was much that both 'sides' disagreed with in the Belfast Agreement but the overall settlement offered enough to harness their support. Participants in discourse did not necessarily believe that their issues would be 'handled reasonably' but that in pragmatic terms the type of society which might emerge out of the Agreement could be preferable to the pre-Agreement situation. Dogmatic positions were engaged in the peace process and remain today – they do not block discursive relations, they are in themselves part of those relations.

Habermas is aware that in any society there will be obstacles to ideal forms of communication, but he contends that this does not negate his theory if politics can be organised in such a way as to overcome the fact that 'structures of the public sphere reflect unavoidable asymmetries in the availability of information, that is, unequal chances to have access to the generation, validation, shaping, and presentation of messages' (Habermas 1996a: 325). The important point here is that Habermas sees no reason why a disorganised public sphere should not be held together by a formal, procedural political system. Thus, he understands that even where conditions are favourable (presumably where social differences are not too disputatious and where there are broadly accepted modes of political discourse), no contemporary complex society could meet the requirements of communicative social relations. However, this is only problematic if we adopt a position which assumes 'a society without law and politics and projects the democratic idea of self-organization onto society as a whole' (Habermas 1996a: 326). Here we can see that the separation of politics and society is the crux of Habermasian theory; indeed it is upon this boundary that it stands or falls. In other words, because the ideas that animate the procedure of legal discourse emanate from civil society discourses, politics is already above those conflicting positions in civil society:

The basic rights and principles of government by law can be understood as so many steps toward reducing the unavoidable complexity evident in the necessary deviations from the model of pure communication. We can see this reduction of complexity still more clearly when such rights and principles are spelled out in constitutional law and when procedures of deliberative politics are institutionalised ...   (Habermas 1996a: 327)

Thus, Habermas accepts that there will be a wide range of positions in society and that the more complex a society is, the more conflicting perspectives there will be. However, political discourse is exempted from the inertia of conflict in the public sphere because it 'can be converted into political power only if it passes through the sluices of democratic procedure and penetrates the constitutionally organized political system in general' (Habermas 1996a: 327). Politics then is protected from dogmatism and closure because the democratic procedures filter out viewpoints and arguments which are not conducive to dialogue and compromise. The main criticism which can be directed at Habermas is that this perspective emasculates politics. In basing his system around agreement on legal procedures, he marginalises the possibility of challenges being raised against those procedures. Thus, oppositional viewpoints which invoke criticism of the political system may be filtered out by the sluice gates of democracy. It is highly likely that civil society will throw up more substantial challenges to the political system than the Habermasian theory of social complexity allows for.

Recent political history in Northern Ireland demonstrates the limitations of the Habermasian approach. For many years there political progress was hampered by the absence of legitimacy in the procedures and institutions of the state in the eyes of a sizeable section of society. Nonetheless, those institutions remained in place for many years and arguably it took the intervention of the British and Irish governments to kickstart the process of change. However, the institutions and procedures agreed through the Belfast Agreement are not universally supported and it is possible to discern growing dissatisfaction with them, especially in some parts of the unionist community. The point here is that it is extremely difficult to establish the universal support for political and legal mechanisms which Habermas relies upon. An open polity must accommodate the right for individuals to dissent against the political system and afford them the possibility of changing the prevailing procedures. In many respects the peace process in Northern Ireland has involved changes of just this kind. The danger of Habermasian theory is that the sluices he supports to safeguard politics and the law might filter out the ideas of those who oppose the dominant regime. This is a recipe for political stagnation rather than the kind of change which many people in Northern Ireland think necessary.

To conclude this section then, it is important to summarise the main difficulties which have emerged from the Habermasian version of deliberative democracy. The major problem noted by many commentators is that Habermas 'cuts political processes too cleanly away from cultural forms of communication' (Benhabib 1996: 7). In Northern Ireland this problem is manifest in the way in which political positions are closely bound up with issues of culture, religion and so on. To divest politics in Northern Ireland of these features would be to emasculate it and deny it the substance of social diversity. The central point that results from this methodological approach is that the Habermasian ideal-type attempts to build 'a *cordon sanitaire* around political discourse such as to block off the articulation of issues of collective identity and visions of the good life' (Benhabib 1996: 7). This strangling of politics is unjustifiable in any supposedly open polity which appreciates complexity and social diversity. In Northern Ireland, where collective identity and visions of the good life are the lifeblood of politics, such a notion of political organisation would render politics impotent in dealing with the very real conflicts and disputes that animate culture and society.

Dryzek's model of discursive democracy

With the publication of *Deliberative Democracy and Beyond* (2000), John Dryzek has offered a different version of deliberative democracy which may be more attuned to the realities of Northern Irish politics. Having noted how the term deliberative democracy is used to mean different things by a variety of thinkers, Dryzek wants to differentiate between deliberative democracy and his preferred term 'discursive democracy'. He argues that deliberation can be a personal process rather than being necessarily social and intersubjective like his model of discourse. Moreover, deliberation also implies calm, reasoned argument rather than a discursive process which can include 'unruly and contentious communication from the margins' (Dryzek 2000: vi). Clearly, in my comments above, I have contended that a realistic theory of deliberation for Northern Ireland must recognise the existence of political conflict and Dryzek's model seems more coordinated with this position:

Discursive democracy should be pluralistic in embracing the necessity to communicate across difference without erasing difference, reflexive in its questioning orientation to established traditions (including the tradition of deliberative democracy itself), transnational in its capacity to extend across state boundaries into settings where there is no constitutional framework ... and dynamic in its openness to ever-changing constraints upon and opportunities for democratization.   (Dryzek 2000: 3)[4]

In Dryzek's eyes then, the deliberative turn involves a search for democratic authenticity which demands both reflection and the potential for change. Whilst this seems a feasible position for Northern Ireland, his pursuit of authenticity also demands an absence of domination and coercion. This is, of course, a worthy objective, but it is difficult to achieve in any polity let alone one rife with the kind of conflict which exists in Northern Ireland.

Like Habermas, Dryzek wants to differentiate his position from that of traditional liberal theories. In the latter he argues that the deliberation which exists has traditionally been within the parameters of liberal political institutions: 'deliberation about the meaning and applicability of rules is central' (Dryzek 2000: 13). In the traditional liberal model this deliberation has basically taken the form of dialogue in parliaments, through the law courts and so on. Many liberals and other political theorists have begun to recognise the limited nature of such a conception of deliberation and its élitist foundation. One attempt to grapple with this came from Rawls, but Dryzek criticises the Rawlsian model because it sees deliberation primarily as an individual process – it is only social in the sense that all individuals deliberate in the same way: 'Rawlsian public reason is singular, and produces consensus. Given that reason is singular, no interactive process is necessary to enable it to produce its conclusions' (Dryzek 2000: 15). Not surprisingly, Dryzek sees this as an extremely thin understanding of deliberative democracy and notes that it has an 'anti-social – and so anti-political – approach to deliberation' (Dryzek 2000: 16). In this sense, Dryzek disputes the Rawlsian pursuit of consensus and argues that the best that can be hoped for is some kind of mutual respect and a *modus vivendi*. His problem with political liberalism has been its failure to understand the depth of power and the favourable position held by some interests in society. Where this is the case, certain discourses will be viewed as more acceptable than others and this may be reflected in the forms of deliberation which are established in any given polity.

Dryzek differentiates this liberal approach to deliberative democracy with an approach which he links with the critical theory tradition. Where liberal constitutionalism has often been ignorant of political economy and associated inequalities of power, traditionally critical theory was more aware of the problems which economic relations might cause for free, open dialogue. In the critical theory tradition, Dryzek refers in particular to the early work of Habermas and the way in which he established his theory of communicative rationality as the counterpoint to the instrumental rationality of the system (state, economy, and so on). Of course, for Habermas, the instrumental rationality of the system has impeded the development of communicative rationality in the public sphere. However, Dryzek wants to point out how this separation of the system from the public sphere has led to numerous assumptions about the sphere of communicative rationality. Thus, he notes how, against the Habermasian ideal-type, the public sphere is inhabited by all sorts of groups such as racists and religious fundamentalists and not just the 'progressive' groups such as the new social movements which seem to be the focus for Habermas. Thus, Dryzek is more sceptical and realistic about the implications of the renewal of civil society and rejects the separation of system and life world which characterised Habermas' earlier work. Moreover, Dryzek contends that Habermas has little to say about political structures (except that they distort communicative rationality):

> under communicative rationality – especially in its counterfactual extreme of the 'ideal speech situation' – the only force that applies is that of better argument. Decision is ideally secured by consensus; implementation of the decision is secured only by the commitment of the individuals involved to the content of that consensus; and subsequent compliance relies on free consent. Such a sequence is not easily related to real-world political institutions and processes, especially those in complex and plural societies.   (Dryzek 2000: 24).

For Dryzek, Habermas rectified some of these problems in *Between Facts and Norms,* but the price he had to pay was that he ended up with a position much closer to the liberal constitutionalist view of deliberative democracy. In his later position Habermas wants the state to be structured in such a way as to support and protect civil society. To do this there is 'a set of human rights inscribed in law. Thus law is treated as the main prop for moral and political discourse, not just the force for social control which an earlier Habermas would have stressed' (Dryzek 2000: 25). However, for Dryzek, this appears to be an accommodation with an older juridical democratic theory and the results are very similar to liberal constitutionalism. Thus there 'is no sense that the administrative state, or economy, should be democratised any further. All that matters is that they be steered by law, itself democratically influenced. Habermas has turned his back on extra-constitutional agents of both democratic influence and democratic distortion' (Dryzek 2000: 26). For Dryzek, the Habermasian approach is no longer then a critical theory insofar as it accepts the main institutional structures of existing liberal democracies. Indeed, they are ascribed a legitimacy which was questioned in Habermas's earlier work. This shift is reflected in much work on deliberative democracy which has been increasingly subsumed within liberal orthodoxy and, with the exception of a few notables, the radical dimension has been squeezed out.[5]

We have noted already the difficulties of political liberalism and Habermasian theory in the context of Northern Ireland. What then does Dryzek have to offer us in his version of discursive democracy? Interestingly, in his refutation of social choice and rational choice theories, he notes how actors in deliberation are not merely strategic actors who behave in predictable, almost pre-determined, fashion. Indeed, Dryzek (2000: 40–1) uses Northern Ireland during the peace process as an example of how participants may make decisions which cannot be reduced to pure strategic interest. Negotiations on such matters are normally more complex than simple strategic interest allows and so are never straightforward. An example from the Belfast Agreement is the controversial scheme for the release of paramilitary prisoners. This provision was agreed by the two governments and many constitutional parties with a heavy heart and, in an ideal world, they would probably have been happy to see the prisoners remaining in jail. Nonetheless, the negotiations were highly contingent and imperfect and, in the interests of the overall agreement, most participants accepted the provision as a *quid pro quo*. This is a reminder of the importance of the complexity of choice and that, despite perceptions of a zero-sum game, when it comes to political deliberation numerous compromises have to be made. Of course, as noted earlier, some within groups will agree with compromises and some will not. The important reminder here is that, despite the difficulties of deliberation and compromise, ultimately decisions have to be taken even where there is not widespread consensus. Thus, Dryzek is keen to remind us that even deliberative democrats who appeal to consensus such as Habermas and Cohen have to resort to voting and elections in the end, which would suggest that consensus has not been reached:

> In Habermas's communicative theory, under ideal, distortion-free conditions, given long enough to debate, consensus would be achieved on matters of both morality and truth. What distinguishes consensus from mere agreement is that individuals support the outcome for essentially the same reasons. Of course, real-world exigencies and time constraints would in practice get in the way, as Habermas himself recognizes ... But consensus remains the regulative ideal, an orientation to which real-world arrangements could aspire, though never actually reach.   (Dryzek 2000: 48)

Dryzek is correct that it is this concern for consensus that worries some commentators who might otherwise be attracted to the Habermasian ideal. This would not be a substantial problem if consensus was a side issue for Habermas but, as we saw earlier, it is actually essential to his normative conception of the political and legal domain.

The other group of theorists that Dryzek challenges is the loose group he identifies as theorists of 'difference democracy'. In this group he includes theorists such as Iris Marion Young and William Connolly who build their arguments around opposition to the pursuit of consensus in most deliberative models. Thus, '[w]here social choice theorists see dangerous variety, difference democrats see dangerous uniformity' (Dryzek 2000: 58). By this he means that difference democrats envisage democracy as a permanent contestation of conflicting identities. The position of Connolly, for example, is described as one where 'identities and their associated differences should be treated as a matter for continuous exploration, receiving at best only conditional and contingent statement. Democratic politics in this light should involve the creative questioning of identities through encounter with disparate others' (Dryzek 2000: 58). Dryzek recognises that Connolly sees little of this in the real world where identity and difference are often accompanied by dogmatism and closure. In a sense this is nowhere more apparent than in Northern Ireland. However, Dryzek rejects the focus on rights for minority groups in difference democrats such as Young. For the former, if we enshrined rights of veto for minority groups, we would end up with political stalemate. Of course, this is precisely what happened in the Belfast Agreement where the need for parallel consent for Assembly legislation was put in place to prevent the unionist majority from implementing policies which were not supported by nationalists. Whilst Dryzek has a point that this can lead to politics where legislation only comes from issues where there is consensus, we have to recognise that there is no consensus on issues which come out of the Northern Ireland Assembly. Rather, all legislation requires is a majority of both of the major designations for laws to be passed. A simple majority of both groups in no way presumes consensus and, as such, in no way does it induce stalemate.[6] Whilst it may be a very blunt instrument, parallel consent does not lead to the outcomes which Dryzek identifies.

This misconception aside, Dryzek is at pains to point to the problems that can emanate from the construction of democracy around the idea of different identities. The danger is that difference democracy, which ostensibly subverts essentialist conceptions of identity, may create new essentialisms. In other words, the issue is one where old political categories such as social class are replaced by new ones focusing on things like gender or sexuality and that the problems of the old categories are merely being replicated. Thus, where difference democrats may object, for example, to the way in which class may overlook important sources of difference around age or geography, they run the risk of doing the same around categories such as gender or sexuality. Here we can see that some difference democrats such as Young are wary of couching their concerns in terms of 'identity' precisely because it can essentialise fixed ideas of groups.[7] Dryzek argues that if we are to build democracy around difference we should do so in terms of competing discourses rather than identities. This is designed to circumvent any sense in which the source of conflict is prescribed by a particular identity, that who we are will automatically programme our response to specific political scenarios. However, where Dryzek differs from Young is in the way in which the latter conceives of the deliberative process. She argues that the particular forms of deliberation which deliberative democrats favour are not necessarily open to all – she contends that deliberation tends to be conceptualised in a rather masculine form. Thus, as deliberation emerges in the work of Rawls and Habermas, Young feels that there are too many strict rules and procedures about what kind of communication is acceptable for rational political engagement. She rejects these models because they favour formal legal and political mechanisms and understandings of rationality over the use of rhetoric or storytelling, for example, as a legitimate form of political expression. Dryzek is more accommodating of these alternative sources of communication but he notes that they can generate political problems too. Ultimately this is not such a difficulty for Dryzek because he does not envisage deliberation as a process of pursuing unity; indeed his model of discursive democracy welcomes the increased diversity which may result from an opening up of more sources of political engagement.

Before concluding, it is worth summarising Dryzek's thesis on discursive democracy. He wants to promote a democratic engagement which is open to numerous forms of communication, although he contends that communication should not be coercive and that the particular must have a bearing on general political concerns. These communications must also be applicable to the rational resolution of problems but he allows space for dissent in a way that many deliberative democrats do not. Indeed, Dryzek goes so far as to allow sectarian positions into his dialogue on the grounds that '[d]eliberative democrats are those who have faith in the powers of deliberation itself to root out bad arguments and sectarianism; to deny their advocates admission into the forum is to reveal a lack of confidence in the efficacy of deliberation' (Dryzek 2000: 169). Sensibly, he also permits bargaining although he feels it can be unedifying and such strategic action can lead to distorted outcomes. Nonetheless, it is to be allowed because in some situations (such as in Northern Ireland) there is insufficient trust between the participants and the only way to achieve a collective outcome may be some kind of bargaining. Even here he notes that 'deliberation can still play a useful role by inducing participants to multiply dimensions and options, thus increasing the possibilities for stable and non-arbitrary bargains' (Dryzek 2000: 170). This is a sensible approach to deliberation which recognises that differing reasons propel different participants to the negotiating table. The strength of Dryzek's argument lies in his readiness to dispense with the pursuit of consensus. Instead he prefers 'workable agreements in which participants agree on a course of action, but for different reasons' (Dryzek 2000: 170). He regards this as the deepest, most authentic form of democracy and, insofar as it challenges prevailing forms of liberal constitutionalism, it offers a more applicable model of deliberation for Northern Ireland than is the case with some other exponents of deliberative democracy.[8] However, whilst it does liberate the concept of democracy from the handcuffs of consensus, even then it is a difficult conception to apply in the context of Northern Ireland.

Deliberation, democracy and Northern Ireland

Whilst a 'deliberative turn' has taken place in contemporary political theory, it is possible to identify numerous different manifestations that this concern for deliberation has taken.[9] It has been adopted by political liberals such as Rawls to reinforce their separation of the non-public and political spheres in such a way as to strengthen traditional institutions of liberalism such as parliaments and courts of law. Habermas makes the case for deliberation more substantively in arguing that there need to be formal rules and procedures for political engagement which filter out irrational positions that can emerge in the freer communicative sphere of civil society. Ultimately, though, he too must separate formal politics from a wider cultural politics because his major concern is the pursuit of a decision-making process in which there can be universal support. These approaches can be contrasted with the ideas of Dryzek who, whilst similarly arguing for more deliberation, recognises that this will not lead to rational outcomes or universal support for the procedures. He envisages discursive democracy as a model of engagement which will be more disputatious in nature and less inclined towards consensus or agreement. This model is the most representative of the kind of political realities which emerge in most societies, especially those of a divided nature such as Northern Ireland. However, this approach is more open-ended and tells us much less about how political institutions should be organised on a practical basis. Nonetheless, this leaves greater scope for particular societies to organise their democratic arrangements in the context of the particular political problems which they encounter.

Much of the attraction of deliberative democracy is rather intuitive insofar as the idea of enhancing communication across difference appeals to many liberal sensitivities. On this intuitive level there is much to welcome in increased political communication. Nonetheless we need to be careful not to let this tentative support blind us to the difficulties which can result from this type of engagement. In this sense, if we are to guardedly support deliberative models, it should be on a critical basis whereby we recognise that no such model can override political conflict or simply manufacture consensus. Tentative support for such an approach is provided by Festenstein who cites the work of Jeremy Waldron as the model for his position. Festenstein summarises the position as one where democracy is characterised by citizens engaging in negotiation and attempting to persuade each other of the validity of a particular policy or course of action. He envisages such a system as one where citizens are committed to trying to reach agreement on common issues and this presupposes a deliberative model of democracy in which:

> citizens are thought to share a commitment to continued coexistence and to be reluctant to exercise the option to exit the associ-

ation or to split it. Furthermore, they are thought to have diverse and conflicting goals, opinions and projects, and an interest in shaping political arrangements by reference to these goals, opinions and projects. There is no presumption that they share a moral or religious code, cultural sympathies or ethnic identity ... However, it does demand that they share a commitment to arriving at agreement in cases of social and political conflict through a process of public deliberation and debate.   (Festenstein 2000: 85)

There are, however, some sticking points which Festenstein recognises. He notes the dangers of majoritarianism and the risk that such a model will merely reinforce existing decisions. After all, we do need some mechanism for decision-making if deliberation does not lead to agreement. It is also important to note that we need to be wary of unrepresentative leaders speaking erroneously for whole communities. In this sense, we should remember the critique of essentialism provided by difference democrats and the perils which can come from the focus on different identities as the basis of dealing with conflict and difference rather than different discourses. Following Habermas, Festenstein contends that the processes of deliberation will at least show up fallacious arguments for what they are even if agreement cannot be reached. However Festenstein is ultimately left with only a pragmatic position because he recognises that the model provided by Habermas does not provide a realistic blueprint for dialogue in deeply divided societies.

On pragmatic grounds some of these theories of deliberative democracy could be applicable in Northern Ireland as Habermasians such as O'Neill have shown (O'Neill 2000, 2002; Newey 2002; Little 2003). Several questions remain though which make this application problematic. In Northern Ireland we need to ask who speaks for whom? Deliberation, though common on an individual level, is usually undertaken on a group basis when it comes to resolving conflict or political decision-making. This can lead to much complexity. For example, when it comes to the representation of communities on the Shankill Road, there are numerous sensitivities. There is an elected MP for the area but it is Gerry Adams for whom very few on the Shankill Road will have voted and indeed whom many will revile. At the same time perhaps, we could look to the defeated unionist candidates or Assembly members or council representatives, but this would show up the differences within unionism. Indeed, different parts of the Shankill Road have traditionally been the preserve of different loyalist groups and this has periodically erupted into internecine strife. At the same time many unionists will be opposed to parties linked to paramilitary organisations. This should make the complexity of Northern Irish politics evident when it comes to those who should deliberate on the behalf of different groups. We could state that all those with an interest should participate (and perhaps we should) but this means that we need to recognise that the more participation there is in the deliberative process, the more likely it is that conflict and disagreement will result. It is for precisely this reason that Habermas wants to use the sluice gates of democracy to narrow down the range of formal political discourse. Given the sensitivities in Northern Ireland, though, a more inclusive but more disputatious understanding of politics may be required.

A further problem with the practical realisation of deliberative democracy in Northern Ireland is simply that it asks a lot of its participants. Arguably, deliberative democracy is biased towards those with the appropriate ability and disposition towards the benefits of dialogue. In other words, it requires all participants to have an accommodating attitude towards deliberation with others and implies that those without this attitude are somehow deficient. In terms of democracy we should of course encourage dialogue, but in Northern Ireland this has been contentious. Some parties such as the Democratic Unionist Party reject the right of Sinn Féin to participate in political institutions. Whilst we may argue that they are misguided given Sinn Féin's electoral mandate, it is the issue of perception which undermines deliberative democracy here. Given their opposition to Sinn Féin, the DUP will see any process based on deliberation as inevitably loaded against them given their unwillingness to enter into completely open dialogue. Thus, one need have little sympathy with the latter to realise that in a society like Northern Ireland we cannot assume that all participants have the 'correct' attitude towards dialogue. The DUP may engage in some deliberation for strategic reasons because failure to do so may lead to an even broader range of changes than those they already oppose. However, we cannot simply rule out the participation of certain parties because of their attitude. Just as Sinn Féin has an electoral mandate so does the DUP and we need to recognise that politics in Northern Ireland cannot be limited prescriptively to only those who we deem to have the appropriate disposition towards dialogue. However, if we believe that everyone with a democratic mandate should be able to participate in dialogue, then we can oppose the DUP position. Following Dryzek, we could argue that everyone should be able to participate and that we should have faith in deliberation to root out poor or sectarian arguments. However, this is not a 'rational' decision in the Habermasian sense; rather, it is political in itself and should be recognised as such. Decisions about who is included and excluded will always have some kind of political foundation and to pretend otherwise is to misunderstand the very nature of politics.

To summarise then, deliberative democracy is attractive to liberals for intuitive reasons but it is extremely difficult to put into practice. This difficulty becomes harder to resolve the more complex or divided a society itself. Whilst Northern Ireland is not as complex as some societies, it is undoubtedly divided. These divisions are not merely down a single ethno-national line (important as it may be) but reflect numerous fractures on issues of class, gender, sexuality, ethnicity and so on. This makes deliberation more complicated and will raise questions about the degree of representativeness of participants. Formal politics in Northern Ireland has tended to be driven by élites and this has limited the capacity of decision-making to provide inclusive solutions to the difficulties which prevail there. In the remainder of the book I will analyse theories of democracy that focus on the possibility of opening up the political sphere to enable greater participation by groups which have often found themselves excluded in Northern Irish politics.

5
Social Capital, Trust and Civil Society

In the liberal theories that we have examined so far, the focus has been directed towards rights discourses as the basis of dealing with social diversity. Whilst some liberals have founded their democratic theory around universal rights, others associated with multiculturalism have argued for group-differentiated rights. However none of these discourses of rights have proved capable of providing a model of liberalism which is practically applicable to Northern Ireland. As an alternative the remainder of the book will examine theories that move the focus from individual or group rights towards issues of social structure. In this chapter I will examine recent theories which are less concerned with the relationship between individuals and the state than contemporary liberalism and which concentrate instead on the strengthening of spheres in between the individual and the state. These theories have become increasingly prevalent in recent years and are evident in the renewed interest in concepts such as civil society and social capital. As we saw in Chapter One, these ideas have been prominent in the Northern Irish peace process and were a feature of the Belfast Agreement that set it apart from previous political initiatives which tended to focus mainly on constitutional arrangements and formal political mechanisms and institutions.

Social capital and civil society

Recent political theory has been characterised by the rejuvenation of the concept of civil society (see, for example, Keane 1998; Dryzek 2000; Young 2000). There is considerable variation in the way in which civil society is used but it is commonly thought of as the space in between individuals and the state which is populated by a range of groups, associations and communities.[1] The renewal of civil society is usually depicted as a process of democratisation whereby political relations are enhanced by the empowerment of sub-state actors and institutions. This is a proposal for greater participation in decision-making processes and it is often accompanied in the literature by the promotion of social capital. For Robert Putnam, social capital refers to 'connections among individuals – social networks and the norms of reciprocity and trustworthiness that arise from them' (Putnam 2000: 19). He contends that a range of political, economic and social benefits accrue from the empowerment of the sphere of community and civic interaction. Clearly these strategies are distinctive from the universalist forms of liberalism promoted by commentators such as Brian Barry that concentrate on the protection of individual rights by the state as the foundation of the liberal polity. In civil society and social capital discourses, the universal guarantees of the state are reduced in importance (though still apparent) in order to strengthen the position of different communities to establish a degree of control over the social, political and economic arrangements around them. This chapter will evaluate the extent to which these arguments apply in Northern Ireland and the extent to which they could facilitate a renewal of the Northern Irish polity and society.

Putnam bases his argument in the supposed decline of civility in the United States since the 1950s. He yearns for the more cohesive relations which characterised American society in the post-World War II period. The metaphor he uses to explain why social capital is the cornerstone of cohesive societies concerns bowling leagues. Putnam notes the continued popularity of bowling as a pastime in the United States since World War II but whilst 'more Americans are bowling than ever before, ... *league* bowling has plummeted in the last ten to fifteen years' (Putnam 2000: 112). Whereas in the 1950s and 1960s bowlers in the United States were organised into teams who participated in leagues within their communities, the trend has become one of 'Bowling Alone': that is, individuals participate alone or in informal groups rather than in the organised leagues which helped to make bowling lanes important sources of social capital in the post-war United States. This is a metaphor for a population that has become more individualistic and less connected with each other since the 1960s. Putnam's argument is for a rejuvenation of the fabric of American communities as the basis for broader socio-economic renewal. In this sense we must reverse the individualistic drift and strengthen our communal bonds with each other.

Social capital is not envisaged by Putnam as a set of relations which are contractual or which generate clear benefits to individuals who participate in them; instead, reciprocity is the key to the existence and production of social capital. Thus, Putnam points to social connections which involve mutual obligations as the centrepiece of social capital. Social capital is especially strong when individuals reciprocate not for direct, specific reasons but where there are relations of 'generalized reciprocity':

> A society characterized by generalized reciprocity is more efficient than a distrustful society, for the same reason that money is more efficient than barter. If we don't have to balance every exchange instantly, we get a lot more accomplished. Trustworthiness lubricates social life. Frequent interaction among a diverse set of people tends to produce a norm of generalized reciprocity. Civic engagement and social capital entail mutual obligation and responsibility for action.   (Putnam 2000: 21)

Putnam's argument then is that a range of political, economic and social benefits accrue when individuals are entrenched in networks that ensure interaction and generate bonds of reciprocity. Despite this, he does raise some caveats with regard to the outcomes of social capital. For example, he recognises the possible ways that local networks can be defensive and exclusionary and the ways in which groups can be dominated by power élites with less than altruistic objectives at heart. Moreover, he points to the fact that terrorist groups, for example, and others bent on violence and destruction rely upon the existence of social capital. This point is particularly pertinent with regard to discussions of Northern Ireland. A key distinction in Putnam's thought, then, is between social capital which is '*bridging* (or inclusive) and *bonding* (or exclusive)' (Putnam 2000: 22). In simple terms, bonding social capital refers to the links within various groups that are established between their members but which do not extend beyond the group. This is exclusive social capital insofar as only those who are seen to be part of a group are granted the benefits of interaction in the network and generalised reciprocity. Putnam is not opposed to bonding social capital insofar as he sees it as important to support the bonds which hold groups together. Nonetheless, reciprocity in these circumstances tends to be specific insofar as we know exactly what we can expect from fellow members and we are able to differentiate insiders from outsiders.

Bridging social capital on the other hand is much more significant in terms of broader social cohesion. Rather than the potentially exclusionary associations of bonding groups, bridging social capital alludes to different groups reaching out to each other in inclusive terms. In this sense, the bonds which hold groups together are broadened outwards into wider social relations. Thus, whilst Putnam believes that there are positive dimensions to both types of social capital, '[b]onding social capital, by creating strong in-group loyalty, may also create strong out-group antagonism ... and for that reason we might expect negative external effects to be more common with this form of social capital' (Putnam 2000: 23). The parallels between Putnam's distinction and life in Northern Ireland are clear. Northern Ireland is characterised by high levels of bonding social capital insofar as communities and traditions have coalesced around shared historical, cultural and political events. There is less evidence of a widespread appetite for bridging social capital whereby the different traditions in Northern Ireland extend generalised reciprocity with each other. Thus, insofar as social capital exists in Northern Ireland, it tends to be of an exclusive rather than an inclusive nature.

Having noted Putnam's caveats, it is worth pointing out that there are a number of assumptions underpinning the 'bowling alone' thesis which call into question its relevance for Northern Irish politics. At its heart is an organic view of society which relies on the idea that there is a coherent society that needs to be reconnected. Of course, the situation in Northern Ireland is rather more complex; it is a society that is built around division rather than coherence or uniformity. The problems with the application of Putnam's theory in Northern Ireland are articulated by Feargal Cochrane (2002). He notes that, in the Northern Irish context, 'the normal gravitational forces that underpin [civil society] within more stable polities ... are sharpened to a degree that they can just as easily mutate into uncivil norms and values'. Thus, 'within a divided society like Northern Ireland joining the group or having a strong sense of community can have a wholly different, (and violent) set of outcomes' (Cochrane 2002: 2). According to this view then, Putnam's advocacy of greater participation and civic awareness needs to be contextualised and this means that social capital will manifest itself in distinctive ways in different contexts. For Cochrane, it is not the absence of organisations in civil society or a lack of willingness to participate that has been at the root of Northern Ireland's problems. On the contrary, those problems may have been exacerbated by the desire of individuals to defend their communities. In this sense 'community cohesion, civic activism and the desire for associational life that are the building blocks of civil society, may lead to very uncivil outcomes' (Cochrane 2002: 10).

The important point to recognise here is that there has never been a shortage of 'social capital' in Northern Ireland in the sense that there is a thriving sub-state sector of social and economic activity.[2] When this is coupled with the acute sense of community that prevails there, we can see that there is a well-established civil society in Northern Ireland and that numerous voices emerged from that sector to play a central role in the build-up to the Belfast Agreement and, in particular, the 'Yes' campaign in the subsequent referendum (Oliver 1998; Cochrane and Dunn 2002). But this civil society is comprised of a wide range of organisations, some of which are more civil than others. Whilst many of the people in these groups have been steadfast peace activists, others have come to the civic sphere through either direct activism in paramilitary groups or, for example, in the rehabilitation of released prisoners (the numbers of which increased through the early release scheme of the Belfast Agreement). The point here is that the idea of a singular community which needs to be reinvigorated to provide social capital is a contentious idea in Northern Ireland. The self-perception there of the existence of at least two communities means that there is 'a near obsessional desire to *bowl together* along a fractured and dichotomous community divide. The existence of two separate communities competing for space and power within the region, produced a desire to bowl together separately!' (Cochrane 2002: 12). In Putnam's terms, we can identify bonding social capital within communities in Northern Ireland, but there is less evidence of bridging social capital between these communities. In short, Northern Ireland is characterised by a thriving civil society sector but one that is scarred by tensions and divisions along the traditional communal lines.

Cochrane makes the important point that the renewal of civil society in Northern Ireland is not as straightforward a matter as might be the case elsewhere because social capital is a relational concept that cannot be divorced from the particular context in which it emerges. He notes how many of the newer community activists were previously activists in violent conflict and, more importantly, their motivation for both types of activity was effectively the same: namely, to defend their community. In Northern Ireland, however, there is a degree of hierarchy in the perception of different community groups. Those that are regarded as fronts for particular political parties or which are represented by prominent individuals in the conflict may not be accorded the same levels of respect and civility as others.[3] The danger with this kind of hierarchy is that civil society might become a venue for peace groups, charities, some religious organisations and so on rather than genuinely representing the variety of individuals and associations that comprise Northern Irish society. This is not just a problem in the context of Northern Ireland but permeates the literature on community and civil society more generally in the sense that consensus rather than conflict is often presented as the atmospheric norm (Little 2002a, 2002d). In Northern Ireland it is particularly dangerous as it risks the marginalisation of some groups and this could easily lead to the resurgence of violence. Therefore, it is important to recognise that the creation of social capital or renewal of civil society alone is not a coherent avenue for the social development of Northern Ireland:

> [bowling together] will only be useful within a divided society such as that in Northern Ireland, if an equal amount of effort is put into managing, healing or transcending the divisions between the bowlers! It is the contention here, that in the absence of the latter, the former may do more harm than good, and bowling alone may prove to be the best conflict management strategy available, in the short term at least.   (Cochrane 2002: 13)

A question of trust: Onora O'Neill

Associated with the growth of literature on social capital has been the rise of theories concerned with the concept of trust. A notable contribution to these debates has been provided by Francis Fukuyama who argues that the prevalence of spontaneous relations of trust and co-operation in civil society underpins successful economic relations.[4] For Fukuyama, these spontaneous relations are culturally embedded and thus any attempt to change the economic conditions of any given society cannot be divorced from consideration of its social structure. However, a more recent philosophical attempt to outline the political implications of trust has been provided by Onora O'Neill in her 2002 Reith Lectures. This is a particularly interesting thesis for our purposes because O'Neill explicitly focuses on Northern Ireland as an exemplar of a society where relations of trust and mistrust have broad social significance. She constructs her argument around the relationship between mistrust, fear and terrorism and the potential of a resurgence of trust as a means of exiting a spiral of violence. However, at the same time she is aware of the existence of issues of spontaneity and unpredictability that come with trust: 'trust risks disappointment. The risk of disappointment, even of betrayal cannot be written out of our lives ... Trust is needed not because everything is wholly predictable, or wholly guaranteed, but on the contrary because life has to be led without guarantees' (O'Neill 2002: 24). For O'Neill then, trust can generate virtuous and vicious spirals whereby, if it is reciprocated, it can generate more trust, whereas, if it is betrayed, mistrust can spiral downwards. In this sense then, her vision of trust is permeated by risk but this risk is ever present in all social relations and is all the more threatening in conditions of terrorism and fear.

The problem for theorists of trust is how it is to be engendered when it has been lost or undermined. In the work of Fukuyama, for example, much rests on whether a particular society has an ingrained cultural disposition towards trust and this has obvious ramifications for societies that he deems to have low trust cultures. For O'Neill, the answer to the problem of restoring trust is not to be found in the discourses of human rights and democracy that have characterised the Northern Ireland peace process. Rather, she sees these discourses as being reliant upon a basis of trust and not *vice versa*. In other words, trust engenders democracy rather than democracy providing trust. O'Neill is deeply sceptical about the prevalence of rights discourses in the contemporary world which she regards as often ill thought out and culturally specific. Her major problem with rights is that they are often claimed with no corresponding awareness that they give rise to duties. Thus, she contends that claims of rights are mere rhetoric if it is not incumbent on the rest of us to respect them. In this sense, in order to have our rights respected, others need to have certain duties. Moreover, for O'Neill, if we are to claim rights, we have a duty to others to respect their rights; this dimension, she argues, is rarely evident in contemporary claims of rights. Thus, individuals 'have often been willing, even eager, to claim their rights, but much less willing to meet their duties to respect others' rights' (O'Neill 2002: 30).

For O'Neill, the major problem here is that we usually look to the state to guarantee rights but she believes that many modern states are unable to provide such guarantees. Whilst O'Neill may be right here, in Northern Ireland the case is not just that the state is problematic in guaranteeing rights but that the rights which are claimed conflict with one another. It may well be the case that many rights-claims are erroneous *qua* rights, for example some of those 'rights' claimed by the protagonists in the Drumcree dispute. The potentially contradictory nature of rights-claims is not the main feature of O'Neill's argument however; instead she focuses on the fact that we fail to see how our claims of rights entail having duties to others. Whilst this may well be the case, in issues of dispute like the Garvaghy Road, both sides claim rights but feel that the other side is failing to fulfil their duties. However, to do what the other side believe to be their duty would entail giving up one's rights claim. For example, marchers may perceive residents to have a duty to allow them to fulfil their right to march down the Garvaghy Road. If, however, the residents were to meet this 'duty' they would surrender their own rights-claim to be free from marches outside their houses. In this sense it is not sufficient for O'Neill to merely highlight the absence of duties in the discourse of rights if she does not recognise that rights-claims – whether justifiable or not – often conflict with one another.

O'Neill is persuasive in arguing that the focus on duties makes us think differently about ethics and politics insofar as it asks us 'to begin by thinking about what *ought* to be done and *who* ought to do it, rather than what we ought to get' but is much too optimistic when she goes a step further to contend that '[a]ctive citizens who meet their duties thereby secure one another's rights' (O'Neill 2002: 4). It is one thing to suggest that we need to reassess our approach to ethical claims in politics but quite another to assert on this basis that actively meeting our duties rather than passively accepting our rights will necessarily secure the rights of others. If we recognise the prevalence of conflicts and disputes in societies such as Northern Ireland, then blithe assertions such as O'Neill's are difficult to implement in practice. As the example of the Drumcree dispute alluded to above suggests, where rights-claims conflict, they are unlikely to be resolved simply by an alternative discourse of duties (laudable as that may be in certain contexts). O'Neill invokes Kantian liberalism to demonstrate how a universal concern for duties can form the basis of justice and how terrorism undermines universalism as perpetrators prevent victims from acting freely. Therefore, in O'Neill's eyes, terrorism and victimisation undermine universal liberalism. This much is evident as an exercise in liberal philosophy but it is much more problematic when we try to apply these ideas in practice. Appealing to the better nature of terrorists and perpetrators of violence on the grounds that their individual actions undermine the universal rights of others is unlikely to carry much weight. After all, if we are serious about dealing with violence and terrorism, we need to grapple with the historical and political reasons that generate it. Kantian ethics tell us more about how we ought to be ideally rather than what to do with real political problems. If we understand Northern Irish politics as centred upon conflict based on incommensurable value pluralism, then O'Neill's universalism has value as an aspiration at best but has limited practical application.

What can be done then to implement O'Neill's theory of trust in such inhospitable conditions? She is right to contend that violence and social unrest such as that in Northern Ireland does not preclude the possibility of trust or civility emerging. Indeed she argues persuasively that, if we focus on rights alone, there is not much we can do until others respect our rights. If, however, we adopt an approach that looks at duties, perhaps elements of trust can emerge. O'Neill is not so persuasive though in suggesting that trust is counterposed with conditions of violence. Instead, there is considerable evidence that societies such as Northern Ireland have always contained elements of trust and mistrust rubbing alongside one another. From her elevated position O'Neill sees trust as something that can only be associated with right thinking people:

> Speaking truthfully does not damage trust, it creates a climate of trust. We can stop using euphemisms to placate those who threaten or do injustice; we can refuse to dignify community intimidators by speaking of them as community leaders; we can accord genuine community leaders the honour they deserve. We can stop using vocabularies of community protection and freedom fighting to dignify crimes. We can stop calling for reduced police powers whilst simultaneously demanding stronger police protection. We can set aside the passive outlook, which fantasises that blaming and accusing others contributes to justice.   (O'Neill 2002: 37–8)

The piety with which O'Neill speaks grates in the context of the real problems of Northern Ireland. People will only make the stands that she asks when they believe in them. She wants to wish away the reasons why people hold the beliefs that they do behind the shroud that they are coerced into doing so by terrorists and perpetrators of violence. However, following the arguments of Cochrane in the section above, we have to recognise that it is not simply a matter of the right thinking people being cowed into acquiescence by the power exercised by terrorists. Terrorists frequently do what they do for political reasons and, whilst their actions may be unpalatable, it does not help us to understand and overcome the problem of terrorism by simply positing ethical rights and wrongs. O'Neill speaks as the philosopher (dare I say, in her ivory tower) but politics in Northern Ireland requires a more pragmatic approach.

The main problem with O'Neill's thesis is not in her philosophical diagnosis of the problems of rights-claims but in her assumptions about the meaning of trust in a society like Northern Ireland. She underestimates the need to talk about political institutions including those of the state and the role they can play in engendering trust. She wishes away violence rather than examining ways in which initiatives like the Belfast Agreement can change political violence and the way a society perceives it. No doubt O'Neill would have castigated paramilitaries and their representatives before the Agreement but it is clear that the political process has changed the rather passive stance to the existence of violence that was adopted by some people in Northern Ireland. These kinds of changes do not make people who have shifted their position whiter than white but the political process has brought elements of improvement alongside continuing unrest. This is the nature of pragmatic politics and it is a more realistic way of generating trust than right-thinking rhetoric about ethical conduct. O'Neill is right to point to the beneficial contribution that trust can make to social relations but wrong in arguing that in 'the wake of terror, trust spirals downwards' (O'Neill 2002: 38). In Northern Ireland trust has often been generated in the wake of some heinous acts of terrorism; it is often manifest as a sign of communities coming together to articulate their rejection of terrorist methods. It is also the case that some of the worst acts of terrorism in Northern Ireland have occurred when politics is working relatively well (albeit away from the public eye). In short, O'Neill's thesis is not sufficiently political. It does not comprehend the sometimes conflicting existence of trust and mistrust and the ways in which politics and violence cross-cut each other in societies like Northern Ireland. Whilst her advocacy of a peaceful vision of trust is worthy, the reality of Northern Ireland is likely to be less than ideal and more complicated than the picture she draws.

Civil society in Northern Ireland

Having examined some of relevant theories of social capital and trust, it is important to analyse the role of civil society in Northern Ireland and the peace process in particular. What is clear is that the concept of civil society has been increasingly prominent in the literature on Northern Irish politics in recent years where it is often presented as an antidote to élite-driven, centralised formal politics. Where the theoretical discourses of civil society often advocate its resurgence or renewal, there has never been any doubt in Northern Ireland that activism in civil society is an important feature of contemporary life. Northern Ireland has been characterised by a thriving community sector although, of course, many groups and activists have focused on one or other side of the political divide. Moreover, many of the activities undertaken in the name of 'the community' have not been particularly civil if that is thought to pertain only to well-meaning actions that are beneficial to society as a whole. However, in the recent political debates, civil society has been advocated as a space and a set of institutions in which a multiplicity of voices can be heard. Some of these voices are rather marginal to the formal political system and, as such, civil society is presented as a more diverse and inclusive sphere in which a greater range of opinions and arguments can emerge. As we will see, however, many of these arguments adopt a rather uncritical reading of civil society in which the conflicts and disagreements of everyday life in Northern Ireland are replaced by groups working together for the common good. In short, if Northern Ireland is a politically divided society, then it is no surprise that these divisions are just as evident in the spaces of civil society as in the formal political machinery.

There are numerous types of groups in Northern Irish civil society often working on very different assumptions. These range from traditional civil society groups reflecting, for example, trade unionism, organised business interests, charities and religious organisations, through to groups which exist to help to bring about peace and conflict resolution (Cochrane and Dunn 2002). At the same time, there has been a substantial tradition of political activism within nationalist communities which have eschewed the formal political institutions of the Northern Irish polity, because they were either dominated by unionists or reflected an extension of British state jurisdiction over Northern Ireland. It is interesting then that one of the few attempts to build a civil society approach into the traditional political architecture of Northern Ireland has come from Norman Porter in his advocacy of civic unionism (Porter 1996). Porter rejects the kind of culturalism that appears in many unionist discourses, such as that of Ian Paisley which presents a unified homogeneous vision of Northern Irish unionism bound up with an historically derived sense of identity and Protestantism. At the same time, Porter is wary of contemporary liberal unionist approaches such as that of Arthur Aughey which he regards as insufficiently focused on the benefits of dialogue and too closed to the potential benefits that could accrue to everyone in Northern Ireland from limited concessions to nationalist demands. As Porter (1996: 170) himself realises, such a civic unionist approach 'lies beyond the horizons of most unionists' and has, not surprisingly, aroused considerable critical commentary from both cultural and liberal unionists. It is important nonetheless though, because it attempts to wed some of the assumptions promoted by civil society theories (and, in particular, civic republicanism) to some orthodox aspirations of unionism.

Porter's vision of civic unionism builds upon what he sees as the shared cultural heritage that has been bequeathed to residents of Northern Ireland. As such he rejects exclusivist approaches that focus merely on Britishness or Irishness, and instead points to the intermingling of a range of factors that 'provide a vastly under appreciated stock of common background meanings which many of our practices presuppose and bear at least implicit traces of' (Porter 1996: 173). From this perspective, whilst it is important to recognise the different claims of diverse groups in Northern Ireland, we must also try to build upon the shared cultural factors that have emerged there. Thus, Porter's unionism rejects the appeals to both Ulster Protestantism and Britishness as the totality of unionist identity and argues instead for a recognition of the influence of Irishness. This flows into an argument that a political settlement in Northern Ireland must not be exclusionary in its appeal to a particular cultural heritage. In institutional terms this requires bodies that:

> safeguard a public space that is constituted by inclusiveness and dialogue. And this extends to the life of civil society, where scope should be given to institutions and practices that express the diversity of individuals, associations and groups – except those entailing a victimisation of others – and where the toleration of difference is central.   (Porter 1996: 179)

This is an important statement of the objectives of civic unionism. It envisages the engagement of people across difference and the establishment of new institutions that can command cross-cultural support. However, it is loaded with the usual assumptions of liberal theories of civil society. Porter preaches inclusivity and yet establishes caveats that groups must not victimise each other and must be tolerant of the claims of others. Arguably, this could rule out the participation of important actors in Northern Irish civil society who are perceived by their opponents to be intolerant and willing to victimise them. Nowhere is there any explanation of how we go about excluding some groups and including others. One is left with the feeling that Porter's civil society is one built upon the participation of middle class liberals rather than groups that are more likely to conflict with one another. This is an oft-raised objection to ideas of civil society in Northern Ireland but it remains pertinent. If groups in conflict do not tolerate each other, then, according to civic unionism, they cannot participate in civil society institutions. This emasculates civil society and neuters its capacity as a forum for the management of conflicts. It narrows the parameters of debate unnecessarily and runs the risk of excluding those that are actually involved in conflictual situations. Consequently, the capacity of civil society to make a meaningful contribution to the management and containment of conflict is limited.

Like many unionists, Porter is sceptical of the parity of esteem agenda as it has emerged in Northern Ireland. He regards parity of esteem as problematic as it asks people to esteem cultures which they regard as a challenge to their own identities and promotes an unquestioning assumption that traditional identities are equally worthy (Porter 1996: 188).[5] Instead Porter puts forward an argument for 'due recognition' rather than parity of esteem as a way of dealing with the diverse claims of identity in Northern Ireland:

> To give identities their due ... is a reasonable request which encourages deliberation and informed judgements about what individual, cultural and political identities are entitled to given the different types of claims they imply and the historical context in which they are made. And 'recognition' is a less loaded term than 'esteem', one that is capable of facilitating the affirmative dimension conveyed by the latter without leaving us hamstrung in the face of obnoxious facets of certain identities.   (Porter 1996: 190)

In this vein 'due recognition' is put forward in civic unionism as the basis of a politics freed from domination and coercion where the identities of groups and individuals can be recognised. But this begs important questions: Who decides which group and individual identities are to be recognised? Who decides what is due to all those making recognition claims? How are we to define the 'obnoxious facets of certain identities'? The answer to these questions in Porter's analysis is the kind of deliberative democratic processes evaluated in the last chapter. Thus, by engaging in a free, inclusive and tolerant discussion we will be able to decide what is appropriate recognition for different claims. In so doing we will be able to agree on what is obnoxious and to be excluded. Of course, what is missing here as in other deliberative democratic theories, is a focus on power and the way in which existing power relations will affect the structures of civil society and democratic engagement. When we place power within the equation, it becomes much clearer that the questions above will be matters of political disagreement and conflict. Different groups will not agree on what is due to others or what is obnoxious. In short, civic unionism, whilst ostensibly a well-meaning attempt to provide a framework for an open and inclusive unionism, falls back on a number of questionable assumptions about the capacity of dialogue to resolve deep-seated disputes. The entrenched reasons why these disputes occur is glossed over in the construction of a wholesome, unified civil society which suffers from its own liberal underpinnings. Moreover, such notions of civil society are a staple of liberal theories and this brings into question the extent to which Porter's civic unionism differs from the liberal approaches he criticises.

The limitations of civic unionism relate to the way in which it is ultimately reliant on the outcomes of rational deliberation to achieve the 'good life'. There is, however, one strand of Porter's argument for civil society that is particularly pertinent in the Northern Irish context. He rejects cumbersome attempts to set out some kind of blueprint of even-handedness where everyone can be recognised as a basis for future political engagement. Instead he contends that any establishment of unity in civil society must be regarded as 'the product of a delicate balancing act ... [U]nity should not be considered as a constant, as a once-and-for-all achievement. Through the state's receptivity to the diversity of civil society, rather, the form of unity remains open to reformulation and revision' (Porter 1996: 206). Whilst the pursuit of 'unity' in civil society is inherently problematic, Porter is nonetheless correct to point out the contingent nature of any agreements that are generated through the mechanisms of civil society. Civil society, by definition, is not an aspiration in itself but is instead a space where political disagreements and conflicts are negotiated, resolved or merely contained. It is not static or sealed off from the broader political context but will instead reflect the wider political environment. As such, any difficulties that hamper politics more generally will also be manifest in the politics of civil society. In this sense, it contains the potential for incivility as well as the more benign, wholesome behaviour that Porter advocates in his pursuit of reconciliation (Porter 2003). These points hold true for all analyses of civil society and raise fundamental questions about the way in which civil society has been regarded in the peace process in Northern Ireland. Too often liberals have eulogised civil society and failed to recognise the contested nature of relations within the spaces of civil society.

The role of civil society in the Northern Ireland peace process has been analysed by Adrian Guelke (2002). Guelke notes many of the initiatives to which civil society groups have contributed but contends that there are structural problems for them which emanate from the way in which the Belfast Agreement has been constructed around a consociational agenda that focuses on political élites. Here he recognises that there has been a resilient scepticism in Northern Ireland regarding the levels of political awareness and understanding within civil society groups. Moreover, he also points to a tendency within republicanism to query the independence of civil society groups because some of them have links to the British state. However, for Guelke, there was a key role for civil society groups in the peace process and, in particular, he points to their role in the campaign for a 'Yes' vote in the 1998 referendum on the Agreement despite the tendency in Northern Ireland to focus politics on élites and the leaderships of the main political parties.[6] Thus, for example, he challenges the view that civil society is weak in Northern Ireland by arguing that such a position is only tenable if we define civil society narrowly to exclude organisations such as the Orange Order. Such a definition is clearly erroneous because, as critical civil society theory reminds us, civil society is comprised of a multiplicity of groups and organisations which reflect the divisions and conflicts which exist within a given society. Importantly then, Guelke recognises that civil society does not have a 'special role' in challenging sectarianism insofar as it will actually contain organisations which may be sectarian. In this sense Guelke's analysis reminds us that support for civil society should not entail its elevation into a privileged position that is somehow 'above' (or, indeed, 'below') politics.

The most important feature of Guelke's argument concerns the way in which civil society has been marginalised since the Belfast Agreement, despite the provisions of the document which reflected some of the wishes of third sector groups and paved the way for the establishment of the Civic Forum. One of the reasons for this has been the way in which political parties have been 'suspicious of both liberal opinion and the third sector' (Guelke 2002: 12), but he also contends that another factor in the decline of civil society groups was their own lack of foresight:

> it seems evident that the groups in civil society that facilitated dialogue among the parties, promoted the idea that a negotiated settle-

ment was possible and mobilised to secure popular endorsement of the settlement when it was achieved, assumed that with popular endorsement of the agreement among the parties their work was done.   (Guelke 2002: 12)

In this sense, the difficulty of civil society groups on the ground was that they clearly had a legitimate role in promoting peace but, for Guelke, their responsibility when it came to implementing the Agreement was much more debatable. Notwithstanding the existence of the Civic Forum, politics after the Agreement became largely driven by élites (and indeed obstructed by political élites). The problem here was that, as Chapter One demonstrated, the consociational element of the Agreement promoted moderation and consensus from the leaderships of political parties above all else in the maintenance of peace. Thus, it was the institutional design embodied in the Agreement which would act against a strong role for civil society groups. As such, Guelke contends that 'in the Agreement as a whole too little attention has been paid to the drawbacks of consociational settlements, not least their implications for the entrenching of divisions and the reduction of the influence of cross-community groups and civil society more generally on the political process' (Guelke 2002: 13). However, whilst Guelke's analysis is persuasive, we should also add that the Agreement's focus on the Civic Forum was predicated upon a more harmonious interpretation of civil society than was ever likely to be the case in practice in Northern Ireland. It employed a narrow understanding of civil society which failed to recognise that the nature of conflict in Northern Ireland entails a civil society that will contain sectarian groups and indeed some people who may engage in uncivil activities.

There are also some problems in the way in which the Civic Forum itself was constructed. As a means of involving people in a participatory process to counteract the focus on the political élites in consociational approaches, a lot was being asked of the Civic Forum. The composition of the Forum was always designed to be representative with a balanced membership in areas such as gender, age, community background and geographical location. However even these aspirations would be difficult to achieve:

Many would view the composition of the forum as imperfect. It appears to attempt to include all sections of society – an impossible task which only serves to draw attention to the fact that many

> interests have not been included. The forum is dominated by the voluntary/community sectors: the traditional social partners have fewer seats between them. There is a grave danger that business and the trade unions will look elsewhere for their primary engagement with government.   (Woods 2001: 81)

Here the problem emerges that the underpinning desire to involve the community sector in the politics of Northern Ireland has entailed the marginalisation of groups such as unions and business which usually play a pivotal role in corporatist political arrangements. According to Woods, the failure to provide a significant enough voice for these traditional partners is likely to mean that they will invest more time in lobbying ministers, for example, rather than focusing on the Civic Forum. He sees this as all the more galling given that elements within both the business community and the trade union movement were such strong supporters of the peace process. These reservations about the composition of the Civic Forum aside, though, Woods articulates several benefits from its institutionalisation. For example, he notes how it has encouraged innovative forms of political participation when, traditionally, 'the political' in Northern Ireland has been dominated by party politics, usually organised along traditional communal divisions. Thus, rather than reinforcing this top-down, hierarchical organisation of government and politics in Northern Ireland, the Civic Forum is intended as a new stratum of governance that will work by 'marrying the skills and knowledge of the sectors it represents with those of elected representatives, public administration and the wider society' (Woods 2001: 82).

However, it should also be recognised that the advocacy of contentious issues as suitable topics for the Civic Forum to discuss would be likely to generate greater conflict and disagreement within the Civic Forum than would be likely over other areas of culture or policy. This is not to say that the Forum should not focus on contentious issues, but rather that we should expect it to reflect the conflicts and divisions characteristic of wider society in Northern Ireland. In this sense, there is a need for civil society to provide a suitably disputatious voice in Northern Irish politics to ensure greater accountability for the political élites. It is important that the Civic Forum is not merely a reactive institution that responds to Assembly initiatives; instead, it must be able to raise issues that are not being dealt with appropriately within the Assembly. There is a need then for empowerment of the Civic Forum to act as a suitable check and balance on the Assembly: the 'nature of four-party coalition government may ... take consensus too far and there may be a danger of reducing policy to a lowest common denominator – the Civic Forum could be an important foil to such a tendency' (Woods 2001: 84). According to this view, it is not the role of civil society to provide institutions that reinforce the status quo or harmonise otherwise disputatious relationships in society. A healthy civil society is one that grapples with social problems and divisions in a thoroughgoing and transparent fashion. Nonetheless, elsewhere Woods appears to take a somewhat optimistic view of the role of the Civic Forum in negotiated governance:

> All the social actors needed to investigate some of the most challenging problems facing our society are present in the forum. The assembly would know that proposals achieved by consensus within the forum would have been negotiated between the traditional interest groups and could count on the cooperation of the sectors represented in the forum in implementing them.   (Democratic Dialogue 1999: 4)

Not only does this view overlook the issue of the representativeness of community 'leaders' and major figures in the business and trade union sectors, but it also relies too heavily on the capacity of those 'leaders' to carry their various constituencies with them. What it ignores then, is the possibility that community leaders can become detached from the communities that they are supposed to represent and that the former may be prepared to make compromises in negotiations that they are then unable to sell to their members. Whilst consensus may be possible on certain issues (and the importance of negotiated governance should not be dismissed), the assumptions underpinning the Democratic Dialogue paper need to be challenged. Members of the Civic Forum may well be representative at any given point of time but equally they may not. In such a scenario it is dangerous to assume that proposals agreed in the Civic Forum 'could be sold to the electorate'. Perhaps rightly, Democratic Dialogue suggests that the Forum need not be directly representative as that is the role of the Assembly but this also illuminates the problematic nature of the quotation above. After all, if the Forum need not be representative then we cannot have unswerving confidence that its proposals and negotiations will carry the weight suggested.

The Democratic Dialogue position then does not see representativeness as the pre-eminent issue, although it clearly does not disregard it altogether. Recognising the difficulty of having every civic interest represented, it argues instead that members of the Forum should have 'an over-arching commitment to articulate, via a problem solving approach, the public interest' and that 'the overall aim must be to nominate people with the right combination of experience, abilities and qualities' (Democratic Dialogue 1999: 6). This gives the lie to the approach articulated by Democratic Dialogue. At root, its strategy is to construct a body 'designed to produce consensus' through the nomination of members who are the most 'able' and who are committed to the 'public interest'. The difficulty here lies in the potential exclusion of those voices in civil society which articulate an oppositional message, which disagree with the dominant perception of what is in the public interest, which position themselves according to their commitments rather than the pursuit of consensus. This is not to say that consensus is undesirable, but that establishing its pre-eminence in the construction of the Civic Forum and making its pursuit the main aim of members, could lead to the marginalisation of the very groups that the Civic Forum should appeal to because they may not have a foothold in the formal political process. This danger is apparent in the explicit argument of Democratic Dialogue that it is only the commitment to the 'public interest' that makes people 'free to explore innovative options and even to "think the unthinkable" while reassuring the society from which they come that it is the interests of that society which they are committed to serving without favour or prejudice' (Democratic Dialogue 1999: 6). At best, this is a pipe-dream. In other circumstances it is a scheme that would increasingly lead to greater detachment of members from their constituencies as they would not be 'representing' them but the 'public interest'. Moreover, it is profoundly patronising to contend that partisan people are incapable of 'thinking the unthinkable'. Many of the problems in Northern Ireland derive from the alienation from the political process felt by many people across the political divisions – any institution which accentuated that divide whilst ostensibly giving a voice to the marginalised is likely to lose credibility amongst alienated groups. In short, the Democratic Dialogue model is a recipe for a new cohort of the great and the good rather than a genuinely inclusive representation of civil society in Northern Ireland.[7]

The concern of Democratic Dialogue, based on the arguments of Paul Hirst and Rory O'Donnell, is that the Civic Forum must have some power and influence amongst mainstream politicians.[8] Here Hirst's argument that groups with different goals can come together in the process of negotiation seems to be sidelined to a degree and greater weight seems to be given to O'Donnell's prescription of a learning process whereby, through working together, groups learn the benefits of such a co-operative process. Thus, for example, Democratic Dialogue follows O'Donnell's argument that the Forum must aim to achieve consensus:

> While there are important arguments against the pursuit of consensus above all other considerations, it is clear that the forum will be unable to present any convincing solutions to the problems it addresses unless it is on the basis of consensus. Negotiating governance suggests that agreement must be reached if proposals are to be successfully implemented. Thus minority reports are unlikely to be a constructive contribution to the process. Nor is a system of voting likely to play a dominant role in the forum's deliberations. (Democratic Dialogue 1999: 7).

Advocates of civil society, then, must be careful not to lapse into a eulogy of the intermediate sector whereby the pessimistic realism of consociational theorists is replaced by a misplaced optimism about the extent to which civil society actors can effect changes by themselves. The point here is that just as political élites are constrained by socio-political circumstances, so are actors in civil society. The constraints will be representative of the inequalities of power and influence that abound in all liberal democracies. Therefore, to expect civil society to rise above structural inequalities is unrealistic as many of the reproductive factors that maintain power differentials will be grounded in civil society themselves. As Cochrane reminds us, we need to be aware of the possibility that middle class liberal élites can hijack civil society discourses, when, in truth, the intermediate sector is at least partly comprised of individuals and organisations with a long history of 'protecting' their communities, albeit sometimes in violent and illegal ways. This is not to say that we must justify such actions but we do need to understand that structural factors will influence the space that we call civil society and the various individuals and groups who act within that domain. Just as several of the prescriptions of consociationalism are 'normatively distasteful' in democratic terms (Dixon 2002b: 18), so the elevation of civil society above the political fray is equally unappealing. Moving from pessimistic realism to an idealistic optimism does not help us to understand civil society, let alone the role it might be able to play in the construction of a peaceful settlement in Northern Ireland. Ultimately, then, Dixon is correct to argue that we need to 'bring politics back in' both in terms of the formal political arena and the less regulated sphere of civil society (Dixon 2002b: 19).

The argument against viewing civil society initiatives as part of a new 'politics of civility' is articulated most convincingly by Aughey (1999). Instead of the wholesome interpretation of civil society evident in much of the literature, Aughey argues that political change in Northern Ireland is unlikely to bring about the end of a politics of incivility as it will not be able to do away with the widespread antagonisms in Northern Irish society. In discussing a politics of civility, Aughey is dealing with 'a style of politics which acknowledges difference and diversity but also acknowledges a common interest beyond difference and diversity' (Aughey 1999: 123). Using the work of Edward Shils, he notes that the politics of civility accepts pluralism and a diversity of incommensurable values but, instead of trying to abolish these conflicts, it tries to reconcile them. However, for Aughey, there is a tension in Shils's arguments between the promotion of a single common good on one hand, and a set of incommensurable divergent interests in society on the other. Instead he prefers an Oakeshottian conception of civility which is 'historically achieved and contingently preserved' (Aughey 2001: 126) and does not reflect an ideal-typical model of how diverse societies will manage to cohere. Thus, Aughey prefers an imperfect understanding of the workings of democracy because of the limitations of liberal abstraction when we attempt to apply them in political practice. The problem with liberal interpretations of civility is that they make impossible demands of political actors and fail to recognise the necessity of pragmatism in a conflictual society such as Northern Ireland. This is:

> the tragedy of those who aspire to do as they wish (eternal peace) but who end up never getting what they want because of the impossibility of inclusivity without limit … [T]hat is the frustrating danger and the ultimate illusion of a thoroughgoing philosophy of inclusiveness. It has a tendency to lead towards a politics of non-negotiable demands based either on felt need or on communal self-esteem.   (Aughey 1999: 129).

The point here is that the rhetoric of inclusivity which implies that all can be included unproblematically without considerable political conflict must be challenged head on. The nature of inclusion and the criteria for inclusivity will often reflect the established distribution of power in a given society and we should not be 'diverted from the fact of power at the core of the political' which acts as 'a useful corrective to the idealisation of civil society and to the demonisation of party politics' (Aughey 1999: 129). For Aughey then, there is a danger in liberal theories of civil society of wishing away conflict and the construction of a pretence that politics anywhere, let alone in Northern Ireland, can be based upon the elimination of antagonistic forces. Such antagonism is constitutive of 'the political' and it is the way in which politics manages to contain and reconcile antagonistic relations rather than eradicate them which should be the concern of civil society theorists.

From this foundation Aughey goes on to examine the question of whether incivility is inevitable in the context of Northern Ireland. To this end he differentiates between a system of open political conflict and violence such as that which characterised Northern Ireland during the 'Troubles' and the kind of incivility that remains despite political agreements and the peace process:

> even in a situation where active paramilitarism is absent, political incivility can take the form of communal self-assertion and mutual provocation. And it is this pervasive sort of corrosive and purposefully destabilising incivility which has been a characteristic of traditional political life in Northern Ireland even when there has been an absence of violence.   (Aughey 1999: 132)

There is a sense in Northern Ireland then, that such forms of incivility are part of political normality in the province. Indeed it is difficult to imagine a *political system* that could eliminate such deep-seated and ingrained incivility. However there is no clear dividing line between civility and incivility; the existence of incivility will always be a matter of degree as, to some extent, will be open relations of violence in societies such as Northern Ireland. This requires a degree of pragmatism from politicians and the public at large to understand the shifting and contingent dynamics of Northern Irish politics. This is a substantial demand however. In Northern Irish politics on the ground Aughey points to the impasse that has permeated the kind of unionism espoused by Robert McCartney for example, where any sense of compromise with the 'enemy' is regarded as a dilution of the union. However, Aughey also points to a tendency to regard unionism through a narrow and moralistic communitarianism where all unionists share a fatalistic disposition towards peace which is characterised by low horizons. This view, which he links with the work of Porter for example, is criticised by Aughey for providing 'a caricature of the multiple, contradictory and diverse influences which together constitute unionist politics in particular and the situation in which unionists find themselves in general' (Aughey 1999: 137). Instead Aughey posits a unionist community that is both complex and contradictory and, by implication, these characteristics must be attached to nationalism as well.

The importance of this argument is that the conflicting interpretations of the peace process and the resulting incivility are not merely features derived from opposing unionist and nationalist positions. Thus, we need to recognise the incivility that emanates from within the 'two traditions' towards those who are supposed to share their disposition. This point is thrown into sharp focus at times when elections loom in Northern Ireland, where much of the political competition for the major parties takes place within the major ethno-national blocs. In recent years this intra-community competition has focused on attitudes to the peace process especially within unionism. The fault line in unionism has been between those prepared to gamble on the imperfect provisions of the Agreement against those who would not countenance such pragmatism. In Aughey's terms the former had an 'affair of reason' with the Agreement whereas the latter remained driven by the instinct of the heart.

In terms of civility then, the Agreement could not guarantee a new culture which terminated the previous relations of incivility. Arguably it is not within the wherewithal of political initiatives alone to achieve such a fundamental transformation in social and cultural relations. However, what the Agreement did do was to establish a new paradigm for 'the political', and with that a changed context within which social and cultural relations take their shape. Thus, the Agreement did not create a new civil 'consensus' but did establish territory in which the possibility of a less uncivil set of relations could emerge. In this sense, it shifted the horizons of politics but was incapable of establishing a civil consensus. Nonetheless we should bear in mind at this juncture that Aughey's definition of a politics of civility was not supposed to do away with difference and conflict; instead it was concerned with how we manage and reconcile disagreements. In order to do this, the Agreement was established upon a set of 'ethico-political principles' that participants had to agree to. By implication, those who did not adhere to principles such as the sole use of politics to achieve one's ends could be excluded as could those who broke the Agreement in other ways. Thus, beneath the contingency in Aughey's reading of the Agreement there was an understanding that the 'politics of civility must have its own exclusions ... the politics of civility cannot be an empty formula' (Aughey 1999: 142). The interesting point to note here is that virtually all parties and both governments have been accused of breaking the 'ethico-political principles' at the root of the Agreement. When all participants are acting contrary to these principles in whatever fashion, then arguably the principles and with them the politics of civility break down.

In many respects this appears to be a useful lens through which we can understand the faltering nature of the peace process including the establishment, suspension and re-establishment of devolved institutions. The extent to which the participants act according to the 'ethico-political principles' embodied in the Agreement varies over time and according to the political calculations of their opponents. From this perspective, the principles themselves that underpin civility will also be part of a dynamic process of change and redefinition. Given his moderate unionist sympathies, it is not surprising that Aughey identifies the threat symbolised by paramilitary weapons as the major obstacle to the politics of civility. According to the argument above though, the politics of civility has been hindered by the variety of ways, both legalistic and ethico-political, that the spirit of the Agreement has been broken by political parties and governments. Periodically this has caused crises in the peace process but, importantly, it is in the light of these crises that new 'ethico-political principles' are established that will define future inclusions and exclusions.

Conclusion

Civil society theory has provided a useful counterpoint to the liberal theories we have examined thus far because it recognises that a wide range of structural factors will influence the nature of Northern Irish society. Whereas rights-based liberalism has tended to focus on the relationship between the state and individuals or groups, civil society theory focuses on a wider range of associations that can be political actors. As such, it broadens politics to incorporate a diverse range of activities rather than the narrow legalism of procedural forms of liberalism. However, civil society has emerged in sometimes problematic fashion in Northern Irish political discourses. Where it invokes wholesome imagery of consensus and civic virtue, civil society loses its potential for a radical edge. Whilst there will always be exclusions, the consensual view of civil society threatens to expunge a substantial and diverse range of critical voices from political debate. The benefits of strengthening civil society would be nullified by such an approach. Instead the invocation of civil society as a counterpoint to élitist politics must permit critical and oppositional viewpoints to emerge. Civil society, if it is to be worthwhile, must widen the scope of Northern Irish political debate to include those that have been traditionally marginalised. It must be envisaged as a space in which we can develop a much more representative political arena than has hitherto been the case in Northern Ireland. It is important, therefore, that we now turn our attention to one such marginalised group – women – and examine how feminist theories have promoted democratic renewal.

6
Feminism and the Politics of Difference

Politics in Northern Ireland has not been noted for its openness to feminist ideas in general or even the formal political participation of women as elected representatives. There are numerous reasons for this but the peace process has witnessed the increased prominence in political activism of women and a growing impact of feminist ideas.[1] Whilst feminist politics is still evolving in Northern Ireland, the feminist movement as a whole has also witnessed considerable change in recent years. This chapter will evaluate these changing ideas and the ways in which contemporary feminists have argued for an egalitarian politics that is coupled with the promotion of diversity. It is this dynamic (and sometimes tense) relationship between equality and difference that has animated many recent feminist debates and these tensions have filtered through to debates within feminism in Northern Ireland. In what follows I will focus on three main aspects of this debate: firstly, I will examine feminism and the politics of difference with particular reference to the work of Iris Marion Young; secondly, I will evaluate the extent to which feminism in Northern Ireland reflects the broader context of feminist politics; and, thirdly, I will analyse the impact that feminist politics has had on contemporary Northern Irish politics. Before this, however, it is useful by way of an introduction to contextualise debates on equality and difference in feminist politics and their implications for democracy.

Since the Enlightenment feminism has had a fluctuating and complicated relationship with liberal democratic politics. As it emerged through the writings of early theorists such as Mary Wollstonecraft, feminism was concerned with the extension of liberal rights to women on the same basis as men. Thus, for example, Wollstonecraft argues that women had the same abilities and capacities as men but that these were not developed through inequalities in education. Systemic changes could enable women to realise their potential in the same way as men and therefore there was a case for women achieving equal rights to those enjoyed by men in liberal democracies. These ideas would remain (and still are) influential in feminist theory through the struggles for enfranchisement, reproductive rights and so on, but since the 1960s feminist politics has taken on a new dimension. Where traditionally liberal feminism was egalitarian insofar as its primary concern was with rights and women's equality with men, radical feminists began to challenge liberal strategies for the emancipation of women and broaden the scope of feminist theory to grapple with cultural issues and the nature of relations in what had up until this time been designated as the private sphere as well as the public world of politics and economics. Radical feminists of the 1970s began to focus more directly not only on the equality of women with regard to men, but also what it was that differentiated women from men. Thus, the focus shifted from an egalitarian politics to one concerned with difference, albeit without relinquishing the concern for formal equality that had animated earlier feminist politics. Here the spotlight was moved from the shared capacities of men and women to what essentially distinguished women from men, such as the 'ethic of care'. The argument, in short, was that patriarchal society valued masculine values and attributes over and above those that were more feminine. This was reflected in the organisation of both the public and private spheres and resulted in inequality for women. Thus, a schism appeared then between liberal feminists concerned with formal equality expressed through rights and difference feminists who wanted to highlight the distinctiveness of women.

Within the feminist literature this divide generated a new range of problems that have emerged since the 1980s. The heart of the problem lay in the suggestion that there was an essence to womanhood, something that all women shared by dint of their gender which differentiated them from men and which should form the basis of political thinking. Two key debates arose out of this foundational principle. Firstly, feminist writers such as Iris Marion Young criticised this kind of thinking as 'essentialist' insofar as it unified all women under its auspices and failed to recognise that the so-called essence of womanhood was not universal. In other words, for Young, women were different from each other and therefore did not all share characteristics such as a propensity for caring. From this perspective, essentialism homogenised women and hence marginalised those who did not share this constructed 'essence'. The second debate, which complemented the first, was that the essentialist perspective constructed womanhood around the values of white, western, middle class women to the detriment of women in different parts of the world or those from different classes, cultures or ethnic groups. This argument is most commonly associated with black feminists such as bell hooks (1981). The influence of these criticisms of feminist thought moved the debate beyond the focus on equality versus difference and instead highlighted differences within the category of women. Thus, we saw the emergence of a feminism associated with the idea of 'multiple, intersecting differences' which rejected the unitary self of liberal citizenship 'in favour of a conception of identity as multiple, contingent and context bound' (Baumeister 2000: 17). This perspective, often associated with the work of Young, implies that there are numerous sources of identity and forms of social structuration which impact upon the lives of different women. For some, culture may be more important than class and vice versa, and difference feminists have therefore stressed a multiplicity of cross-cutting differences that differentiate and individualise the experience and identity of all women. This translates into an 'anti-essentialism' which rejects the view that all women share a common foundation and that the solution to patriarchal society is to 'feminise' it. However, this anti-essentialism does not relinquish the pursuit of equality; its focus is on how to equalise the position of all women so that they have opportunities to pursue the goals and values which they deem most appropriate to their identity and values.

The irony of the debate on 'multiple intersecting differences' emerges when we evaluate its implications for feminist political strategy. Whilst liberal feminism advocated the pursuit of formal, legal equality as the primary objective of feminism, more radical feminists have sought to address not only legalistic measures but also issues of cultural practice as an area of fundamental political interest. However, many of those who advocate 'multiple intersecting differences' have suggested that the key to furthering feminist objectives is to provide meaningful choices and opportunities for *all* women to pursue conceptions of the good regardless of whether these fit comfortably with pre-conceived ideas of femininity. Arguably this returns us to liberal theories of citizenship where universal rights are supposed to guarantee basic freedoms to enable people to flourish in self-defined activities. The danger here is that everything becomes reduced to the level of the individual with a concomitant fragmentation which undermines a shared sense of citizenship (Baumeister 2000: 23). Aware of this danger, many contemporary feminists would argue that we need to combine the concern for the universal with an understanding that it will lead to particularistic self-expressions (Lister 1997). Commentators like Young (1990) continue to remind us that formal liberal rights are unlikely by themselves to challenge inequalities of power and the variety of sources of oppression which exist within contemporary liberal democracies. Thus, feminists cannot merely resort to traditional liberal strategies but must recognise that political initiatives for freedom and equality must be accompanied by a continued challenge to socio-cultural practices which inhibit the experience of liberal rights for many women. To clarify these arguments it is worth examining the arguments of Iris Marion Young on the politics of difference and their implications for democracy in greater detail.

Young and the politics of difference

With the publication of *Justice and the Politics of Difference* in 1990, Young established herself as one of the primary feminist theorists of democracy. Her central thesis is that we need to develop a theory of 'differentiated citizenship' whereby we understand that the provision of rights of citizenship must enable people to enjoy their rights in different ways depending upon their own lifestyles, identities and experiences. However, rather than merely reducing this to the level of the individual, Young recognises that there are groups in society which have traditionally been disadvantaged and discriminated against. For this reason she contends that there is a need for special group rights to protect the interests of marginalised groups in society. The principle here is that '[c]orrect principles of justice can only be arrived at when all social groups, including those currently excluded, marginalised and oppressed, are enabled to participate in the formulation of such principles' (Phillips 1999: 31–2). In this sense, Young's approach to conceptions of justice in democratic theory suggests that liberalism has been dominated by discourses of injustice which have undermined the very project of liberal democracy (Campbell 2001: 200). Instead Young promotes a form of affirmative action as a strategy for renewing democracy to take account of the demands of marginalised and oppressed groups in contemporary society. Typical of many feminist theorists then, she contends that theories of justice cannot be solely based around issues of distribution and redistribution because the sources of exclusion for women and other marginalised groups are grounded in other issues beyond material factors. Whilst not ignoring the significance of these material factors, Young wants to remind us of the multiple forms of exclusion and oppression that help to reproduce the exploitation of women.

The democratic implications of Young's argument for group differentiation are explained at greater length in *Inclusion and Democracy* (2000). Here she argues that liberal democracies operate according to a rather minimalist definition of democracy that 'entails a rule of law, promotion of civil and political liberties, [and] free and fair election of lawmakers' (Young 2000: 5). The major contention of the book is that our understanding of democracy needs to be deepened if we are to attend to the existence of diversity in contemporary societies and the exclusion of some groups and forms of communication. In Young's view, what emerges in such a deepened form of democracy is greater legitimacy in decision-making as long as the procedures are public and inclusive. Clearly then, justice is about processes of communication as well as distribution and redistribution. Young contends that legitimacy emanates from appropriate processes even though political actors may lose arguments or compromise their beliefs. Deeper democracy then, is based upon the development of processes that enable the inclusion of a wider range of groups in society in decision-making. Young's contention is that such measures would enhance democratic legitimacy beyond the superficiality of arrangements in many liberal democracies where many groups are effectively excluded.

Clearly Young's perspective shares key aspects of the liberal paradigm that we have already examined in the book. As in many liberal theories the nature of just processes is central to her argument, although Young is attuned to the concern of multiculturalists that we understand the different claims of divergent groups in society, particularly minorities. However, rather than focusing on rights as is the case with much multiculturalism, Young is much more concerned with political communication and the ability of civil society to provide a range of venues in which political concerns can be articulated. Where Young's thesis moves beyond the parameters of these perspectives is in her recognition of the multiple forms of exclusion and the extent to which certain groups are marginalised from political representation. Thus, she wants to establish more participatory forms of democracy where citizens can play a full role as political actors despite their differences. For Young, the recognition of group difference should not fragment society – the charge often levelled at multiculturalism – but instead we should develop solidarity based around the basic concept of recognising difference. Citizenship is partially based upon a reciprocal understanding that we should extend the right to express political affinities to everyone on the basis that those groups are prepared to recognise that we are different from them. This would be a more inclusive politics because it envisages 'a heterogeneous public engaged in transforming institutions to make them more effective in solving shared problems justly' (Young 2000: 12). Clearly this presupposes the possibility that there can be agreement on just solutions to problems in diverse societies; as we saw in discussing deliberative democracy, however, such assumptions can be dangerous in societies such as Northern Ireland.

There are sound reasons behind Young's critique of liberal democracy as it has developed in contemporary Western societies. She delineates two main approaches to analysing liberal democracy, namely the aggregative and deliberative models of democracy. The aggregative model is described by Young as one where democracy is regarded as a:

> process of aggregating the preferences of citizens in choosing public officials and policies. The goal of democratic decision-making is to decide what leaders, rules, and policies will best correspond to the most widely and strongly held preferences. A well-functioning democracy allows for the expression of and competition among preferences, and has reliable and fair methods for adding them to bring a result.   (Young 2000: 19)

Not surprisingly, this model of democracy has severe limitations from Young's perspective. Its focus on political élites denigrates the importance of ordinary citizens as political actors and reduces opportunities for active participation. Its majoritarian ethos undermines the importance of attending to the views and demands of minorities. It usually relies on formal, often legalistic political procedures rather than participation and therefore underestimates the dynamism of non-traditional forms of political expression. Young quite rightly notes that this kind of model is constructed according to a pluralist recognition of different groups in society but objects to the rather crude democratic principles that underpin it. This bears similarities to the dominant consociational approach to Northern Irish politics insofar as it treats groups as relatively stable and fixed and focuses on political leadership and élites as the key to democratic politics. Moreover, consociational approaches to Northern Ireland have relied upon the delineation of clear rules for decision-making that encourage legalistic formalism as a means of taking complicated decisions.

Where the aggregative approach to democracy differs from consociationalism is obviously in the simple majoritarianism of the former which is at odds with power sharing initiatives that have characterised the latter. However, both approaches assume that individuals will act only according to thin, individualistic rationality and they both fail to provide incentives for individuals to engage with the perspective of the other. Young articulates clearly the main limitations of this kind of approach to democracy as one that offers:

> a weak motivational basis for accepting the outcomes of a democratic process as legitimate. If even at its best democracy is simply a mechanism for aggregating preferences which are subjective and non-rational, and if the fair outcome reflects which preferences are more widely or more strongly held, then there is no reason why those who do not share those preferences ought to abide by the results. They may simply feel that they have no choice but to submit, given that they are in the minority.   (Young 2000: 21)

Whilst consociationalism tries to get around the issue through formal power-sharing arrangements, it is unable to explain why people who are in the minority on any given issue or set of issues should accede to them. Worse still, in Northern Ireland the tendency of politically excluded groups has often not been the meek submission that Young describes but political violence and terrorism instead.

Not surprisingly, Young is more sympathetic to deliberative forms of democracy but she also criticises some of the dominant deliberative theories. She regards deliberative democracy as based primarily on notions of inclusion, political equality, reasonableness and publicity. Deliberative democracy is stronger than aggregative models in Young's eyes because it understands democratic processes as being more comprehensive than the mere assertion of interests and preferences. Rather, the strength of deliberative democracy lies in its requirement for political actors to be 'open and attentive to one another, to justify their claims and proposals in terms acceptable to all', and in asking participants to move beyond self-regard, this model 'conceptualises the process of democratic discussion as not merely expressing and registering, but as *transforming* the preferences, beliefs, and judgement of participants' (Young 2000: 26). The correlations between this kind of thinking and civil society approaches to the Northern Ireland problem lie in the emphasis placed on communication between conflicting groups, the inclusion of as many groups as possible in political engagement, and the demand that participating actors are reasonable to one another. Both approaches share the optimistic belief that public engagement on issues of concern can lead to transformations in the way that different groups think about each other, and, even more optimistically, that these processes will transform the way groups think about themselves. Quite rightly, the feminist theory of democracy articulated by Young wants to open up democratic processes to excluded groups, and similarly, feminists in Northern Ireland have been eager to stress the extent to which women have traditionally been excluded in Northern Irish politics. However, the burdens of such lofty aspirations as to what deliberative democracy can achieve are very heavy indeed. Thus, whilst it may be an ideal-type model that is worth aspiring towards, it is very difficult to advance such a model in deeply divided conflictual societies like Northern Ireland.

To her credit Young is aware of some of these problems. She understands that one of the major limitations of deliberative democracy is that we envisage it as an all-encompassing source of political justice. Rather than attempting to construct a model of justice that overrides particular views and interests and postulate procedures that allow all to agree on the justness of outcomes, Young wants to view political justice as referring to agreement on ways in which we might communicate better with one another:

> Members of a polity, then, need not seek and arrive at agreement on a general conception of justice in order to argue productively about their problems and come to morally legitimate resolutions. Recognizing this can make political agreement seem less intractable than is sometimes supposed; it is often easier for people facing shared problems or conflicts to agree on a particular judgement about ways to address those problems than to commit themselves to a set of general principles to apply to all their collective dealings. (Young 2000: 29)

What makes Young's take on deliberative democracy a feminist one is her particular focus on modes of communication that have been privileged in liberal democratic processes and the ways in which women have traditionally often used alternative communicative methods. Thus, much of her analysis focuses on the way in which we should change the traditional basis of political communication during the process of agreeing just ways of communicating across difference. In this sense, she criticises those models of deliberative democracy that focus upon face-to-face interaction within a given setting such as a town meeting or courtroom. Instead, Young is concerned with the heterogeneous nature of politics and the wide variety of settings in which political views need to be articulated. Consequently, the idea that deliberative democracy should only involve strictly formalised rules and procedures within a given setting is anathema to her understanding of democracy. Indeed it is just such procedures that have impeded the articulation of the political voice of many women. Young is forthright in rejecting 'political moves to restrict discourses or their mode of expression to formal argument, appeals to a common good, or to those that some label as moderate and civil' (Young 2000: 51).

Young's view of democracy then is predicated upon what she refers to as 'inclusive political communication'. Here she differentiates between two main ways in which individuals and groups of people can be excluded from the usual forms of political engagement in liberal democracies. The first she describes as external exclusion which entails the overt exclusion of certain people from political debates or the domination of political processes by certain groups. The second type she refers to is internal exclusion which is perhaps a more subtle form of exclusion that keeps groups of people out of the decision-making process because, for example, 'the terms of discourse make assumptions some do not share, the interaction privileges specific styles of expression, [or] the participation of some people is dismissed as out of order' (Young 2000: 53). From this viewpoint, the role of feminist argument is to focus on the opening up of political dialogue to a wider range of discourses through embracing different types of communication. As Young notes, much contemporary democratic theory focuses on external exclusion as the major deficiency to be addressed and deliberative democracy has been at the forefront of attempts to establish more inclusive processes that are less prone to domination by certain privileged groups in society. Young's feminist concern is to raise the prominence of internal exclusion and present ways in which it might be challenged. To do this she examines particular forms of communication that are often disregarded in formal political settings – namely greeting, rhetoric and narrative – and shows how the neglect of these forms of communication has led to the exclusion of certain groups in society. Moreover, she aims to show how the recognition of these types of communication could lead to more inclusive political processes. Thus, we should not be hung up on formal processes requiring standards of articulacy or the absence of emotion for example:

> A more complete account of modes of political communication not only remedies exclusionary tendencies in deliberative practices, but more positively describes some specific ways that communicatively democratic processes can produce respect and trust, make possible understanding across structural and cultural difference, and motivate acceptance and action.   (Young 2000: 57).

Young's focus on greeting refers to the importance of public acknowledgement and recognition as a sign of the acceptance of the right of individuals and groups to contribute to a deliberative process. Greeting is seen as important insofar as it represents a sign of respect for others in the situation of public discourse as well as an indicator of political equality and an element of trust. Thus, Young contends that even where such gestures are formal and superficial, they play an important symbolic role in according status to all participants. This is an important argument in the context of Northern Ireland where symbolism is so important. Greeting has often been absent even on a symbolic level during the Northern Irish peace process which has been evident in the refusal of the DUP to recognise Sinn Féin and the open mockery of the Northern Ireland Women's Coalition by the former. In short, many feminists point to the gendered nature of the dominant forms of political dialogue.

Young's idea of the affirmative uses of rhetoric is not always evident in Northern Ireland but similarly we can identify signs where it is used. She promotes rhetoric as a form of political communication unlike many theorists of deliberative democracy like Habermas who see only 'rational' forms of speech as applicable to formal political intercourse. By establishing a role for rhetoric, Young asserts the value of discourses with an emotional tone, discourses that use figures of speech, the use of signs and symbols as well as speech, and discourses formulated to suit a specific audience. This is because she argues that 'the role of rhetoric in political communication is important precisely because the *meaning* of a discourse, its pragmatic operation in a situation of communicative interaction, depends as much on its rhetorical as its assertoric aspects' (Young 2000: 65). In Northern Ireland there is no shortage of rhetorical flourish in political discourse to both the benefit and detriment of political engagement. Young's point is that this is important precisely because rhetoric helps to establish the meaning of a discourse. Deliberative theories that try to denigrate such discourses deprive the political of key sources of meaning and hence of understanding. Moreover, Young believes that frequently it is rhetoric that establishes an issue on the political agenda, that in certain public spheres 'rational' formal language is not the most appropriate form of communication, and that rhetoric helps us make political *judgements* which is not always the case with formal political engagement. This is important in Northern Ireland where dialogue across difference frequently requires these kinds of political judgements – to suggest that this can only take place in a sphere of dispassionate formality damages politics precisely because opinions and beliefs are often matters of passion and commitment. The ability to communicate these passionate beliefs is central to a genuine understanding of the motivations behind political conflicts.

The third aspect of Young's thesis of inclusive political communication involves 'narrative and situated knowledge'. This refers to political situations which are too divided to establish a shared understanding of the communicative model. In this scenario groups can be excluded because their beliefs and values are at variance with the dominant idea of public discourse. Young believes that groups that face such exclusion need more than arguments to challenge the dominant paradigm. Instead, another 'mode of expression, narrative, serves important functions in democratic communication, to foster understanding among members of a polity with very different experience or assumptions about what is important' (Young 2000: 71). Thus, any inclusive polity needs to provide avenues for groups to express their concerns even where they differ from the dominant paradigm. Young argues that storytelling is a vital mode in which excluded groups can articulate their views and the reasons why they differ from the normative model in operation in any given society. Although this is not a perfect recipe for cohabitation in divided conflictual societies, it is a means through which:

> Members of a polity with very different histories and traditions than others in it, for example, often find things important to them that have no meaning or which seem trivial to others ... Those facing such lack of understanding often rely on myths and historical narratives to convey what is meaningful to them and why, to explain 'where they are coming from'.   (Young 2000: 75)

The point here is that just because a particular conception of the public operates in any given society, this does not mean that this is necessarily the most appropriate system. Young, and others who promote storytelling and narratives, see it as a part of a process of teaching and learning whereby dominant groups can be educated as to the reasons why weaker groups and minorities differ from the dominant paradigm. The contention is that narrative is a more appropriate way of communicating these differences than the 'rational' and controlled modes of communication that characterise formal political spheres.

The most notable feature of contemporary feminist discourses on democracy has been the way in which commentators such as Young have established an anti-essentialist perspective that stands in stark contrast to the advocacy of group rights within multicultural theory. Where contemporary feminists tend to focus on the problems of attributing rights or any other political characteristic to particular groups, multiculturalists tend to group people together depending on their culture. This, according to many feminists, is an essentialist agenda that denies the differences that exist within these groups of people. This throws up numerous issues but, in terms of feminist theories of democracy, it is important to ask how theories that reject any essentialisation of groups are to ensure that minority groups are not exploited. In other words, anti-essentialists, in their denial of the uniformity of groups, must explain how the rights of people who are part of those groups are to be protected. Whilst there is considerable criticism of feminism in this area, there is nothing to prevent feminists arguing that rights should be provided for certain groups such as women but at the same time recognising that the experience of those rights will be variable for different women. In other words, the formal attribution of rights does not entail that they are substantively experienced in the same way by everyone within a particular group or category. Thus, feminists need to couple their identity politics with a recognition that equal rights of a universal nature can be pursued and achieved on a formal level but that it is impossible for those rights to be experienced universally by all. In this sense, it is still possible for feminists to champion equality but to remain anti-essentialist and respectful of difference. There is, then, still scope to support equal rights without lapsing into essentialism.

Whilst recognising these issues, Nancy Fraser directs her critique of contemporary feminism at the way in which it is constrained within the domain of identity politics. Thus, she argues that it is deeply problematic to separate the pursuit of recognition and issues of political economy. She refers to 'the Gordian knots of identity and difference' and contends that we need a process of 'resituating cultural politics in relation to social politics and linking demands for recognition with demands for redistribution' (Fraser 1997: 174). Thus, she argues that feminists, and other anti-essentialists, have concentrated too heavily on issues of culture and identity at the expense of substantive issues related to welfare and the distribution of resources. In this vein she contends that anti-essentialists need to revisit concepts such as justice and equality that have been surrendered to some extent to the prevailing discourses of liberalism. Fraser's argument is that feminists have embroiled themselves in debates surrounding the relationship between equality and difference (both between men and women and among women themselves) and that this has led them away from the path of coupling a politics of recognition with a politics of redistribution. To be fair, she feels that Young has gone further than most feminist commentators in attempting to establish a link between cultural politics and the issue of justice which clearly involves debates over political economy. Thus, whilst Young's argument is not wholly persuasive on several issues, Fraser sees it as an advance towards the coupling of recognition and redistribution.

Young's perspective is multi-layered in its understanding of the operation of power and oppression. For this reason she has tended not to dwell explicitly on the issue of redistribution and debates within political economy because, as she rightly argues, economic distribution is not by itself the sole source of inequalities of power in the contemporary world. As Fraser notes, Young talks critically of the 'distributive paradigm' and the assumptions that underpin it. Instead she seeks a more sophisticated understanding of the sources of oppression and inequality but retains a 'bifocal' position that involves issues of distributive justice. However, recognition and 'the politics of difference' tend to predominate over redistribution in Young's schema (Fraser 1997: 190–2). Indeed Fraser argues that there is a tension in the way in which Young's definition of oppression embraces a bipartite position where oppression occurs because groups are not only undervalued in terms of culture but are also exploited in the sphere of political economy. The problem here is that recognition of the culture of oppressed groups does not grapple with the political and economic reasons why that culture is exploited. For Fraser, we need to go beyond recognition if we are serious about tackling oppression and create 'opportunities for self-development' (Fraser 1997: 194).

Alongside her critique of Young's definition of oppression, Fraser also takes issue with the way in which Young theorises social groups. This, as we shall see, is pivotal in understanding social division in Northern Ireland. Fraser notes that in Young's argument individuals are oppressed because they are members of certain groups who face prejudice and inequality. Importantly, these groups are seen to be constitutive of individual identities insofar as they entail specific cultural practices or ways of life and people feel an affinity with those who share these practices. Moreover they define those who are not members of these groups as the 'Other'. For Fraser, this a further reflection of Young's bifocal approach insofar as groups are made up of people who culturally 'recognise' one another and collectivities such as social classes which are established in political economy. Whilst Fraser is attracted to the way in which Young treats these different types of group under one umbrella, she worries that such a model may not do justice to the claims that these divergent groups may make. Thus, Fraser argues that the tendency to use ethnic groups as the exemplar in debates over recognition has come to predominate in subsequent analyses at the expense of groups such as social classes. Indeed she contends that Young's claims for the recognition of ethnic groups are sensible but become much more problematic when they are applied to other types of affinity group. Not surprisingly, Fraser argues that groups who face inequality on the basis of social class, for example, are more likely to find their needs served better by political economy rather than cultural politics.

Fraser goes on to analyse the understanding of oppression in Young's thesis and, in particular, her separation of oppression into five main categories: exploitation, marginalisation, powerlessness, cultural imperialism, and violence. These are treated separately in Young's thesis but Fraser argues that we can still identify Young's bifocal approach. Thus, the categories of exploitation, marginalisation and powerlessness are 'rooted in political economy', whilst cultural imperialism and violence relate to culture and an absence of recognition. To tackle the second set of oppressions, it is necessary to promote cultural pluralism and challenge the establishment of a uniform set of cultural norms, whereas the first group would be remedied by a reworking of the division of labour. It is at this point that Fraser identifies a problem with Young's schema:

> Each of these remedies seems well suited to redress its respective oppressions ... [b]ut there is a potentially disabling tension between them. Whereas the remedy for the culturally rooted oppressions promotes group differentiation, the remedy for the economically rooted oppressions may undermine it. In some cases, consequently, the effects of the two remedies will be contradictory   (Fraser 1997: 199).

The example Fraser uses to clarify this point is the issue of cultural imperialism. Following Young, we might argue that cultural imperialism emanates from the universal domination of culturally rooted practices but Fraser contends that it can also develop as a result of the economic domination of specific cultural groups. To tackle the problem as Young sees it would require policies to affirm cultural difference whereas Fraser's explanation would require 'political-economic restructuring' in which the politics of difference may be counterproductive. In other words, where Young's position requires a particularistic pluralism, Fraser's focuses more on an egalitarian universalism because recognition might negate efforts at redistribution. Fraser has a valid argument in identifying the ways in which a politics of difference could act in such a way as to counteract redistribution to groups that are being oppressed in one way or another. However, Young does not really differentiate between the groups that require recognition and those that need redistribution and so Fraser's criticism hardly invalidates her argument. Nonetheless Fraser's warning that we need to understand that neither recognition nor redistribution alone may be a strategy to challenge oppression is important. The fault line appears to be that Fraser focuses as much on the redistributive angle as Young does on the strategy of recognition.

Fraser summarises her critique of Young by putting forward what she calls a *critical* theory of recognition. Her starting point is the realisation that the politics of difference is not universally applicable as a method of challenging oppressions. Fraser argues that different groups have various requirements when it comes to the exclusions and inequalities that they experience. Where Young sees differences as merely expressions of human diversity, Fraser sets out a position where there are 'different kinds of difference', some of which should be abolished (for example, the construction of stereotypes to reinforce racism), some of which should be universalised (for example, notions of 'feminine nurturance'), and, lastly, some of which should be enjoyed (e.g. cultural variations). The advantage of Fraser's perspective on difference is that it provides a safeguard against relativism. Instead of merely identifying difference, it enables us to engage politically with diversity and to make judgements about the differences that exist. Not only is this healthily political in its outlook on difference, but it is also a more accurate reflection of what we frequently do with differences anyway. In other words, rather than trying to establish blanket rules regarding differences that can encapsulate our approach to them all on the same basis, Fraser's position implies that we need political engagement with differences to ensure that they receive appropriately different treatment. This implies that:

> we can make normative judgments about the relative value of alternative norms, practices, and interpretations, judgments that could lead to conclusions of inferiority, superiority, and equivalent value. It militates against any politics of difference that is wholesale and undifferentiated. It entails a more differentiated politics of difference.   (Fraser 1997: 204)

Whilst these are worthwhile sentiments, we also need to recognise that such a position does not tackle the fact that those who are making decisions about 'inferiority, superiority and equivalent value' may well be groups of people in power with an oppressive, sectarian or racist agenda. However, according to Fraser, when this differentiated conception of recognition is accompanied by a radical politics of redistribution to empower those groups that are oppressed through political economy, then sectarians or racists will not find it so simple to assume positions of power and responsibility. Although this argument has its merits, we also need to remain aware that it will not always be clear how different differences should be addressed and that the decision of how to tackle differences will, in itself, generate political disagreement and tension. Thus, Fraser provides us with a useful critique of Young but not a strategy for eliminating conflicts of power within contemporary democratic politics. The remainder of this chapter will examine the ways in which feminist debates about difference, recognition and redistribution have been played out in Northern Ireland.

Feminism and identity politics in Northern Ireland

Until recent years feminism has had a very limited impact on formal politics in Northern Ireland. This is not to say that there has not been political activism from women but rather that they have been marginalised in Northern Irish political debates and have found it difficult to progress within the main political parties. The difficulties for feminism and women in general in Northern Ireland relate to a political culture dominated by ingrained patriarchal attitudes. Moreover, many of the issues raised by feminists have had a limited impact due to the perception that politics in Northern Ireland is primarily concerned with 'bigger' issues of sovereignty and constitutional status.[2] Thus, whilst there was never an absence of feminism or political activism around issues of particular concern for women, it has struggled to have a major impact on the political landscape in Northern Ireland. As a result feminist politics there have often seemed somewhat underdeveloped in relation to the wider debates within feminism. Due to the structure of political culture in Northern Ireland, feminists have often had to employ a strategy of 'necessary essentialism' in order to demonstrate the exclusion of women from politics. In recent years however, there have been signs that this strategy has made greater headway with, for example, an important role in the dialogue leading to the Belfast Agreement and a growth in representation by women in the main parties and in the form of the Northern Ireland Women's Coalition. There are signs then that the role of women in Northern Irish politics is changing and that some of the traditional obstacles are breaking down. However, it is wise to remember the ingrained nature of many of these obstacles and the difficulties that remain in opening up political culture in Northern Ireland in the various ways that feminists advocate. As a result, contemporary feminism in Northern Ireland remains bound to elements of an essentialist strategy. Although the discourses of 'multiple intersecting difference' are becoming more influential, their impact on current practical politics in Northern Ireland are more limited.

One sign of the impact of feminism on political debates in Northern Ireland has been evident in the nature of the peace process with a recognition that lasting peace in Northern Ireland was not just about reaching agreement amongst political élites (as cruder versions of consociationalism might suggest). Feminists have been at the forefront of debates about deliberative democracy and the importance of multi-layered dialogue has been evident in recent politics in Northern Ireland. Feminists have also been forthright in debates promoting civil society. This has been particularly important in Northern Ireland due to the relative lack of women in party politics compared to those active in civil society politics. Not surprisingly then, the Northern Ireland peace process bears the implicit imprint of feminist thinking.[3] However, it is worth noting that much political activism by women in Northern Ireland has not been indicative of a liberal view of civil society. Instead, given the communal divisions in Northern Ireland, much community politics has reflected the prevailing schisms in wider society. When this is viewed in the light of the traditional élitist dimension to Northern Irish politics where the middle and upper classes have prevailed, it is clear that community politics has often involved the reaction of the working class to their exclusion on both sides of the communal divide. Following the work of Cynthia Cockburn, McCoy notes that many women have entered politics in response to 'political neglect, poverty and violence':

> Overcoming the first of these has been the inspiration for the involvement of the majority of women in community groups. Frustrated at the ignorance of and indifference to the economic and social problems of their communities shown by policy-makers, women have tried to find ways to make public these problems and possible solutions.   (McCoy 2000: 17–18)

What is not particularly clear from this analysis is its relationship with essentialist feminist positions. There has been a tendency to support increased activism by women in Northern Irish politics on the grounds of changing the nature of political engagement. Thus, some women have used the example of groups such as the Peace People in the 1970s to contend that women are more likely to be receptive to cross-community enterprises. This essentialist position suggests that women are less likely to be imbued with sectarianism or that women are, by their nature, better equipped to engage in dialogue across communal divides due to a greater communicative capacity. A similar approach advocates political activism by women because they are more able to see past the traditional schisms of Northern Irish politics to realise the problems of everyday life. Thus, many women have been active in the politics of everyday life – a 'situated' politics – that differs from the usual political battlegrounds in Northern Ireland (Porter 1998; McCoy 2000). In essentialist commentaries this kind of activism is used as a symbol of the ability of women to provide a positive contribution to the normalisation of Northern Irish politics.

This is not to say that feminism in Northern Ireland is inherently essentialist; indeed many of the essentialist discourses emanate from strategic requirements rather than whole-hearted commitment to female essentialism. One of the most fluent expositions of this kind of approach is Roulston (2000). In her coverage of variants of feminist thought, she accepts the limitations of earlier forms of feminism and points to the advantages of approaches characterised not by a simple differentiation between men and women but rather the existence of diversity amongst women. In evaluating the work of commentators such as Young, Phillips and Lister, she notes the importance of understanding democracy in terms of a differentiated universal citizenship. It is interesting, given the discussion above, that Roulston sees parallels between Young's advocacy of group differentiation leading to group rights and the consociational strategies that have reinforced communal identities in Northern Ireland. In the light of this it is worth noting that, in a brief reference to Northern Ireland, Young speaks approvingly of aspects of the Belfast Agreement because it 'aims to recognize the distinctness of peoples, but also aims to define their governance relationally in the context of wider interlocking institutions' whilst aiming to 'protect the rights of individuals and groups with little or no affiliation with the two major groups' (Young 2000: 262). Thus, she supports the Agreement on the grounds of the idea of 'relational autonomy':

> The institutional design of the 1998 agreement offers a good example of relational autonomy. The agreement recognizes all the inhabitants of the territory known as Northern Ireland as a self-determining people with their own government. It also recognizes that there are two main groups with historic relations to that territory and whose fates have been intertwined for centuries, and gives each of them special rights in the governance structure, on terms that aim to recognize a 'parity of esteem' between them.   (Young 2000: 262–3)

The links between group differentiation and consociational thinking here are clear. However, as Roulston argues, the important difference between consociationalism and Young's group differentiation lies in Young's concern for inequalities of power and their impact on democratic arrangements. Thus, whilst 'consociational theories stress elite accommodation, Young is suggesting that governments and states should create mechanisms which would allow all oppressed or minority groups to meet, discuss and formulate policy' (Roulston 2000: 34). This is a substantive difference because, where Young wants to challenge and undermine élitism and hierarchy, consociationalism reinforces it. In this sense the similarities are illusionary when placed in the context of the underpinning principles which structure the two positions. More crucial problems in Young's thesis emerge in the light of Roulston's discussion of Phillips and Mouffe, who both warn against the dangers of essentialising groups in society in the process of establishing differentiated group rights. The problem of establishing group rights lies in the danger of reifying arbitrary categories and suppressing the differences within groups.

To overcome these dangers, Roulston, like many feminists in Northern Ireland, professes an attraction to theories of deliberative democracy linked with commentators such as Seyla Benhabib (1996). As we saw in earlier chapters, there are numerous problematic assumptions that underpin deliberative democracy although these do not invalidate arguments for greater dialogue in places like Northern Ireland. Roulston, however, articulates a case for deliberative democracy in relation to the establishment of coalition politics in Northern Ireland. She cites the establishment of the Northern Ireland Women's Coalition as an example of what can be achieved through a commitment to deliberation. Using difference feminisms, she contends that in Northern Ireland there is a need for a 'transversal politics' in which 'one can learn about different perspectives without abandoning one's own identity'. This transversal politics is described as a process whereby:

> women enter into dialogue with a commitment to try to uncover a fair solution to the conflict which divides them. They are all rooted in a particular community, but make no claim to represent it, or even any particular subgroup within it. In the process, they aspire to learn about and respect the situations of women from the 'other' community ... Both 'rootedness' and the capacity to 'shift' are regarded as equally important if all are genuinely to learn about their differences.   (Roulston 2000: 41)

The difference, then, between this approach and that of Young is that the former requires a more committed form of public engagement between different groups and an open disposition towards changing and reforming one's beliefs through a recognition of the beliefs and demands of the 'Other'. Where some critics have accused Young of reinforcing group identities in a way that is problematic in divided societies, transversal politics require individuals to engage with each other in a less dogmatic fashion. Nonetheless Roulston's transversal politics implicitly recognises that the process of deliberation and political engagement will sometimes not change the beliefs of groups in divided societies. The problem then emerges of what to do in the light of continued disagreement and conflict. Whilst transversal politics aspire to deliberation in establishing elements of agreement and coalition, it simultaneously recognises that it cannot guarantee such a process. Whilst this may be a feasible strategy in less divided societies, this is problematic in Northern Ireland where transversal politics will encounter some intractable conflicts that dialogue may be incapable of surmounting. This is not to say that transversal politics is undesirable. However, we do need to recognise that it faces larger obstacles than some of its advocates suggest and provides no clear strategy for tackling some issues. It is no accident that the Northern Ireland Women's Coalition has sometimes had to overlook its internal differences in the process of formulating a coherent political message (Little 2002b).

In line with a general shift in feminist thinking in the last few years, feminists in Northern Ireland have focused on the need to open up spaces for engagement and dialogue (Porter 2000). This opening up of political deliberation is envisaged as a necessary challenge to the power hierarchies in the Northern Irish public sphere. Not surprisingly then, many of the difficulties in deliberative democracy are also reflected in feminist discourses on the potential of deliberation in the Northern Irish context. A useful example of this approach is employed by Elisabeth Porter who demonstrates a sound understanding of the challenges feminists face in Northern Ireland, but appears to see deliberative democracy as a way to surmount these obstacles. In her analysis she explains how the predominant 'two traditions' model of Northern Irish politics cannot provide sufficient space for the articulation of a coherent feminist politics. Therefore, she is aware that when it comes to issues of political identity, we need to recognise that 'cultural, national and political identities are multiple, negotiable and gloriously rich, not singular, fixed and exceptionally limited' (Porter 2000: 149). Clearly then, a feminist politics in Northern Ireland needs to construct a more robust conception of difference than has hitherto been the case. Moreover, this is underpinned by a heterogeneous understanding of communities and the diversity that exists within them. For this reason Porter wants to open political dialogue across difference rather than rely upon the closed notions of community that prevail in many political discourses in Northern Ireland which she sees as conservative and potentially exclusionary. Whilst Porter is clearly aware of the divisive way in which community emerges in much political discourse, she also recognises that identity politics can provide clearer voices for groups such as women that have traditionally been excluded or marginalised.

Why then does Porter see deliberative democracy as a particularly useful method of changing the nature of political dialogue in Northern Ireland? Her argument focuses on the need to create 'transitional spaces' in which Northern Irish politics can be redeveloped to take account of changing political demands. Thus, she contends that the process of engaging in political discussion can generate greater solidarity whereby, even if groups agree to disagree with each other, there will at least be a higher level of mutual understanding and a commitment to talking through problems. In this vein Porter contends that it is through political dialogue that coalitions emerge as groups and can see beyond the narrow parameters of their own perspectives to encompass the views of others. This potentially enables us to accommodate the 'Other' and encourages us to reconstruct our own political position. Quite properly, she sees such coalitions as contingent and negotiable; they are not set in stone and the values, principles and policies that are agreed upon are always subject to change. Thus, whilst she promotes and supports the work of the Northern Ireland Women's Coalition, her perspective suggests that the foundations of that coalition are alterable and dependent upon the broader political context at any given time and the shifting political identities that exist within the coalition. This implies that Porter regards the feminist contribution to politics in Northern Ireland as not only transformative of the nature of political dialogue, but also as where the articulation of the many voices of women are liable to shift the foundational principles upon which the coalition was formed.

What then are the difficulties of this feminist perspective on deliberative democracy in the context of Northern Ireland? There are four main areas of criticism: firstly, Porter makes numerous assumptions about separating deliberative politics from other forms of politics in Northern Ireland; secondly, she makes too many demands on the participants; thirdly, she adopts an overly optimistic position on what deliberation can achieve; and, fourthly, there is an underlying female essentialism that suggests that women are naturally more adept at this kind of engagement than men. The first problem is evident in her explicit point that she is only dealing with debates on democratic participation. Whilst this is understandable, it can be argued that in Northern Ireland there is a need to engage in deliberation with those who perpetrate or have perpetrated violence in order to achieve a firm understanding of their reasons for doing so. Moreover, the construction of deliberative institutions can hardly be seen as a model for Northern Irish democracy if there is no attempt to engage with those who have no faith in these bodies. In short, the reality of conducting politics in Northern Ireland can never be wholly separated from the violent legacy that has bequeathed the political conditions that prevail there. The second difficulty relates to her description of the disposition of participants in deliberation. For example, in taking issue with the thesis of Jane Flax, Porter contends that one of the 'most positive contributions individuals, groups and institutions can make is to confront "the other" without suspicion, in a spirit of open equality' (Porter 2000: 148). As desirable as this may be, Porter must heed her own warnings that suspicion and distrust permeate divided societies and this is obviously the case in Northern Ireland. To wish away such conditions is to divorce theoretical prescriptions from the real conditions in which dialogue could take place. Thus, whilst a decrease in hostility *may* be an outcome of democratic deliberation, in no sense can it be established as an *a priori* principle in the context of Northern Ireland. Similarly, her invocation of Habermasian communicative ethics and the work of Simone Chambers to argue that participants in dialogue should not attempt to deceive each other flies in the face of the practical conditions in which political actors can enter dialogue (Dixon 2002a). Certainly, deliberative democracy is purposively idealistic, but this kind of condition renders it impotent in terms of guiding *realpolitik*.[4]

The third criticism of Porter's feminist theory of deliberative democracy is evident in what she expects such dialogue to achieve. Where political engagement in Northern Ireland has generated contingent messy compromises that have sometimes generated further animosity and conflict in the longer term, Porter argues that what must be recognised is the need for sound political judgement. Thus:

> Judgement assumes difference and conflict, but refuses the notion that disagreement must lead to antagonism and continual political blockage. Rather, through reasoned debate, and motivated by the urgency to deliver a resolution that is acceptable to all different parties, judgement allows citizens and political representatives to listen, talk, consider other's views and allow themselves to be persuaded of the need to change.   (Porter 2000: 159)

Here the issue is not so much with her diagnosis of the problem but in her prescription of possible outcomes. Porter is correct to contend that the existence of difference need not manifest itself in antagonism or political stagnation (even if, in Northern Ireland, it frequently does). Nonetheless the view of the dialogic process as one that persuades participants of the need to change is somewhat optimistic. The reality of political engagement in Northern Ireland is one where judgement tends to manifest itself in terms of calculating the most beneficial outcome for a party and their constituency. Frequently this judgement involves reinforcing rather than changing ideas. Thus, political judgement in Northern Ireland is exercised more in terms of strategic calculation rather than being a process where political actors are persuaded of the error of their ways by their opponents. The deliberative model envisages a degree of openness that is very rarely the case with any political actors let alone those trying to negotiate pathways through conflicts as divisive as that in Northern Ireland. This stands in stark contrast to the picture depicted by Porter who contends that where political engagement 'is lacking in goodwill there can be no reconciliation' (Porter 2000: 157). Reconciliation can be just as much a strategic decision as one abounding with goodwill.[5] Where reconciliation founded on goodwill *might* be desirable and beneficial in the long-term, it is not necessarily fundamental to workable political agreements. Indeed consociational politics has to some extent been predicated upon a situation where such goodwill is in short supply.

The last critical reflection on Elisabeth Porter's approach is the unfortunate tendency to make essentialist remarks amidst the protestations that women should be viewed as a heterogeneous and diverse group. Thus, even though she is aware of anti-essentialist arguments and even demonstrates some sympathy with them, Porter makes a few remarks that betray a more traditional feminist approach. For example, following a passage in which she rejects the idea of corralling women in Northern Irish politics into areas that have traditionally been viewed as 'women's interests', she states that women have 'prime nurturing roles, adopted through choice, coercion and/or socialisation [that] require women to be flexible, accommodating and compassionate' and that we should 'value highly those traits traditionally associated with femininity, like cooperation, non-hierarchical modes of operating, adaptability and nurturance' (Porter 2000: 143–4). Porter correctly notes that these traits are not a matter of essence insofar as they can be acquired in a number of different ways, but nonetheless it does seem a rather sweeping statement to generalise about the existence of these capabilities in the broad category of women and by implication the absence of these characteristics amongst many men. Similarly, in highlighting Young's advocacy of storytelling as an important source of communication that is often marginalised from what is seen as political communication, Porter remarks that:

> Women constantly share each other's life stories and the myriad of details that make up mundane ordinary lives, shared over the telephone, when walking the children to school, over coffee when

> borrowing a household item or clothes. Talking through our narratives with those who come from different traditions, communities and regions is crucial to break the barriers of distrust that too often are based on fear cultivated through ignorance.   (Porter 2000: 158)

The second sentence contains much wise counsel but the specification of women as a general category in the first sentence is much more questionable. The idea that women 'constantly' share each other's lives is surely debatable and it is quite possible in Northern Ireland to engage in the activities outlined above without dealing in any kind of substantive way with people from 'other' communities. Apart from a rather stereotyped, general image of the lives that women in Northern Ireland lead, there is also little attempt to grapple with the reality that men engage in some of these activities as well. Of course, it is the case that men take part in those activities listed by Porter much less than women do. Clearly though, there may be numerous examples of social interactions which tend to be dominated by men, or in which men participate equally, where they may 'share each other's life stories'.[6] However, the point is that Porter serves her argument poorly in making sweeping generalisations about the lives women lead and, by implication, that they are rather different to the life experiences of men. Arguments about storytelling are important ones but they are not well served by examples that rely heavily upon such generalisations. To be clear, Porter does not see these traits as a matter of essence but her argument that women as a group are different to men in these respects leads her towards assumptions that are broadly similar to those that might be made by essentialist feminists.

An alternative feminist approach that avoids some of the pitfalls of Porter's argument is the chapter by Eilish Rooney (2000) in the same volume. Rooney is at pains to stress that, despite some shared understandings of the ways in which women have been excluded from Northern Irish politics and the reasons behind these exclusions, it is vital to grasp the importance of difference in Northern Ireland. Thus, she implies that not only are there significant differences between the experiences of women in different religions or other communal groupings based around political outlook, but it is also crucial to understand the diversity within each of these categories. In this sense Rooney wants to challenge feminist arguments that imply universal experiences for women or essentialist viewpoints as to what comprises the identity of women. In short, against theories such as Porter's that postulate equality without grappling with inequalities of power, Rooney contends that 'difference matters'. Indeed where Porter proposes a transversal politics built around the experience of women, Rooney argues that:

> Gender-inscribed forms of political agency are an ideological and political resource within unionism and within nationalism, and are utilised by all political parties in the North of Ireland. The notion that women's active participation in politics is necessarily or essentially progressive or emancipatory for women *qua* women is fallacious. Women evidently see their political activity as valuable in promoting the interests of their collectivity.   (Rooney 2000: 168)[7]

This is an important rebuttal to the dominant themes in feminist literature in Northern Ireland which usually depict women as inherently part of a progressive transversal politics. Whilst many women are involved in such strategies, the value of Rooney's approach lies in the reminder that many women are active within the traditional parameters of party politics in Northern Ireland. Moreover, even where female political activists are involved in the sphere of civil society or community politics, this does not mean that their beliefs transcend the communal divisions of everyday life in Northern Ireland. Rooney's key contention is that a political strategy that extracts people from the everyday social context of life in Northern Ireland tends to underestimate the ways in which the experiences of the conflict have varied. This refers not only to the 'two communities' but also, for example, the widely differing experience of working class and middle class communities especially in cities such as Belfast. Indeed, we might add the differences that have emanated from the urban struggles to conflicts in rural areas around the border. For Rooney, the danger in neglecting these differences is that we end up making prescriptions about people that contradict their own conceptions of what conflicts are about and ways to address them. Thus, in noting the work of Iris Marion Young, Rooney points out how inequalities of power may result in a skewing of the territory in which deliberative democracy can take place. This reflects the problems of establishing the ideal-type conditions advocated as a model by deliberative democrats. Ultimately, for Rooney, the bottom line is that the exclusion of women in Northern Irish politics has been uneven and therefore the process of dealing with inequalities and exclusions is much more complicated than some less sophisticated feminist analyses might have us believe.

Conclusion

Feminist theory has traditionally had a negligible influence in mainstream debates in Northern Irish politics but its relevance is increasingly evident. It provides a powerful reminder of the perils of essentialism and the limitations of viewing Northern Ireland in terms of the 'two traditions'. Moreover, by using recent theories of 'multiple intersecting differences', we are better able to understand the variety of forms of identity and exclusion that exist. At the same time though, it is important to point out how feminists understand 'the political' and the reasons why they have been drawn towards deliberative understandings of democracy. Earlier in the book we saw that, whilst deliberative democracy contains many worthy aspirations, it is a difficult model to operationalise in deeply divided societies like Northern Ireland. Not surprisingly then, some feminists have fallen into a similar trap by expecting too much of political actors or demanding reasonableness and reconciliation. It is the contention here that a more radical model of democracy needs to be articulated to understand the complexities and conflicts of Northern Ireland. This approach has clearly been informed by feminist arguments but takes a more realistic view of the capacity of democracy to resolve political conflict.

7
Radical Democracy

In the liberal theories examined so far in the book, we have seen the problems that emerge from abstract individualism, discourses of rights and the overly prescriptive drawing of boundaries between the public and non-public or private spheres. However, in recent theories of civil society and social capital we have witnessed more attention being paid to context and issues of social structure, whilst feminism (and identity politics more generally) has raised questions about the need for contemporary polities to recognise social and cultural difference. If any kind of synthesis can be formulated from these critiques of liberalism, it is that we need to understand the tensions between liberalism and democracy and the way in which those tensions undermine the universal models that tend to emanate from liberal theory. Democracy, then, is a much more complicated and chaotic phenomenon than it appears in most theoretical ideal-type constructions.[1] Whereas orthodox models of liberal democracy attempt to simplify and negate this diversity and complexity in the political sphere, a radical approach to democracy must recognise and build upon the complicated relations of diverse societies. This chapter will explain and critically evaluate radical democratic understandings of democracy and the extent to which they offer alternative perspectives that could be applied to Northern Irish politics.

The extent to which any of the strategies employed during the peace process can be justified as genuinely democratic is open to question. Paul Dixon (2002a), for example, notes how the process was largely driven by political tactics far removed from the ideal-type democratic models which have been discussed thus far in this book. Amongst the methods employed by Northern Irish politicians and the two governments have been numerous 'political skills' that have sought to mislead rather than inform people on the ground in Northern Ireland as to the real processes taking place away from the public eye (Dixon 2002a: 732–7). Examples of these 'political skills' have included pragmatic zigzagging by the two governments to appeal in turn to unionist and nationalist agendas so as not to appear to favour one side over the other. Another strategy has been what Dixon calls 'constructive ambiguity' whereby the various documents that have punctuated the peace process have all been open to interpretation in different ways by the various interests in Northern Irish politics. Indeed we noted in Chapter One how ambiguity was a central element of the Belfast Agreement itself. Dixon's analysis is based upon an examination of the rectitude of the role of élites and 'dirty hands' in politics. From this basis, we can assess the extent to which politicians are justified in misleading or misinforming the general public if their pursuit of a worthwhile objective is likely to be accentuated by the 'dirty hands' strategy.

In answering the question of the acceptability of deception, Dixon outlines a schema involving three main approaches: absolutist, realist and democratic realist. The absolutist position on lying and deception depends on a 'common sense' approach which suggests that misinformation and other dubious strategies are inherently wrong and democratically unjustifiable. Dixon notes how many critics of the peace process have adopted an absolutist position in their opposition to the political élites arguing that '[l]ies are unnecessary, sincerity and honesty with the party and electorate stands a better chance of winning popular support for ideological and political change' (Dixon 2002a: 737). The absolutist approach, then, accuses politicians of breeding a culture of mistrust and disrespect.[2] The realist approach challenges the absolutist perspective as naïve and ignorant of the practicalities of political engagement in complex societies. As Dixon notes, realists contend that absolutists tend to be less than pure themselves and that at least realists are aware of the deceptions they are carrying out. Moreover, the latter contend that absolutists underestimate the practical and structural constraints in any given situation and fail to differentiate between different types of 'political skills'. The fact is, then, that some 'political skills' may be more appropriate and acceptable to particular political processes and situations than others. However, the realist approach can be criticised itself for its élitist nature and the underpinning assumption that the leadership of political parties know better than ordinary people about the 'correct' course of action in any given situation. These élites may harbour all kinds of vested interests – not least the desire to get re-elected – and this may result in less beneficial outcomes from political engagement than would be the case if these vested interests were not in place.

Dixon notes that some commentators have justified the élitism of realists in Northern Ireland on the grounds that politics is a 'dirty business and deception and manipulation are justified on the grounds that they promise peace and a lasting settlement' (Dixon 2002a: 738). Clearly in Northern Ireland there have been occasions when choreography and different forms of deception have been deemed necessary but it is stretching credulity to suggest that élites in Northern Ireland have always acted as they have on the basis of achieving peace. If realists ask us to accept that politics is a dirty business, then they cannot ask us to suspend our suspicions at their own motives for behaving in the way that they do. If politics inevitably involves 'dirty hands', then exponents of these dark arts cannot simply claim purity when their actions do come under public scrutiny. Democracy is a messy business and perhaps it is best that all involved make this as clear as possible rather than relying on a pretence of the best interests of all which no-one really subscribes to anyway.

From this analysis we can understand that open and honest communications would be preferable, all things being equal. However, in democratic politics these conditions rarely prevail and inevitably politics will involve engagement which is not part of open, public communication.[3] Faced with these realities and structural constraints, Dixon indicates his support for a 'democratic realist' position. His main problem with the absolutist and realist approaches has been that 'little attempt has been made to *persuade* rather than *manipulate* important sections of the population to support the peace process ...' (Dixon 2002a: 739). Thus, whilst he acknowledges that there can be a fine line between persuasion and manipulation, Dixon argues that the choreographed development of the peace process has generated mistrust and scepticism amongst the wider public. The population of Northern Ireland remains divided and insufficient attempts have been made to bridge these gaps. Indeed one could argue that the consociational arrangements of the Belfast Agreement have accentuated those divisions between the general public and the political élites. From this perspective, Dixon argues that there is good reason for a realist approach in the particular context of Northern Ireland insofar as we cannot change the world simply from what it is to what it ought to be.

Dixon's vision of a 'democratic realist' position promotes a narrowing of the 'credibility gap' between the public face of politics and the realities behind the scenes. Indeed, he sees this as necessary because he argues that the longer this gap prevails, the more counterproductive are the attempts of the élite to manipulate politics. This critique of the élite politics which have driven the Northern Irish peace process is convincing, given that he acknowledges that structural constraints necessitate a degree of realism. Nonetheless it is not clear exactly what a democratic realist approach would involve. Dixon's idea of democratising contemporary politics in Northern Ireland is attractive in the light of the élite-driven and top-down nature of political parties and institutions there. A radical democratic approach might argue for greater participation by a more representative group of people than is currently the case, or promote reformed, democratised political institutions. However, Dixon appeals for a politics where the political élites that have hitherto manipulated the population of Northern Ireland become more open and candid in their actions. This aspiration, whilst understandable and legitimate, appeals to an absolutist vision tinged by a realist understanding of the political situation. As such, it remains within the established parameters of understanding democracy in Northern Ireland. Perhaps an alternative approach to democracy in Northern Ireland needs to embrace more radical considerations of politics and democracy.

Radical democracy invokes a model that asks us to conceive 'the political' differently and which challenges the ethical presumptions which underpin liberal conceptions of democracy. Radical democratic theory is a rather loose body of work which has yet to attain a clear identity as a coherent position but this is partly due to the nature of the ideas that radical democrats embrace. According to Fraser:

> to be a radical democrat today is to appreciate – and seek to eliminate – two different kinds of impediments to democratic participation. One such impediment is social inequality; the other is the misrecognition of difference. Radical democracy ... is the view that democracy today requires both economic redistribution and multicultural recognition.   (Fraser 1997: 173–4)

In the work of commentators such as Chantal Mouffe (2000) a radical variant of pluralist theory is advanced. It recognises that there is a wide variety of social and political perspectives in contemporary Western societies which emanate from a range of different sources of individual and collective identity. Mouffe argues that these sources of identity cross-cut one another which leads to their manifestation in a multiplicity of different ways. Thus, identities are not merely prescribed by simple accidents of birth or the 'communities of fate' that we belong to without choice. Rather identity is a complicated mixture of fate and choice that is constructed out of the relationships which individuals have with a range of different collective identities. According to this view of identity then, we need to be careful about making prescriptive definitions of what individuals from any given community will believe or how they will act. The beliefs and actions of an individual within a community will not be defined simply by the fact of membership of that community because that individual will also be a member of other communities as well. It is through the interaction of these different (and sometimes conflicting) sources of the self that individual identity emerges. For example, each individual will emerge differently out of the complex interaction of sources of identity such as class, gender, ethnicity, religion, nationality, sexuality and so on.

What, then, are the political ramifications of this pluralist under-standing of identity? Clearly it gives rise to a 'politics of difference' insofar as any democratic settlement must be capable of containing a wide degree of diversity within a pluralistic society (Baumeister 2000). However, as we have noted thus far, this throws up a number of problems for the political organisation of contemporary societies. The 'fact of multiculturalism' has generated considerable controversy within contemporary political theory and the two most influential perspect-ives in dealing with this pluralism, the theories of Rawls and Habermas, have been deficient in providing persuasive models of accommodating diversity. Both of these theorists have been subject to considerable criticism from other liberals who regard their theories as insufficiently aware of the complexities and incommensurability of value pluralism (Baumeister 2000; Crowder 2002; Gray 2000), and communitarians who argue that the likes of Rawls neglect the social context and attachments which impact upon the interaction of indi-viduals, groups and the state (see Little 2002a). As Baumeister (2000, ch. 7) notes, however, there is a tradition within liberalism which recognises the incommensurability of value pluralism and therefore the challenges that emerge to those attempting to forge a democratic model which can accommodate such diversity. This is the territory upon which radical pluralists such as Mouffe have articulated a model of democratic politics which is critical of the ideas of Rawls and Habermas, but which also presents a radical variant on communitarian thinking (Little 2002d). Before discussing the implications of such value pluralism, it is worth outlining Mouffe's ideas on radical demo-cracy in more detail.

Chantal Mouffe and *The Democratic Paradox*

Mouffe originally set out her argument for radical democracy in collaboration with Ernesto Laclau in their book *Hegemony and Socialist Strategy* published in 1985.[4] Influenced by post-structuralist theory, Laclau and Mouffe set out a post-Marxist perspective that rejected both the universalism of Habermas and the post-modernist particularism of Jean-Francois Lyotard. Where Habermas provides a model of political engagement that potentially emasculates political discourse, Lyotard's particularism makes meaningful political engagement virtually impossible. For Laclau and Mouffe, both of these perspectives misunderstand the nature of antagonism and its relationship with democracy. This is where the post-Marxist credentials of their argument become apparent for they regard the emergence of ideas built around consensus as inherently problematic. This perspective sees the pursuit of the 'radical centre' by the Left since the 1980s as profoundly anti-political and rejects the view that this entails 'progress' in the way that many on the social democratic Left see it. For Laclau and Mouffe, radical democracy is built around 'a profound transformation of the existing relations of power' in which 'the objective was the establishment of a new hegemony, which requires the creation of new political frontiers, not their disappearance' (Laclau and Mouffe 2001: xv). Where the social democratic Left has surrendered the essence of politics in seeking to establish consensus by removing antagonisms, Laclau and Mouffe see such antagonisms as constitutive of the political:

> there are a variety of possible antagonisms in the social, many of them in opposition to each other. The important problem is that the chains of equivalence will vary radically according to which antagonism is involved; and that they may affect and penetrate, in a contradictory way, the identity of the subject itself. This gives rise to the following conclusion: the more unstable the social relations, the less successful will be any definite system of differences and the more the points of antagonism will proliferate. (Laclau and Mouffe 2001: 131)

What this argument suggests, then, is that the pursuit of consensus in liberal democracy emasculates politics. Laclau and Mouffe agree with deliberative democrats like Habermas that the aggregative model which characterises many contemporary liberal democracies does not grasp the way that political ideas are 'constituted and reconstituted through debate in the public sphere' (Laclau and Mouffe 2001: xvii). However, they disagree with the idea of resolving conflicts through the kind of 'rational' dialogue which inspires deliberative democracy and argue instead that 'without conflict and division, a pluralist democratic politics would be impossible' (Laclau and Mouffe 2001: xvii). In this sense, a radical democratic politics is one that recognises the existence of antagonisms and attempts to grapple with them. This stands in stark contrast to liberal theories of democracy which do not recognise the essentially contested nature of the principles upon which it is founded. In Laclau and Mouffe's terms these principles are 'contingent social logics' (Laclau and Mouffe 2001: 142).

From these foundations Chantal Mouffe has constructed a radical pluralist position within contemporary debates in democratic theory that is most cogently expressed in *The Democratic Paradox* (2000). What makes Mouffe's contribution distinctive and radical is the way in which she grapples with the political complexities which emerge from the idea of value pluralism. Rather than disengaging with the political, as arguably 'doctrinal postmodernist' or relativist approaches to diversity imply, Mouffe's 'post-Marxist' model is focused upon the ways in which we might generate democratic renewal from the conflict and disagreement that value pluralism might entail. According to this model, we should reject liberal theories which attempt to reach some kind of rational or impartial consensus between conflicting groups and, instead, build upon the multiplicity of diverse perspectives that exist in complex modern societies. Thus, Mouffe opposes liberal impartialism and Habermasian discourse ethics as well as extreme pluralist positions which neglect the political dimension that inevitably arises when diverse groups of people have to live alongside one another. When it comes to dealing with the reality of pluralistic societies, 'what is really at stake is power and antagonism and their ineradicable character' (Mouffe 2000: 21). This statement is vital. It recognises that the existence of diversity and value pluralism in no way equates to a position of equal power between different groups. On the contrary, contemporary societies are characterised by vast differentials in power and, thereby, a situation in which the values and beliefs of certain dominant groups come to prevail over those of the less powerful. Thus, we should be careful to avoid falling into the trap of regarding the existence of different groups in society as an indicator of equality of power or worth. It is for precisely this reason that traditional liberal pluralism must be challenged for failing to engage with differentials of power. Mouffe provides a justification for renewing the democratic process to construct spaces for the expression of political difference.

This model of democratic renewal provides a fundamental challenge to the more orthodox liberal theories of Rawls and Habermas. Mouffe criticises Rawls for asserting the 'fact of pluralism' and then constructing a political model that attempts to override the plurality of views by reducing them to effectively private or 'non-public' differences which do not impact upon the public sphere. On the contrary, Mouffe argues that:

> from an anti-essentialist theoretical perspective ... pluralism is not merely a fact, something that we must bear grudgingly or try to reduce, but an axiological principle. It is taken to be constitutive at the conceptual level of the very nature of modern democracy and considered as something that we should celebrate and enhance. (Mouffe 2000: 19)

According to this radical pluralist position, we must recognise and embrace the conflict and antagonism that such pluralism makes inevitable. This is the very stuff of 'the political': it stresses that difference must be tackled in the public sphere rather than being viewed as something which should (or can) be hived off in the private domain to avoid conflict and tension. This is the centrepiece of Mouffe's critique of Rawls's political liberalism. She criticises Rawls for constructing a model based upon 'reasonable pluralism' whereby we attempt to build an overlapping moral consensus based on an agreement on liberal principles in the public sphere. For Mouffe, the Rawlsian position entails the non-public sphere being the space for the expression of difference, whilst the public domain would be characterised by liberal principles such as neutrality and tolerance. Mouffe's objection is that this is, in itself, a political decision that places liberalism in a pre-eminent position whereby it is the superior political ideology for the organisation of the political sphere. This provides a closure of the political – there is no space in Rawls' thought for argument about the principles which should govern the public sphere or the rules of political engagement. These kinds of differences are relegated to the private sphere and are not constitutive of political debate. In short, there can be pluralism within society (in the non-public domain) but not pluralism about politics (how we should engage with one another). As Mouffe notes, if we follow Rawlsian liberalism we are left with a rather circular form of political argument: 'political liberalism can provide a consensus among reasonable persons who, by definition, are persons who accept the principles of political liberalism' (Mouffe 2000: 26).

From the radical democratic perspective, the problem with Rawlsian political liberalism is the assumption that individuals and groups can maintain their fundamental differences on religion, nationality, culture and so on and yet will reach consensus on the nature of political engagement. It is the ease with which Rawls divorces politics from other aspects of individual and collective identity that is perhaps the most impractical aspect of his thought. Pluralistic societies are divided not just on the basis of religious or ethnic difference but also on the ramifications that those differences have for political relations. Rawls attempts to prescribe what the acceptable face of the political is, when the reality of pluralism is that there is likely to be much more contention and conflict about political engagement and organisation. In short, for radical democrats, we cannot assume a rational or impartial consensus on the nature of politics. Where Rawls has attempted to construct such a position, it reflects his own preordained model of what liberalism in practice would look like and it therefore tries to preclude conflict and debate about how the political should be constituted.

Mouffe's alternative radical democratic model (which she terms 'agonistic pluralism') emerges out of her critique of deliberative democracy and Habermasian discourse ethics. Habermas' model moves beyond that of Rawls insofar as his preferred normative structure, communicative rationality, allows for participants to critically question the basic procedures of political engagement. However, his thesis relies upon the procedural rules whereby all individuals or groups with a relevant interest in any given topic can enter political debate on a fair and equal basis with other affected persons. Such a procedure is not merely concerned with *reaching* consensus but also focuses on following a certain rule-bound type of engagement which will make such a consensus *universal* and *morally impartial*. This will provide decisions made through following such procedures with a greater legitimacy than is apparent in the decision-making processes of contemporary liberal democracies. Whilst Habermas succeeds in articulating a position that does not rely on the clear-cut and unachievable separation of the public and non-public which emerges in Rawlsian thought, Mouffe agrees with Rawls that Habermas' 'approach cannot be as strictly procedural as he pretends. It must include a substantive dimension, given that issues concerning the result of the procedures cannot be excluded from their design' (Mouffe 2000: 91). Thus, even though Habermas doesn't employ a strict private/public divide, he does attempt to circumvent the irreconcilable differences which emanate from liberal value pluralism by differentiating between issues concerned with ethics and those of morality. Issues of ethics, such as disputes about the nature of the good life, are separated from the moral sphere in which universal legal procedures must apply to allow a rational impartiality to develop. For radical democrats like Mouffe, Habermas falls into precisely the same trap as Rawls (albeit in a different way) by failing to recognise that the different ethical perspectives which people hold will impact upon the nature of their engagement in the moral-political procedures. Therefore, we need to recognise that the varying substantive positions of value pluralism will affect the design and operation of our decision-making processes.

The radical democratic argument put forward by Mouffe suggests that we need to be more realistic about what we can achieve through democratic systems. In complex pluralistic societies we should be considering how we open out political spaces to enable more engagement and a clearer reflection of the multiplicity of identities, communities and attachments that we have. However, if we take incommensurable value pluralism as the foundation of political space, then we need to recognise that liberal strategies such as those of Rawls and Habermas designed to reach an impartial or rational consensus are likely to end in failure. For radical democrats, the strategies of Rawls and Habermas both lead to political closure whereas a radical democratic position should seek to open out opportunities for political engagement. This position is cogently expressed by Mouffe who believes that Rawls and Habermas want to deny:

> the paradoxical nature of modern democracy and the fundamental tension between the logic of democracy and the logic of liberalism. They are unable to acknowledge that, while it is indeed the case that individual rights and democratic self-government are constitutive of liberal democracy ... there exists between their respective 'grammars' a tension that can never be eliminated ... [T]his does not mean that liberal democracy is a doomed regime. Such a tension, though ineradicable, can be negotiated in different ways. Indeed a great part of democratic politics is precisely about the negotiation of that paradox and the articulation of precarious solutions.   (Mouffe 2000: 93)

To summarise the radical democratic position then, the problem of liberalism is in trying to construct a rational, impartial position from the complexity and contradictions of pluralistic societies. If values are incommensurable, then such impartiality is difficult to achieve. If that is the case, then the 'rational' position in any given society on any particular issue is likely to represent the particular views and interests of certain sectional groups. For this reason, democratic politics should be concerned with the process of teasing out different confrontations and the sources of disagreement and engaging in dialogue and debate about them. However, unlike the dominant trends in contemporary liberalism, that does not mean that we should expect such debates to generate consensual agreement, let alone agreement which is impartial or rational. Participants in such discussions will bring their own rationalities to the table (if there is a democratic process at work) and negotiate with those with whom they are in conflict but a radical democratic position will not expect that some kind of agreement will always ensue. Conflict and disagreement are the very essence of democratic politics and liberals do us few favours by attempting to sidestep such differences through theoretical models which base themselves upon imagined divides between the public and the non-public or the ethical and the moral. For radical democrats, these approaches foreclose space for political dialogue rather than opening out democratic debate.

The question remains as to the contribution that radical democratic theory can make to our understanding of politics in Northern Ireland. Clearly the centrality of conflict and antagonism to radical democracy gives it a foothold in trying to grapple with the well-known difficulties there. Indeed it could be argued that the political practice in Northern Ireland is ahead of the game compared to the dominant liberal theories of democracy insofar as the peace process has been an example of contingency, pragmatism and the fluid nature of politics. However, radical democracy relies heavily upon a multiplicity of cross-cutting constructions of identity which are subject to change through the constant interaction with other sources of the self. In Northern Ireland, however, efforts to deal with diversity have been built around a much narrower understanding of diversity and an assumption, at least in documents like the Belfast Agreement, that the identity and self-understanding of conflicting groups is much more fixed than radical democrats would have us believe. In this sense, a radical democratic perspective on Northern Ireland not only tries to normalise the conflict that exists there, but also critically implies that a healthy polity in Northern Ireland would recognise a greater capacity for diversity and change with regard to the major sources of identity. Thus, radical democracy can claim to provide both a theoretical position from which we can adopt a pragmatic approach to political conflict in Northern Ireland, whilst at the same time establishing a radical challenge to the prevailing understanding of culture and identity which dominate the understanding of diversity there.

Perhaps the most notable aspect of radical democratic theory is the critique of consensus as it is traditionally understood in contemporary politics. As we shall see, ultimately all variants of liberal democratic thought, even radical versions, must operate with some understanding of consensus (however limited). Nonetheless radical democrats are clearly sceptical of the promotion of consensus as a normative good *per se*. Rather, they tend to see consensus as a political necessity of a kind but not something that should be understood as healthy in itself for any given society. After all, a majority consensus could be highly exclusionary of small minorities and could discriminate against groups in society for all kinds of arbitrary reasons. This is why radical democrats believe that we should treat the pursuit of consensus and harmony with a degree of scepticism. Before we go on to discuss political consensus and its role in finding a feasible politics for Northern Ireland, it is important to discuss the implications of value pluralism in radical democratic theory and the extent to which the diverse values that exist in Northern Ireland can be regarded as incommensurable or irreconcilable.

Value pluralism and incommensurability

The radical democratic perspective on the problems of organising politics in diverse societies is based upon the existence of value pluralism and a degree of incommensurability between different values. This perspective is not necessarily divergent from liberalism insofar as most contemporary liberals build their theories around the existence of diversity and the fact that different individuals or groups will hold a variety of values in democratic societies. However, what liberals do not all recognise is that this diversity of values might entail *incommensurable* value pluralism whereby different viewpoints are irreconcilable with one another. The most frequently discussed liberal view of incommensurability can be found in the work of Isaiah Berlin and these ideas have been adapted by radical democratic theorists to sustain their argument for a more open and diverse democratic engagement.[5] The argument for the existence of incommensurability in value pluralism has also emanated from romantic nationalism which has tended to regard different national cultures as incompatible with one another because there is no transcultural standpoint from which they could be compared with one another or which can provide a suitable paradigm for interaction (Barry 2001: 264). In the context of Northern Ireland, as Thompson has argued, there is a similar view of the relationship between culture and politics in romantic nationalism and cultural unionism whereby the appeal is always to one set of political institutions and affiliations rather than arrangements which could successfully accommodate both traditions (Thompson 2002).

John Gray describes value pluralism as an approach that claims that there are 'many conflicting kinds of human flourishing, some of which cannot be compared in value. Among the many kinds of good lives that humans can live there are some that are neither better nor worse than one another, nor the same in worth, but incommensurably – that is to say, differently – valuable' (Gray 2000: 6). Although this perspective is not of itself inherently liberal, it is true to say that many of the implications of this perspective have been played out within liberal political philosophy. Here Berlin's perspective on value pluralism has been highly influential but his ambiguous position with regard to the implications of value pluralism for liberalism has also been cast into a sharp light:

> Value-pluralism merely tells us that we have to choose between competing goods; it cannot circumscribe the choices we make. The problem for liberal pluralists is that value-pluralism cannot prevent us choosing values beyond the liberal value-set. Indeed it implicitly requires us to do so. Liberal pluralists are therefore required to accept the validity of anti-pluralist and anti-liberal conceptions of the good. Once they do so, it is less clear that the liberal polity is the most appropriate regulative framework within which the competing claims of these groups can be managed.   (Kenny 2000: 1035)

What is clear, then, is that the attempt to marry value pluralism with liberalism is not necessarily consistent; indeed, following Kenny's line of argument, it may lead to incoherent conclusions. Like most forms of liberalism analysed here, liberal value pluralism struggles to justify itself in its own terms. For Berlin, it was his intuitive attraction to liberal values and opposition to many radical perspectives which provided the foundation for his marriage of liberalism and value pluralism. However, more recently, George Crowder has attempted to justify a liberal approach to value pluralism in a more systematic fashion.

Crowder argues that it is important to differentiate between the recognition of value pluralism and ethical relativism. Whereas ethical relativism insists on the absence of any firm or universal ethical criteria whereby we can adjudge different claims of value, Crowder (2002: 45) contends that value pluralists maintain some universal human values, albeit at a high level of generality. The key to his argument lies in the tradition of Aristotelian particularism whereby, in making judgements between competing claims, we use specific 'covering values' which pertain in the particular area under discussion. This is the 'context of choice' whereby to 'choose rationally among plural values is to specify what matters most to the chooser in a particular context' (Crowder 2002: 60). Rather than asserting universal moral claims as the basis of making such judgements then, Crowder argues that the context in which we make decisions provides the backdrop to which particular value we invoke in making a judgement.[6] This ethical position is established upon four key premises of value pluralism. Firstly, Crowder contends that value pluralism does not preclude universal values. Thus, we can recognise things like basic human rights whilst simultaneously understanding that they sometimes manifest themselves in alternative ways in different contexts. Secondly, human values are themselves plural. In this sense human needs, though they may be universal, are experienced and valued in different ways.[7] Thirdly, Crowder contends that value pluralism involves incommensurability insofar as competing values may not always be judged against one another because their claims are not always comparable, measurable or rankable. Crowder claims that the third of these forms of incommensurability is the most appropriate for a liberal interpretation of value pluralism on the grounds that it implies a 'particularist approach to ethics, one that requires us to decide value-related questions by attending to the particular circumstances of the case rather than to the guidance of abstract rules' (Crowder 2002: 53). Lastly, and in line with radical democratic thinking, he contends that not only are values sometimes incommensurable but they will frequently conflict with each other. The point is that it is not just a matter of the existence of different values in any given society; the conflictual nature of disagreements requires judgements and political decisions. This is, then, a highly political understanding of the implications of pluralism.

Crowder's advocacy of an Aristotelian particularist approach is persuasive and it is important to recognise his point that value pluralism does not preclude us from making reasoned value judgements or entail a lapse into ethical relativism. Nonetheless there are problems with his invocation of liberalism as the most coherent set of values that can deal with the challenges which emanate from value pluralism. Ultimately, as with Berlin's disposition towards liberal values, Crowder's position is an almost intuitive defence of liberal values. It might well be that liberalism and value pluralism are complementary in certain instances, but it is clear that more will have to be done to convince non-liberal groups and minorities about the rectitude of the liberal values which Crowder wants to defend. Ultimately, where liberal value pluralism and a more radical approach differ is the neglect in the former of discussions of power and the ways that socio-economic and cultural inequalities can inhibit the political recognition of the claims and values of those with less power. In radical democratic theories, the existence of power relations in every social domain provides the dynamism for challenging the dominant order in liberal democracies. As such, radical democrats do not accept the claims of impartiality which underpin the political outlook of many liberals. Decision-making will always reflect value judgements on the part of those with the power to decide. It is only through democratisation and an opening out of decision-making processes that excluded and marginalised voices will be able to contribute to judgements over conflicting value claims. One further point of differentiation between liberal and radical democratic versions of value pluralism also needs to be elucidated. Where liberals tend to talk about pluralism in terms of a range of groups with fixed identities based on culture, religion, nationality and so on, radical democrats stress the complexity of individual identities and the cross-cutting nature of the factors which comprise our identities. In the view of the latter then, individual identities will often be inherently contradictory and sometimes conflictual. Such an approach renders it extremely difficult to outline a set of institutional premises upon which a liberal value pluralist theory can be grounded. Instead, it implies that all the values underpinning democratic institutions are inherently questionable and contingent.

A more critical analysis of liberalism and value pluralism has been provided in the recent work of John Gray (2000). Like Crowder, Gray is keen to point out how the existence of value pluralism does not preclude the existence of universal values such as human rights. However, what it does imply is that how those universal values are interpreted may be different. In this sense, value pluralism does not contradict universal values but what it does oppose is a universal morality. The point here is that conflicting interpretations of value are part of the human condition: 'human needs make conflicting demands. The idea of a human life that is without conflicts of value runs aground on the contradictions of human needs' (Gray 2000: 9).[8] For this reason Gray sees value pluralism as an 'account of ethical life' rather than a justification for liberal democratic politics. This stands in contrast to Crowder who is concerned with the ways in which value pluralism can *generate* a case for liberalism (Crowder 2002: viii). For Gray, the best that can be hoped for in linking liberal politics with value pluralism is the kind of 'agonistic liberalism' that he identifies in the work of Berlin. But, even then, the former is not persuaded that a coherent case has been made. Like J. S. Mill, Berlin's position fails to deliver the goods because, given that the latter is well aware of multiple – sometimes conflicting – understandings of liberty and the problems of ranking them, it becomes impossible to base a society on the maximisation of liberty. Once again, then, the failure to justify a universal value of liberty that is not interpreted differently by different groups provides a damaging blow to liberalism and its conception of democratic politics.

Gray's position also focuses on the ethical implications of incommensurability in value pluralism. Like most commentators, he recognises that value pluralism need not always imply incommensurability. Indeed, there may be many circumstances in which people with different claims of value are able to reconcile their claims or at least reach some kind of compromise. Nonetheless, for Gray, the evidence of late modern societies points to the fact that some claims of value will be incommensurable with one another and he cites Ulster as one such example. He understands the roots of incommensurability in three ways: firstly, specific values may be sacrosanct in some cultures which prevents them being traded off in any kind of compromise; secondly, where varying cultures may share certain values, they may differ in their interpretation of how those values are to be realised; thirdly, different cultures may believe in different values; what 'some praise as virtuous others may condemn as a vice' (Gray 2000: 35). In Northern Ireland all three kinds of incommensurability are sometimes evident. The first can be seen in the claims of some groups to be able to use their own minority languages or others to march in traditional fashion. Rather than being transient cultural phenomena, these are often claimed as fundamental to cultural traditions. The second type of incommensurability is also apparent in Northern Ireland; discourses concerning the 'universal' values of justice, equality, freedom and rights abound in Northern Ireland, but they are interpreted radically differently depending on the political agenda of their exponents. The third type of incommensurability is clearly linked to the first and in

Northern Ireland manifests itself in the rejection by one side of the cultural traditions of the other. Thus, for example, the freedom to march may be regarded as a good on one side of the political divide, but an objectionable expression of triumphalism on the other. Clearly, then, following Gray, there is evidence that *at least some* of the conflicts in Northern Ireland demonstrate the existence of incommensurable value pluralism.

One final point with regard to Gray's argument is worth noting. He is eager to argue that value pluralism does not entail ethical relativism: 'to claim that some values are incommensurable does not mean all values are equally valid' (Gray 2000: 41). Indeed, radical democratic theory would imply that incommensurability requires us to construct ethical standards on which we can make political decisions. However, those decisions can never be fixed, they are contingent upon changing circumstances and the different viewpoints which will emerge out of democratic engagement. Interestingly, Gray makes a brief allusion to Northern Ireland in his outline of the ramifications of value pluralism. In pointing out how value pluralism is based upon competing interpretations of justice, he states that:

> The communities that are locked in conflict in Israel and Ulster may claim that they invoke the same principles of justice. Yet their judgement of what is just and what unjust in the context of their contemporary conflicts are deeply at odds. In part, this reflects their different interpretations of their shared history. Partly, no doubt, it is also an expression of the fact that their interests are in many ways opposed ... Where interests are at odds and political power is at stake, shared principles of justice are likely to yield incompatible judgements of what justice demands.   (Gray 2000: 7)

The key point to recognise here is that the foundational principles of liberal democracy are shared in the Northern Ireland polity. All politicians pay lip service to objectives such as justice, equality, freedom and rights. However, Gray argues that the way in which those concepts are interpreted will vary substantially and that this can sometimes make value claims irreconcilable with one another. Moreover, radical democrats such as Mouffe would contend that not only are interpretations of these concepts likely to vary, but that the very concepts themselves may contradict one another. For Mouffe, the democratic paradox lies in the conflictual demands of liberty and equality and the inability of liberal democracies to totally reconcile the two.

Conflict in Northern Ireland is difficult to challenge through the sphere of institutional politics because the antagonisms are much more complex than the simple mechanisms of liberal political agreement. It was therefore sensible that the Belfast Agreement did not attempt to achieve the unachievable by pretending that politics could change ingrained cultural attitudes. Certainly politics and agreement have a role to play in such a process but only in accordance with a broader cultural politics that understands the deep-seated nature of antagonism. As Ruane and Todd have argued, conflictual issues in Northern Ireland:

> tap into personal feelings and memories of pain, loss, intimidation and humiliation, forged in the heat of violent struggle. The Agreement did not – and could not – dissipate those feelings or memories; for many, particularly those who had suffered irreparable loss, the Agreement rendered them all the more acute, isolating them from those who could now enjoy the peace ... If it was simply a matter of emotions, this problem might ease as time passes and peace holds. But the emotions are reinforced by the logic of the conflict.   (Ruane and Todd 1999: 23)

Democracy, consensus and political change

As we noted earlier, the ideal of consensus has animated many contemporary liberal theories but we have also seen in earlier chapters how theories such as multiculturalism can buck the trend of pursuing consensus. The latter, along with radical democratic theories, argue that there are difficulties with theories of democracy which have emerged in the social contract tradition, because of what Barry Hindess calls the 'presumption of uniformity'. The problem with theories that presume commonality and universalism is how we are to deal with diversity because the implication of uniformity is that we should all be treated the same. Hindess notes how even liberals like Kymlicka who attempt to grapple with the differences of minority groups have an attraction to uniformity. In Kymlicka's case this uniformity exists within national minority groups and not necessarily wider society. For Hindess, this leads Kymlicka to suggest that:

> the presence of distinct peoples in the one polity does not sit easily with the presumption that the rule of uniformity has its foundations in the culture and way of life of a singular person. Multiculturalism

> operates within the limits of this view of culture and aims to finesse
> the tensions that it produces: to maintain the rule of uniformity
> while nevertheless ensuring that citizens who belong to minority
> peoples are not substantially disadvantaged.   (Hindess 2001: 96)

Hindess criticises Kymlicka's thesis, and many other multicultural theories, for focusing too heavily on culture and ethnicity as the basis of
rights. Instead he promotes the approach of Iris Marion Young who
sees the politics of difference as not only concerned with the exclusion
of ethnic or cultural groups but also notes how 'the exclusive character
of the dominant way of life in most Western societies discriminates
also against women in general, blacks, gay men, lesbian women, and
others who are seen as having deviant lifestyles' (Hindess 2000: 96).

Hindess notes how the rule of uniformity can impact on minority
groups. For example, he cites David Miller as an example of someone
who believes that granting minority rights can ossify differences and
undermine the common nationality which he sees as paramount to a
democratic politics. In Northern Ireland though, such pretensions to a
common nationality are relatively rare. Rather, the peace process has
been animated by attempts to construct a democratic polity in which
two competing national allegiances are explicitly recognised. In
Northern Ireland Miller's position, even if it were true that there is
some kind of inherent link between nationality and democracy, is
simply not a workable option for an internal settlement. The dangers
in the pursuit of uniformity are shown up when these theories are
applied to the case of Northern Ireland and there is a clear tension
between the liberal impetus which has underpinned the peace process
and the universalist tendencies of most variants of liberalism. Another
important critical point to be raised against universalism and the
pursuit of uniformity is that it tends to gloss over differences within
different groups or communities. Hindess uses the example of
Australian Aborigines to show the way in which attempts to protect
collective group rights can serve to disguise the diversity which exists
within both majority and minority groups. Similar warnings can be
sounded with respect to Northern Ireland. For example, the experiences of working class Protestants in North Belfast cannot be assumed
automatically to be the same as those who live in rural Fermanagh.
Geography and social class are but two of many categories which can
differentiate the political make-up within a larger group. We can
perhaps predict that newer generations of unionists may have different
interests and strategies from those that developed politically whilst the

Stormont regime was in place or under direct rule. Similarly, the primarily political approach adopted within the republican movement in recent years raises new questions and challenges for those who remain wedded to an older military ideal. This suggests that the pursuit of uniformity is methodologically flawed and that any kind of consensus which can be established is transient rather than fixed.

One further issue raised by Hindess in relation to Australian Aborigines is the way in which collective group rights may be articulated by 'community leaders' who are not necessarily representative of those they are deemed to represent. Indeed, as in the Australian case, governments may be suspicious of and try to undermine 'community leaders' by questioning their representativeness (Hindess 2000: 98). Again these warnings are applicable to Northern Ireland where gifted political activists may become figureheads for their communities but over time they may lose the respect or support from community members. Similarly, it may be convenient for governments or opponents to deride the representativeness of 'community leaders', especially when the views those leaders articulate do not correspond with their own point of view. As an example, a frequent discourse in Northern Ireland is the claim that the politicians are all at fault and that 'ordinary, decent folk' have no truck with the conflict and violence. This is an attempt to homogenise diverse groups of people and establish a logic of consensus and uniformity around the idea of decency. This endeavours to circumvent the reasons behind political conflict in Northern Ireland by imposing an over-arching value that is clearly not shared universally. Following Young, Hindess claims that this 'empire of uniformity' can only be undermined by a different foundational value for democracy such as equal respect: 'this ... appeals to an image of overarching cultural unity, but it is a unity that is considerably less substantial than that suggested by most received understandings of democracy' (Hindess 2000: 100).

According to radical democratic thinking, the pursuit of consensus and uniformity is a dangerous phenomenon in any liberal democratic regime, let alone one as divided as Northern Ireland. This is not to say that we can do without foundations on which to build political institutions or that they do not require a modicum of agreement to achieve popular legitimacy. Radical democrats, such as Mouffe, contend that basic agreement is indeed required but that this demands a different understanding of the nature of political agreement. In this sense we need to contemplate the ways in which agreements are transient and that changing circumstances might impact upon the degree of agreement. Social, cultural and economic developments can have fundamental ramifications for our political outlooks especially in increasingly complex societies. Thus, when political agreements are forged, we must constantly question their legitimacy over the course of time. The Belfast Agreement is a perfect example of this point. Since 1998, the Agreement's legitimacy has been questioned by many parties and individuals. At different times its provisions have been broken by a range of different signatories including the governments. Some groups have withdrawn and reinstated their support for the Agreement, whilst others have been expelled from political institutions on the basis that the behaviour of their members or supporters transgresses acceptable boundaries. It should be clear then how a radical democratic perspective on the nature of 'the political' corresponds with the practical problems encountered by those who frame and try to maintain political agreements in the real world. However, one could argue that this pragmatic approach has a conservative heritage rather than being radical. The question that remains to be asked is what is so radical about the radical democratic approach?

A radical democratic approach?

Having identified the way in which radical democratic theory establishes itself on the territory of value pluralism, incommensurability and the rejection of uniformity and consensus, it is important to differentiate it from liberal or conservative theories which can also make use of these ideas. Initially this chapter suggested that the way in which radical democrats embraced political conflict set them apart from most orthodox theorists of democracy but, as noted above, they also point to a need for levels of agreement albeit on a radically contingent basis. However, the point is not just that radical democrats see conflict as potentially constitutive of politics but that the disputatious voices which they want to promote are those which are most frequently excluded from mainstream political debates. Thus, radical democracy contends that liberal democracies tend to reflect the interests and beliefs of hierarchies and established political élites. The political institutions which are established tend to emanate from those bearing the greatest power in society. Moreover, the procedures and rules of engagement in democratic processes often exclude forms of communication that may well be the favoured forms of those marginalised from the established political processes. Where radical democrats mark themselves out as radical is in encouraging us to understand democracy as a process in which oppositional voices are able to challenge the dominant order. Rather than relying on a somewhat artificial, 'established' consensus, radical democrats see a healthy democratic polity as one in which political opposition can be freely articulated both within political institutions and against political institutions.

The key to understanding the centrality of conflict in radical democratic politics lies in Mouffe's advocacy of a shift from antagonism to agonism. Whilst she recognises that relations of antagonism will always prevail in any complex society, the radical democratic imagination advocates a dynamic polity in which relations are not between foes or enemies but instead adversaries who recognise the legitimacy of the different viewpoints which their opponents hold. As such, democracy is not based upon the search for consensus or unity but instead it promotes a recognition and acceptance of political difference. Thus radical democrats must simultaneously recognise that political conflict will continue, albeit, hopefully, in a less violent and aggressive fashion than has been the case for much of the history of Northern Ireland. Radical democracy, then, strives for a more inclusive democratic politics in which imposed obstacles to participation such as gender, class, ethnicity, disability and so on are broken down. This is not to say, of course, that a polity can ever be totally inclusive – to some extent, exclusions will always take place. Nonetheless, for radical democrats, those exclusions cannot be arbitrary as in contemporary liberal democracies but must be based upon political decisions. This means that exclusions must be justified on political grounds but that they need not be permanent. Thus, as groups or individuals change their views over the course of time, it may well be the case that they are able to re-enter the political domain.

Again, Northern Ireland is an excellent example of this kind of process in action, albeit one that is blighted by élitism and the domination of 'the political' by relatively small groups of people. A radical democratic reading of events since the Belfast Agreement could recognise many key aspects of the theory although frequently they emerge in less than perfect form. This is not the problem for radical democrats as it is for some political liberals, multiculturalists, deliberative democrats and civil society theorists because radial democracy is never conceived in ideal-typical form. Instead, democratic relations and the institutions they produce are always contingent, contextualised and subject to change. In Northern Ireland there have always been exclusions from the political process but at various times politics has been more inclusive than at others. For example, the exclusion of representatives of the republican movement from the political mainstream for so long was difficult to defend on purely democratic grounds in the sense that they had an electoral mandate. Nonetheless, and many would say problematically, this exclusion represented the hegemonic position in Northern Ireland at the time. That said, with a more open polity in which republicans have a more substantial role to play, exclusion has not gone away altogether. Fringe elements of the republican movement such as the Real IRA and Continuity IRA have been excluded because of their uncompromisingly violent opposition to the political process as it has developed and similar measures have been taken against loyalist paramilitaries at various stages. At the same time some groups have excluded themselves in various ways. Whilst the DUP has participated in the governance of Northern Ireland when devolved institutions have been running as established in the Agreement, their participation has been limited. Similarly, groups such as the Ulster Democratic Party (as was) or the Progressive Unionist Party have withdrawn support from the process as it has progressed. A radical democratic position sees these shifting dynamics as inevitable but also recognises that the withdrawal or removal of a party need not be permanent: the party may later shift its position, as Sinn Féin has gradually done over the last twenty years, or political institutions may change in such a way that allows previously dissenting voices to be reincorporated into the political process. These examples demonstrate the way in which parts of the radical democratic approach are already evident amongst those dealing with the practicalities of political conflict in Northern Ireland.

There is one further argument that needs to be discussed in analysing the radical nature of radical democratic approaches. This is the critique of Nancy Fraser who, despite considerable sympathies with much of the radical democratic agenda, argues that within radical democratic theory there is a 'tendency to focus one-sidedly on cultural politics to the neglect of political economy' (Fraser 1997: 174). As we saw in the previous chapter, this is a situation which has emerged out of the debates on difference within feminist theory and finds its contemporary manifestation in discourses of 'multiple intersecting differences'. What this requires, according to Fraser, is a more developed version of radical democracy that couples the concern for difference with a broader understanding of the social and economic issues which can impact upon the way in which we experience our differences. As such, she contends that we need to move beyond a narrow concern with identity to address issues of distribution. If the radical democratic project does not do so, it 'will not be genuinely democratic. It will not succeed in forging democratic mediations among "multiple intersecting differences"' (Fraser 1997: 181). In this sense, Fraser argues that we need to move beyond the 'culturalist' impasse that emerges from the argument between anti-essentialist radical democrats and multiculturalists concerned with group rights. Thus, she rejects both the tendency of radical democrats to view all differences as contingent and exclusionary as well as the multiculturalist argument that all differences are worthy of recognition and celebration.

Fraser recognises that important advances have been made by anti-essentialist theorising, not the least of which is the understanding that identities are not fixed or given but rather are constructed discursively. However, she rejects the view that this necessitates a negative 'deconstructive' version of anti-essentialism whereby we cannot make any meaningful political statements about group identity. Ultimately, there are real political exclusions, inequalities and hardships that need to be addressed and these will often be linked with group differences. For Fraser, the tackling of these problems can never be achieved through a negative, 'deconstructive' anti-essentialism. The problem with this type of thinking is the failure to understand 'how a given identity or difference is related to social structures of domination and to social relations of inequality' (Fraser 1997: 183). Thus, if deconstructive anti-essentialists are incapable of linking identity and difference to social inequality, then they are not in a position to establish a political economy that would couple recognition with redistribution. On this basis Fraser contends that a deconstructive anti-essentialism is inherently problematic because its contention that all identities are 'fictions' renders it incompetent when it comes to 'distinguishing emancipatory and oppressive identity claims' (Fraser 1997: 184). This makes the claims of such a position to be either radical or democratic deeply suspect in Fraser's eyes.

However, the failings of this deconstructive model should not lead us down the path of a multiculturalism where all differences are reified. Fraser regards this type of multiculturalism as the offspring of the American pluralist tradition whereby 'difference is viewed as intrinsically positive and inherently cultural' (Fraser 1997: 185). Such an approach is antithetical to a radical democratic approach because of the extremely limited understanding of difference it implies and, as with the deconstructive model, it establishes obstacles to the linkage of redistribution and recognition and ignores important questions of power and inequality. This reinforces identities as they are and negates the notion that those identities are subject to change and, indeed, may require change. Hence, for the radical democrat, there is a need to recognise the conflict which may emanate from pluralistic difference: 'affirming some identities – or some strands of some identities – requires transforming others. Thus, there is no avoiding political judgments about better and worse identities and differences' (Fraser 1997: 185). From this perspective pluralist multiculturalism is no more successful than deconstructive anti-essentialism in the establishment of a workable democratic model for complex, diverse societies.

What then does Fraser see as a more viable understanding of the radical democratic project that does not fall into the traps identified above? Not surprisingly, she advocates a strategy of establishing and understanding the link between social differences, a politics of recognition and a socio-economic programme of redistribution. In this sense she wants to articulate the link with the politics of social justice and the pursuit of social equality. Hence these arguments over cultural difference cannot be divorced from debates surrounding social structure. In the context of Northern Ireland this would mean relinquishing any simplistic differentiation of 'two traditions' as nationalist/unionist, Catholic/Protestant, and so on. Fraser believes that we need to learn from the advances of the 'multiple intersecting differences' thesis without lapsing into a deeply relativist anti-essentialism or an equally relativist multiculturalism which suggests that cultural difference is paramount and that all should be equally recognised. Instead, for Fraser, 'we should develop an alternative version of antiessentialism, one that permits us to link an antiessentialist cultural politics of recognition with an egalitarian social politics of recognition' (Fraser 1997: 187).

The argument then, when extended to Northern Ireland, suggests that we need to understand how Northern Irish society is comprised of 'multiple intersecting differences' which resist simple classification into the orthodox categories and divisions that have hitherto dominated political analysis of the problem. This is not to say that there are not schisms along these traditional lines but that society is too complicated to expect us to be able to achieve political solutions within these limited parameters. Instead we need to understand how a greater focus on issues of distribution and redistribution can empower many of those who have been marginalised from the political system in Northern Ireland, potentially enabling them to contribute more effectively and to have their voices heard. This will not necessarily facilitate political agreement but it would entail a radical reworking of political debate in Northern Ireland and provide a more accurate reflection of the demands of democratic politics. Radical democracy suggests a move away from élitist democratic politics and, whilst it is feasible that this may increase political conflict, it would provide a clearer picture of the problems that Northern Ireland has to manage. It is in this practical example that we can understand the radical democratic demand for coupling recognition with redistribution.

Conclusion: radical democracy and the ethics of democracy

Radical democracy is not a systematic, coherent body of thought; instead it is primarily a way of rethinking 'the political' and the ethical parameters within which democratic debates take place. This engenders it with both strengths and weaknesses. The most notable of the latter are the danger of losing our focus on issues of political economy as noted by Fraser above, and the fact that radical democracy does not provide us with a clear picture of the way in which democratic politics should be organised in divided societies. Nonetheless this last point can also be depicted as a strength: rather than establishing unworkable blueprints of democratic institutions, radical democracy encourages us to see that all institutions are highly contingent and dependent on the political context in any given society. As such, radical democracy encourages us to move away from the utopias of contemporary liberalism, although it is clearly still open to the charge that it fails to guide us on issues of institutional design. The point made here is that this is intentional. The question to be asked is 'how do we proceed to debates on institutional design if we do not have a sufficiently mature conception of democracy?' Until we understand the conflictual nature of values in complex societies, our conceptions of democracy will be merely theories with little practical applicability.

In terms of Northern Ireland, radical democracy helps to explain both some of the developments that have taken place in recent years and some of the impediments to the construction of an agonistic polity. It highlights the contingency of political agreements and institutions in any complex society especially one as divided as Northern Ireland. At the same time however, it highlights the élite nature of politics in many liberal democracies where many are excluded from decision-making apart from the limited opportunities at the ballot box. Like civil society theorists, radical democrats want to encourage an opening out of politics so that more informal bodies and institutions have a greater substantive role to play. However, where civil society theory sometimes seems too focused on consensus and agreement, radical democrats see a broadened polity as one that involves more conflict and dissent. In Northern Ireland, this approach would involve much greater participation for working class people and the bodies that represent them as well as some groups and people with former links to paramilitary organisations for example. This is the inevitable outcome of a widening of the political in Northern Ireland.

The final point to make is that the radical democratic project challenges us to rethink our perceptions of 'the political' and the meaning of democracy. Its rejection of consensus provides a substantial rebuttal of the liberal orthodoxy and undermines many of the assumptions made about the organisation of complex societies. In its critique of liberalism, radical democracy asserts the inevitable conflict which will emerge from contradictory claims of liberty and equality. As such, the legitimacy of liberal democratic institutions will always be open to question. This is not to say that they will be abolished but that there will always be a dynamic movement of critique and change within any system of liberal democracy. Unfortunately this is not often recognised in liberal theories. As such, it would appear that radical democracy moves us beyond the liberal paradigm into a new ethical framework which posits political conflict at the heart of democracy. This is a lesson not only for divided societies like Northern Ireland but all complex societies where a plurality of values renders consensus unachievable.

Conclusion

The rethinking of the nature of democratic politics has profound implications for Northern Ireland. Political change there in the last fifteen years has been enormous despite many of the political debates taking place within an environment dominated by the traditional values of liberal democracy. Nonetheless the willingness of many political actors in Northern Ireland to take brave and selfless measures in the cause of advancing the peace process should not go unrecognised. In so doing they have demonstrated the ways in which practical politics sometimes demands actions that extract us from the ideal-typical surroundings of normative political philosophy. In showing the necessity of such actions, these participants have made evident the contingent nature of politics and the changing shape and ethical frameworks of democracy.

If we reject the ideal-type projections of liberal theories of democracy in our understanding of 'the political', what alternatives can be employed in the development of democratic politics in Northern Ireland? The argument here has suggested that we need to jettison some of the assumptions of liberals, such as prescriptions about political procedures and rational deliberation. Indeed, we have seen how much contemporary political liberalism, derived from the work of Rawls, is excessively procedural in such a way as to make its practical realisation appear unfeasible. Although Habermasian theory has avoided *some* of these problems, it is too concerned with rational consensus and suffers from the presumption that rational debate will always trump the non-rational in political dialogue. Whilst these ideas have been influential in political thinking in Northern Ireland, it is fair to say that the construction of political institutions has been more determined by consociational theory. As we saw at the outset of the book, however, consociational theory has reinforced an élite-driven political system in a society that was already extremely hierarchical in political terms. Thus, whilst consociational solutions might be more attuned to political practicalities than the promised lands of liberalism, it has exacerbated numerous problematic elements of Northern Irish politics. Not least of these is the augmentation of the hegemonic status held by the 'two traditions' paradigm. This has been accompanied by a growing lack of trust between politicians and ordinary citizens and the continued marginalisation of many deprived communities from the benefits that have derived from the peace process since the 1990s.

It is in the light of these criticisms of the dominant consociational model that an increasing number of political commentators have been advocating approaches to Northern Ireland that concentrate more on the social structures within which politics takes place. These approaches have identified problems of exclusion and inequality related to phenomena such as gender, class, ethnicity and so on. This is not to say that all liberals are unaware of these issues, but that their prescriptions for political institutions to combat them often seem inadequate in dealing with the embedded social structures that support these exclusions. Part of the problem here is that contemporary liberals have tended to grapple with these issues in solely political terms as if political institutions alone can rectify inequalities and divisions. Following the lead of Nancy Fraser, I have argued that political change is insufficient on its own and that we need to couple struggles for recognition with strategies to tackle socio-economic inequalities. In short, we need to resurrect the redistributive paradigm and recognise its centrality to democratic politics in Northern Ireland. As we have seen, with these challenges to liberalism and consociationalism in mind, civil society theorists, feminists and radical democrats have been able to mount substantive critiques of the traditional understandings of Northern Irish politics.

The promotion of civil society, and the arguments of some feminists and many on the Left that we tackle social inequalities and exclusions from the public sphere, has challenged the dominant understanding of politics in Northern Ireland. In so doing they have reinforced the critique of the hierarchical, élitist political system. However, despite these advances it remains the case that there is a drive for consensus in many of these theories. In varying ways they have tended to argue that the recognition of diversity and increased engagement in more or less formal types of politics will transform Northern Irish society and enable us to transcend our differences. The contention as this book has progressed has been that this pursuit of consensual politics, whilst perhaps understandable given the conflict in Northern Ireland, runs the risk of emaciating 'the political'. Thus, there is a danger that a well-meaning desire to establish a more harmonious political environment may exclude those who might be critical of particular decisions, procedures or institutions.

Although feminism has hitherto had a rather low profile in Northern Irish debates, much has changed during the last ten years or so. Not only is there a clearer political voice espousing the concerns of women in the form of the Northern Ireland Women's Coalition, but there is also evidence that women are getting more opportunities to participate in other political parties as well. That said, there is clearly a long way to go in challenging the ingrained patriarchy of Northern Irish politics. However, perhaps the most substantive contribution of feminism in Northern Ireland has been to dispute the parameters of political debate. For too long Northern Irish politics has been conducted as if constitutional issues and the border were all that mattered. Feminism, on the other hand, has alerted us to issues such as abortion, the role of the churches and domestic violence as legitimate topics for political analysis. The experiences of women in Northern Ireland have also informed this broadening out of 'the political'. Thus, for example, feminism informs us that when we talk about violence it is not merely perpetrated by paramilitaries and the state, but that it takes place on other levels as well, such as in the domestic domain, where it might be much more pernicious.

Radical democratic theory builds upon this critique of the narrowing of 'the political'. Whilst it recognises that there will always be some forms of exclusion in liberal democracies, it suggests that we need to open out politics to be more inclusive of oppositional voices. Thus, there should be scope for alternative voices to challenge the political system and raise objections to the dominant order. This has fundamental implications for democracy in Northern Ireland. Rather than envisaging an inclusive polity as one which facilitates the needs and demands of 'two traditions', it contends that we need to recognise the differing viewpoints held within those two traditions. Indeed, it provides a substantive challenge to the 'two traditions' model and the hegemonic position it has acquired in the analysis of Northern Irish politics. It is fair to say that some of the foundations of this kind of understanding already exist in Northern Ireland. For example, there is little suggestion that rejectionist unionists should not be able to articulate their opposition to unionists who support the political arrangements established through the Belfast Agreement. At the same time it may well be the case that there should be exclusions from the political process for groups such as the Real IRA which continue to use violence as their primary form of political expression. The point that radical democracy drives home is that these inclusions and exclusions are always contingent. As society changes different inclusions and exclusions may emerge. Those who were once excluded may be welcomed into the fold and others may – by their changing demeanour towards political developments – be excluded or may exclude themselves. For the radical democrat, this is the essence of a dynamic democratic politics although the more inclusive a polity is the better. The point here is that radical democracy understands the fluctuating and contingent nature of democratic politics better than liberal or consociational theories of democracy.

The pre-eminent idea emerging from radical democrats such as Mouffe is that of a 'conflictual consensus'. This refers to the fact that there do need to be some basic levels of agreement about democracy for a society and a political system to cohere. Radical democratic politics, however, does not see this as consensus in terms of everyone coalescing around institutions and procedures and accepting their outcomes uncritically. Instead it posits 'the political' as a sphere of conflict and disagreement where we are able to challenge the workings of democracy and voice opposition to the outcomes of political processes. Where it differs from liberal conceptions of democracy is in its acceptance of conflict as constitutive of democratic politics. However, just because there is conflict, this does not mean that we must question the legitimacy of those with whom we disagree. Instead a 'conflictual consensus' is one where we accept the legitimacy of our opponents and understand how their perspectives embrace a different way of thinking to our own (although this does not mean that we have to accord all views equal validity). Thus, the outcome of political engagement is not a rational consensus; instead a political decision is an indicator of one argument having prevailed over others. This is not necessarily a 'rational' decision because the policy implemented may prove to be erroneous or harmful. For radical democrats, this is the nature of democracy and it makes it vital that there is ample opportunity to voice discontent and challenge political decisions. This is a more dynamic view of politics than any of the major variants of liberalism which have informed contemporary thinking on the meaning of democracy.

This book has outlined the ways in which Northern Ireland helps to illuminate the radical democratic critique of liberalism whilst simultaneously arguing that radical democracy provides an alternative explanation of Northern Ireland to those that have dominated the literature hitherto. Although the focus has been on one specific society, the general critique of liberal democracy expounded here is intended as one that can be applied to all liberal democratic polities in diverse societies. Whether one accepts the critique of liberal theories of democracy or not, the example of Northern Ireland throws up all kinds of questions for political theorists that need to be addressed more explicitly in the literature.[1] How are we to accommodate competing rationalities? What are the political options when different perspectives prove to be irreconcilable? What is to be done when deliberation is incapable of generating agreement? Where do we draw the line with regard to the continuation of political violence? These are the kinds of ethical questions that radical democratic theory leads us towards and that liberals struggle to answer within their ideal-type prescriptions. Nonetheless, they must be addressed if political theorists are to offer better insight into Northern Irish politics. This book is an initial step in understanding the ethical framework within which these questions must be tackled and my main contention is that it takes us beyond the boundaries of the liberal paradigm. It signifies a point at which we start to debate rather than being an attempt to resolve these issues. The challenge is for political theorists to demonstrate that they can offer fresh insight into Northern Irish politics which might enable the wider conceptual debates in democratic theory to inform everyday politics in Northern Ireland. This book is intended as such a contribution. It clearly does not answer all the questions it raises but it does demonstrate that an engagement between political theorists and commentators on Northern Ireland is both necessary and desirable.

Notes

Introduction

1. Some of the authors I deal with in this book have already started this process. I am thinking in particular of Alan Finlayson (1997, 2001), Glen Newey (2002), Shane O'Neill (2000, 2002), Norman Porter (2003), Joseph Ruane and Jennifer Todd (2002), and Simon Thompson (2002).
2. This point was raised by Alan Finlayson in a panel on political theory and Northern Ireland at the Political Studies Association conference at the University of Leicester in April 2003.
3. I am thinking here of the work of people such as O'Neill (2000) who advocate Habermasian discourse ethics to resolve conflicts such as that at Drumcree. Elsewhere I have defended utopian political theory on its own terms. See Little (1996: Chapter Seven).
4. I am grateful to Paul Dixon for this point.
5. An example would be the changing ethics of political actors in accepting the release of paramilitary prisoners as part of the Belfast Agreement.

1   Explaining the Belfast Agreement

1. The two representatives of the Northern Ireland Women's Coalition also redesignated, one as a unionist and the other as a nationalist.
2. 'The d'Hondt rule means that parties get the right to nominate Ministers according to their respective strength in seats – no vote of confidence is required by the Assembly. It also means that parties get to choose, in order of their strength, their preferred ministries' (O'Leary 1999: 71).
3. The following range of twelve issues are listed in an Annex to this section of the Agreement as ones that *may* be a basis for co-operation and implementation: agriculture, education, transport, environment, waterways, social security, tourism, relevant EU programmes, inland fisheries, aquaculture and marine matters, health, and urban and rural development. For a fuller definition of what may come under these headings, see The Agreement (1998: 13).
4. The Ministers representing the DUP decided, not surprisingly, not to attend the Council. Whilst this was seen to contravene the Agreement, there was an ambiguity based around the likelihood that the DUP would hold ministerial position. This allowed the leadership of the Executive to make alternative arrangements should such a boycott take place. As Wilford (2001: 119–120) notes this was politic but seemed contrary in the light of consociational theory.
5. On the idea of parity of esteem, see Thompson (2002).
6. For my reflections on some of these issues, see Little (1998: Chapter Three).

7. This is not to say that these issues are irrelevant to other liberal democracies. Paul Dixon has pointed out how there are generalised lessons to be learned about the trade-off between violence and democracy, for example.
8. There is much diversity within the literature on consociationalism but the main theoretical foundations can be found in Lijphart (1968, 1969, 1977), whilst a critical response is provided by Barry (1991, Chs. 4 and 5). Consociational ideas are applied to Northern Ireland in Lijphart (1975, 1996) and O'Leary (1999). For critical analysis of the prospects of consociationalism in Northern Ireland which ultimately argues that the Belfast Agreement is not actually consociational, see Dixon (1997a, 1997b, 2002b).
9. The view that the Belfast Agreement amounted to 'Sunningdale for slow learners' is not accurate when the context of the two agreements is evaluated despite the similarities in the proposed institutional framework. These contextual differences are noted in Ruane and Todd (1999: Chapter One).
10. In 1999 O'Leary predicted that Ulster Unionists would be drawn into a 'phoney legalism' that involved an 'adversarial and petty-minded interpretation of the Agreement' whereas Sinn Féin would employ a 'hard legalism' based on extracting 'the full letter of its contract with the UUP' (O'Leary 1999: 94).
11. Many commentators argue that these objections are over-stated. See, for example, O'Leary (1999) who sees these criticisms as utopian, myopic and cloaked in tacit partisanship and Evans and Tonge (2003) who argue that they are naïve and exaggerated.
12. See Chapter Five of this volume.

2   Political Liberalism

1. There is a vast literature on *A Theory of Justice* which I cannot do full justice to here. For my own reflections on its concerns, see Little (2002a). The discussion here focuses more heavily on his more recent perspective articulated in *Political Liberalism*. The references to *Political Liberalism* are to the 1996 edition of the book which also contained the 'Reply to Habermas' in addition to the original text.
2. Electoral support for the anti-Agreement Democratic Unionist Party has generally increased since the Belfast Agreement at the expense of the Ulster Unionist Party which is divided on the outcomes of the peace process.
3. See de Wijze (2002) for further discussion of the theoretical limitations of reasonableness.
4. For analysis of political constructivism, see McKinnon (2002).
5. For more discussion of the right of exit, see the analysis of associative democracy in Little (2002a).
6. For more detail on the Drumcree controversy and liberal approaches to it see O'Neill (2000, 2002), Newey (2002), and Little (2003).

3   Multiculturalism and the Politics of Difference

1. I leave aside here the fact that Taylor can be seen as part of the liberal tradition and that a clear dividing line between liberals and communitarians is

   difficult to draw. For further detail on my stance with regard to these issues, see Little (2002a).

2. Taylor illustrates this point by examining the debate around the publication of Salman Rushdie's *The Satanic Verses* and points out that it is difficult to separate the private and the political. Thus, for Taylor, liberal institutions reflect one particular postreligious view of the world that is at odds with the way in which many Muslims conceive of the political.

3. There is insufficient space here to go into detail on the problems that can emerge when the discourses of culture and community are combined in this way. Parekh indicates that he is aware of differences between his understanding of culture and differing conceptions of community as voluntary associations. For my own position on these questions see Little (2002a).

4. See Little (2002a) for a discussion of different understandings of state neutrality in liberal theory.

5. Barry is using the work of Peter Jones (1998) here.

6. For further discussion of the Millian basis of Barry's thesis, see Kelly (2002).

7. Barry (2001: 265) criticises Charles Taylor in particular on this issue.

8. Eagleton notes approvingly that *part* of the work of the Field Day group was to form a 'constructive intervention' which has 'tried to couple questions of cultural identity with questions of material politics'. This he counterposes with a traditional nationalism that erroneously believed that 'a new culture could be born merely by booting out the landlords and Dublin Castle' (1998: 133).

4   Deliberative Democracy and Democratic Communication

1. Following the 'deliberative turn', there has been substantial growth in the theorization of deliberative democracy. One of the most recent volumes that contains essays by several important commentators is Fishkin and Laslett (2003).

2. There is now a wealth of literature on Habermas. Recent discussions that analyse his theory of democracy and discourse include Baumeister (2000) and Leet (1998).

3. For a discussion of Barber's idea of a 'civic forum', see Little (2002c).

4. Dryzek's thesis also contains an important ecological dimension. Whilst I do not have sufficient space to discuss this aspect in detail here, I have analysed his position in Little (2000).

5. Dryzek includes himself amongst those who have maintained a more radical tradition alongside Benjamin Barber, Seyla Benhabib, David Miller and Nancy Fraser.

6. Note the redesignation of Alliance members as unionists to enable David Trimble to stay in power in November 2001 (Evans and Tonge 2003).

7. Young's thesis and other forms of identity politics will be discussed in Chapter Six.

8. See, for example, the Habermasian argument put forward by O'Neill (2000, 2002) and the critical responses of Newey (2002) and Little (2003).

9. For a critical appraisal of deliberative democracy from a unionist perspective see Porter (2003). Porter ultimately supports a deliberative approach as one that can facilitate reconciliation in Northern Ireland but he has reservations about the Habermasian and Rawlsian approaches to deliberation.

5   Social Capital, Trust and Civil Society

1. For further analysis of the concept of civil society see Little (2002a, 2002c).
2. See Cochrane (2001) and Cochrane and Dunn (2002) for a discussion of the role of non-governmental organisations in the Northern Irish peace process and society more generally.
3. The Drumcree dispute has been prolonged in one way by the unwillingness of the local Orange Order leaders to engage in talks with the leader of the Garvaghy Road residents because of his background in the republican movement.
4. See Little (2002a: Chapter Five) for further discussion of the economic implications of Fukuyama's thesis.
5. There is a growing literature on parity of esteem in Northern Ireland. Unionists objections are articulated in English (1995) whilst a supportive argument is constructed by Thompson (2002, 2003). More recently, Porter (2003: 71–82) has differentiated between a more palatable form of parity based on 'accommodation' and a negative version that gives rise to claims of 'extreme entitlement'.
6. Guelke discusses the political activism of the Opsahl Commission in the peace process and the campaign for a 'Yes' in the referendum at some length. For more detail see also Pollak (1993) and Oliver (1998).
7. It should be noted that Democratic Dialogue retains scepticism about the implementation of its model. It alludes to the lack of clarity in what the Civic Forum is designed to do and too much concentration on who the members are to be. At the early stages this was manifest in the less than clear approach from key politicians and the lack of commitment from traditional 'social partners' such as trades unions and the business sector.
8. For Hirst's arguments see Hirst (1994). A critical reflection on Hirst's position from a radical democratic perspective is provided in Little and Martin (2002).

6   Feminism and the Politics of Difference

1. For some of my reflections on these issues see Little (2002b).
2. The constraints for feminism are addressed in more detail in Little (2002b).
3. The irony of these issues is that 'the majority of women involved in community politics were unlikely to identify themselves as feminists' (McCoy 2000: 14).
4. The distance between theories of deliberative democracy and the political practicalities is apparent when Porter notes that 'greetings like smiles, handshakes, hugs, the giving and taking of food and drink are important preliminaries that establish trust and respect' (Porter 2000: 158). This as it may be but hardly pertains to how some political actors will engage in Northern Irish politics.

5. This is a much more inclusive understanding of reconciliation than that of Norman Porter (2003). Porter claims that, whilst the Belfast Agreement had some reconciling intent, the signatories were behaving strategically. In viewing strategy and reconciliation as diametrically opposed, Porter makes large demands of political actors in divided societies: 'Reconciliation is integral to the process of making Northern Ireland a decent society. And, even though it does ask a lot of us, it need not be elusive' (Porter 2003: 12). My contention is that such an approach makes reconciliation all the more improbable than a less demanding position.
6. I am grateful to Anna Hilton for this point.
7. Rooney uses the term 'North of Ireland' which is a signifier of her position of questioning the legitimacy of the state in Northern Ireland. The exact terminology used in the literature in Northern Ireland is a matter of considerable dispute. The author does not see this as particularly important for his concerns. He has frequently used the term Northern Ireland in this work but where other authors offer alternative conceptions he is happy to use them interchangeably.

7   Radical Democracy

1. I am influenced in this section by the contemporary literature applying complexity theory in the natural sciences to politics. A survey of this literature in relation to contemporary theories of the Third Way can be found in Geyer (2003). An older analysis assessing the implications of complexity for democracy can be found in Zolo (1992).
2. It is possible to view many of the liberal theories in the book as absolutist in terms of their ideal-typical vision of political engagement between conflicting groups. This is particularly problematic, as we saw in Chapter Four, with models of deliberative democracy.
3. An example of these kinds of strategic considerations can be seen at election times in Northern Ireland when the primary rationale for major political parties is to win seats. It has been evident throughout Northern Irish politics in recent years that the leadership of the Ulster Unionist Party has faced a dilemma between adopting a hardline approach aimed at rebuffing the electoral rise of the Democratic Unionist Party and pursuing the more moderate agenda embodied in the Belfast Agreement. In this situation the Ulster Unionists have appeared to try and say different things to different groups of people. Whilst this is strategically understandable, it clearly does not fit with the kind of open communication that many deliberative democratic theorists advocate.
4. In this chapter I concentrate on the work of Mouffe as it is applied more directly to contemporary political situations. Nonetheless Laclau has produced a substantive body of work that has contributed to the development of radical democracy. See, for example, Laclau (1990, 1996). More recently, Laclau has published a collection with two other major contributors to radical democratic thinking, Judith Butler and Slavoj Žižek (Butler et al. 2000). Other theorists to have contributed more indirectly to the development of radical democratic theory are Connolly (1995) and Rose (1999).

5. A useful overview of the recent literature on Berlin is provided by Kenny (2000).
6. Crowder points out that many monists can accept the existence of value pluralism whilst still establishing a universal or rational criteria for making decisions. A similar point is at the heart of my disagreement with Shane O'Neill on the applicability of deliberative democracy to disputes in Northern Ireland (Little 2003).
7. For a more developed analysis of human needs and the particularity with which they are experienced, see Little (1998: Chapter Four).
8. See also Little 1998: Chapter Four; Crowder 2002; Kekes 1993.

Conclusion

1. I intend to address this in forthcoming work on ethical debates in the Northern Irish context.

Bibliography

The Agreement (1998) (Belfast: The Stationary Office).

Aughey, A. (1999) 'A New Beginning? Prospects for a Politics of Civility in Northern Ireland', in J. Ruane and J. Todd (eds) *After the Good Friday Agreement: Analysing Political Change in Northern Ireland* (Dublin: University College Dublin Press).

Aughey, A. (2001) 'Learning from "The Leopard"', in R. Wilford (ed.) *Aspects of the Belfast Agreement* (Oxford: Oxford University Press).

Barry, B. (1991) *Democracy and Power* (Oxford: Clarendon Press).

Barry, B. (2001) *Culture and Equality: An Egalitarian Critique of Multiculturalism* (Cambridge: Polity Press).

Barry, B. (2002) 'Liberalism Egalitarianism, Impartiality and Multiculturalism: An Interview with Brian Barry', *Imprints*, vol. 6, no. 2, 100–7.

Baumeister, A. (2000) *Liberalism and the 'Politics of Difference'* (Edinburgh: Edinburgh University Press).

Benhabib, S. (ed.) (1996) *Democracy and Difference: Contesting the Boundaries of the Political* (Princeton, NJ: Princeton University Press).

Butler, J., Laclau, E. and Žižek, S. (2000) *Contingency, Hegemony, Universality: Contemporary Dialogues on the Left* (London: Verso).

Campbell, T. (2001) *Justice*, 2nd edition (London: Macmillan).

Cochrane, F. (2001) 'Unsung Heroes? The Role of Peace and Conflict Resolution Organizations in the Northern Ireland Conflict', in J. McGarry (ed.) *Northern Ireland and the Divided World: Post-Agreement Northern Ireland in Comparative Perspective* (Oxford: Oxford University Press).

Cochrane, F. (2002) 'Bowling Together Within a Divided Community: Global and Local Understandings of Civil Society – The Case of Northern Ireland', paper presented at the ECPR Joint Sessions, University of Turin, 22–27 March.

Cochrane, F. and Dunn, S. (2002) *People Power? The Role of the Voluntary and Community Sector in the Northern Ireland Conflict* (Cork: Cork University Press).

Connolly, W. (1995) *The Ethos of Pluralization* (Minneapolis, MN: University of Minnesota Press).

Crowder, G. (2002) *Liberalism and Value Pluralism* (London: Continuum).

Dallmayr, F. (1996) 'Democracy and Multiculturalism', in S. Benhabib (ed.) *Democracy and Difference: Contesting the Boundaries of the Political* (Princeton, NJ: Princeton University Press).

Democratic Dialogue (1999) *The Civic Forum and Negotiated Governance* (Belfast: Democratic Dialogue).

Dixon, P. (1997a) 'Paths to Peace in Northern Ireland (I): Civil Society and Consociational Approaches', *Democratization*, vol. 4, no. 2, Summer, 1–27.

Dixon, P. (1997b) 'Consociationalism and the Northern Ireland Peace Process: The Glass Half Full or Half Empty?', *Nationalism and Ethnic Politics*, vol. 3, no. 3, 20–36.

Dixon, P. (2002a) 'Political Skills or Lying and Manipulation? The Choreography of the Northern Ireland Peace Process', *Political Studies*, vol. 50, no. 4, 725–741.

Dixon, P. (2002b) 'Con-sociationalism', paper presented at the Annual Conference of the Political Studies Association of Ireland, Belfast, 20 October.

Dryzek, J.(2000) *Deliberative Democracy and Beyond: Liberals, Critics, Contestations* (Oxford: Oxford University Press).

Eagleton, T. (1998) 'Postcolonialism: The Case of Ireland', in D. Bennett (ed.) *Multicultural States: Rethinking Difference and Identity* (London: Routledge).

English, R. (1995) 'Unionism and Nationalism: The Notion of Symmetry', in J. W. Foster (ed.) *The Idea of the Union* (Vancouver: Belcouver Press).

Evans, J. A. J. and Tonge, J. (2003) 'The Future of the "Radical Centre" in Northern Ireland after the Good Friday Agreement', *Political Studies*, vol. 51, no. 1, 26–50.

Festenstein, M. (2000) 'Cultural Diversity and the Limits of Liberalism', in N. O'Sullivan (ed.) *Political Theory in Transition* (London: Routledge).

Finlayson, A. (1997) 'The Problem of Culture in Northern Ireland: A Critique of the Cultural Traditions Group', *Irish Review*, 20, 76–88.

Finlayson, A. (2001) 'Culture, Politics and Cultural Politics in Northern Ireland', *New Formations*, 43, 87–102.

Fishkin, J. S. and Laslett, P. (eds) (2003) *Debating Deliberative Democracy* (Oxford: Blackwell).

Fraser, N. (1997) *Justice Interruptus: Critical Reflections on the 'Postsocialist' Condition* (London: Routledge).

Geyer, R. (2003) 'Beyond the Third Way: The Science of Complexity and the Politics of Choice', *British Journal of Politics and International Relations*, vol. 5, no. 2, 237–57.

Gray, J. (2000) *Two Faces of Liberalism* (Cambridge: Polity Press).

Guelke, A. (2002) 'Civil Society and the Northern Ireland Peace Process', paper presented at the Annual Conference of the Political Studies Association of Ireland, Belfast, 19–20 October.

Habermas, J. (1984) *The Theory of Communicative Action, Volume One: Reason and the Rationalization of Society* (Boston: Beacon Press).

Habermas, J. (1987) *The Theory of Communicative Action: Volume Two: Lifeworld and System, A Critique of Functionalist Reason* (Cambridge: Polity Press).

Habermas, J. (1996a) *Between Facts and Norms* (Cambridge: Polity Press).

Habermas, J. (1996b) 'Three Normative Models of Democracy', in S. Benhabib (ed.) *Democracy and Difference: Contesting the Boundaries of the Political* (Princeton, NJ: Princeton University Press).

Habermas, J. (1998) *The Inclusion of the Other: Studies in Political Theory* (Cambridge: Polity Press).

Hindess, B. (2001) 'Democracy, Multiculturalism and the Politics of Difference', in R. Axtmann (ed.) *Balancing Democracy* (London: Continuum).

Hirst, P. (1994) *Associative Democracy: New Forms of Economic and Social Governance* (Cambridge: Polity Press).

hooks, b. (1981) *Ain't I a Woman* (London: Pluto Press).

Jones, P. (1998) 'Political Theory and Cultural Diversity', *Critical Review of International Social and Political Philosophy*, no. 1, 28–62.

Keane, J. (1998) *Civil Society: Old Images, New Visions* (Cambridge: Polity).

Kekes, J. (1993) *The Morality of Pluralism* (Princeton, NJ: Princeton University Press).

Kelly, P. (2002) 'The Long Shadow of John Stuart Mill: Brian Barry on Culture and Freedom', *Contemporary Politics*, vol. 8, no. 2, 117–128.

Kenny, M. (2000) 'Isaiah Berlin's Contribution to Modern Political Theory', *Political Studies*, vol. 48, no. 5, 1026–39.

Kukathas, C. (1995) 'Are there any Cultural Rights?', in W. Kymlicka (ed.) *The Rights of Minority Cultures* (Oxford: Oxford University Press).

Kukathas, C. (1998) 'Liberalism and Multiculturalism: The Politics of Indifference', *Political Theory*, no. 26, 686–99.

Kymlicka, W. (1995) *Multicultural Citizenship: A Liberal Theory of Minority Rights* (Oxford: Clarendon).

Kymlicka, W. (2001) *Politics in the Vernacular: Nationalism, Multiculturalism and Citizenship* (Oxford: Oxford University Press).

Laclau, E. (1990) *New Reflections on the Revolution of Our Time* (London: Verso).

Laclau, E. (1996) *Emancipation(s)* (London: Verso).

Laclau, E. and Mouffe, C. (2001) *Hegemony and Socialist Strategy: Towards a Radical Democratic Politics*, 2nd edition (London: Verso).

Leet, M. (1998) 'Jurgen Habermas and Deliberative Democracy', in A. Carter and G. Stokes (eds) *Liberal Democracy and its Critics* (Cambridge: Polity Press).

Lijphart, A. (1968) *The Politics of Accommodation: Pluralism and Democracy in the Netherlands* (Berkeley: University of California Press).

Lijphart, A. (1969) 'Consociational Democracy', *World Politics*, 21, 207–225.

Lijphart, A. (1975) 'Review Article: the Northern Ireland Problem; Cases, Theories, and Solutions', *British Journal of Political Science*, 5, Part 1, 83–106.

Lijphart, A. (1977) *Democracy in Plural Societies* (London: Yale University Press).

Lijphart, A. (1996) 'The Framework Document on Northern Ireland and the Theory of Power-Sharing', *Government and Opposition*, vol. 31, no. 3, 267–274.

Lister, R. (1997) *Citizenship: Feminist Perspectives* (London: Macmillan).

Little, A. (1996) *The Political Thought of André Gorz* (London: Routledge).

Little, A. (1998) *Post-Industrial Socialism: Towards a New Politics of Welfare* (London: Routledge).

Little, A. (2000) 'Environmental and Eco-social Rationality: Challenges for Political Economy in Late Modernity', *New Political Economy*, vol. 5, no. 1, 121–134.

Little, A. (2002a) *The Politics of Community: Theory and Practice* (Edinburgh: Edinburgh University Press).

Little, A. (2002b) 'Feminism and the Politics of Difference in Northern Ireland', *Journal of Political Ideologies*, vol. 7, no. 2, 163–177.

Little, A. (2002c) 'Rethinking Civil Society: Radical Politics and the Legitimization of Unpaid Activities', *Contemporary Politics*, vol. 8, no. 2, 103–115.

Little, A. (2002d) 'Community and Radical Democracy', *Journal of Political Ideologies*, vol. 7, no. 3, 369–382.

Little, A. (2003) 'The Problems of Antagonism: Applying Liberal Political Theory to Conflict in Northern Ireland', *The British Journal of Politics and International Relations*, vol. 5, no. 3, 373–392.

Little, A. and Martin, J. (2002) 'Conflict and Community: Radical Democracy and Associational Theory', paper presented at the ECPR Joint Sessions, University of Turin 22–27 March.

McCoy, G. (2000) 'Women, Community and Politics in Northern Ireland', in C. Roulston and C. Davies (eds) *Gender, Democracy and Inclusion in Northern Ireland* (London: Palgrave).

McIntyre, A. (2001) 'Modern Irish Republicanism and the Belfast Agreement: Chickens Coming Home to Roost, or Turkeys Celebrating Christmas', in R. Wilford (ed.) *Aspects of the Belfast Agreement* (Oxford: Oxford University Press).

McKinnon, C. (2002) *Liberalism and the Defence of Political Constructivism* (London: Palgrave).

Mitchell, P. (2001) 'Transcending an Ethnic Party System? The Impact of Consociational Governance on Electoral Dynamics and the Party System', in R. Wilford (ed.) *Aspects of the Belfast Agreement* (Oxford: Oxford University Press).

Mouffe, C. (2000) *The Democratic Paradox* (London: Verso).

Newey, G. (2002) 'Discourse Rights and the Drumcree Marches: A Reply to O'Neill', *The British Journal of Politics and International Relations*, vol. 4, no. 1, 75–97.

O'Leary, B. (1989) 'The Limits to Coercive Consociationalism in Northern Ireland', *Political Studies*, XXXVII, no. 4, 562–588.

O'Leary, B. (1999) 'The Nature of the British-Irish Agreement', *New Left Review*, 233, January/February, 66–96.

O'Leary, B. (2001) 'The Character of the 1998 Agreement: Results and Prospects', in R. Wilford (ed.) *Aspects of the Belfast Agreement* (Oxford: Oxford University Press).

Oliver, Q. (1998) *Working for 'Yes': The Story of the May 1998 Referendum in Northern Ireland* (Belfast: The 'Yes' Campaign).

O'Neill, O. (2002) *A Question of Trust* (Cambridge: Cambridge University Press).

O'Neill, S. (2000) 'Liberty, Equality and the Rights of Cultures: the Marching Controversy at Drumcree', *The British Journal of Politics and International Relations*, vol. 2, no. 1, 26–45.

O'Neill, S. (2002) 'Democratic Theory with Critical Intent: Reply to Newey', *The British Journal of Politics and International Relations*, vol. 4, no. 1, 98–114.

Parekh, B. (2000) *Rethinking Multiculturalism: Cultural Diversity and Political Theory* (London: Palgrave).

Phillips, A. (1999) *Which Equalities Matter?* (Cambridge: Polity Press).

Pollak, A. (1993) *A Citizens' Inquiry: The Opsahl Report on Northern Ireland* (Dublin: Lilliput).

Porter, E. (1998) 'Identity, Location, Plurality: Women, Nationalism and Northern Ireland', in R. Wilford and R. L. Miller (eds) *Women, Ethnicity and Nationalism: The Politics of Transition* (London: Routledge).

Porter, E. (2000) 'Participatory Democracy and the Challenge of Dialogue across Difference', in C. Roulston and C. Davies, *Gender, Democracy and Inclusion in Northern Ireland* (London: Palgrave).

Porter, N. (1996) *Rethinking Unionism: An Alternative Vision for Northern Ireland* (Belfast: Blackstaff).

Porter, N. (2003) *The Elusive Quest: Reconciliation in Northern Ireland* (Belfast: Blackstaff Press).

Putnam, R. D. (2000) *Bowling Alone: The Collapse and Revival of American Community* (New York: Touchstone).

Rawls, J. (1996) *Political Liberalism* (New York: Columbia University Press), originally published in 1993.

Raz, J. (1986) *The Morality of Freedom* (Oxford: Oxford University Press).

Raz, J. (1994) *Ethics in the Public Domain: Essays in the Morality of Law and Politics* (Oxford: Clarendon).

Rolston, B. (1998) 'What's Wrong with Multiculturalism? Liberalism and the Irish Conflict', in D. Miller (ed.) *Rethinking Northern Ireland* (London: Longman).

Rooney, E. (2000) 'Women in Northern Irish Politics: Difference Matters', in C. Roulston and C. Davies (eds) *Gender, Democracy and Inclusion in Northern Ireland* (London: Palgrave).

Rose, N. (1999) *Powers of Freedom: Reframing Political Thought* (Cambridge: Cambridge University Press).

Roulston, C. (2000) 'Democracy and the Challenge of Gender: New Visions, New Processes', in C. Roulston and C. Davies (eds) *Gender, Democracy and Inclusion in Northern Ireland* (London: Palgrave).

Roulston, C. and Davies, C. (eds) (2000) *Gender, Democracy and Inclusion in Northern Ireland* (London: Palgrave).

Ruane, J. and Todd, J. (2002) *The Dynamics of Conflict in Northern Ireland: Power, Conflict, Emancipation* (Cambridge: Cambridge University Press, 2nd edition).

Ruane, J. and Todd, J. (1999) (eds) *After the Good Friday Agreement: Analysing Political Change in Northern Ireland* (Dublin: University College Dublin Press).

Taylor, C. (1992) *Multiculturalism and 'the Politics of Recognition'* (Princeton, NJ: Princeton University Press).

Thompson, S. (2002) 'Parity of Esteem and the Politics of Recognition', *Contemporary Political Theory*, vol. 1, no. 2, 203–220.

Thompson, S. (2003) 'The Politics of Culture in Northern Ireland', paper presented at the Political Studies Association conference at the University of Leicester, 17 April 2003.

de Wijze, S. (2002) 'The Political Limits of Reasonableness', *Imprints*, vol. 6, no. 2, 171–186.

Wilford, R. (ed.) (2001a) *Aspects of the Belfast Agreement* (Oxford: Oxford University Press).

Wilford, R. (2001b) 'The Assembly and the Executive', in Wilford (ed.) *Aspects of the Belfast Agreement* (Oxford: Oxford University Press).

Wolff, S. (2001) 'Context and Content: Sunningdale and Belfast Compared', in R. Wilford (ed.) *Aspects of the Belfast Agreement*, (Oxford: Oxford University Press).

Wolin, S. (1996) 'Fugitive Democracy', in S. Benhabib (ed.) *Democracy and Difference: Contesting the Boundaries of the Political* (Princeton, NJ: Princeton University Press).

Woods, J. (2001) 'The Civic Forum' in R. Wilson (ed.) *Agreeing to Disagree?* (Belfast: The Stationary Office).

Yack, B. (2002) 'Multiculturalism and the Political Theorists', *European Journal of Political Theory*, vol. 1, no. 1, 107–19.

Young, I. M. (1990) *Justice and the Politics of Difference* (Princeton, NJ: Princeton University Press).

Young, I. M. (2000) *Inclusion and Democracy* (Oxford: Oxford University Press).

Zolo, D. (1992) *Democracy and Complexity: A Realist Approach* (University Park, PA: Pennsylvania University Press).

Index